Snake Pilot

Related titles from Potomac Books

Chained Eagle: The Heroic Story of the First American Shot Down over North Vietnam, by Everett Alvarez, Jr. and Anthony S. Pitch
Dien Bien Phu: The Epic Battle America Forgot, by Howard R. Simpson
Legacy of Discord: Voices of the Vietnam War Era, by Gil Dorland
Long Binh Jail: An Oral History of Vietnam's Notorious U.S. Military Prison, by Cecil Barr Currey
The U.S. Navy in the Vietnam War: An Illustrated History, by Edward J. Marolda
Victory at Any Cost: The Genius of Viet Nam's Gen. Vo Nguyen Giap, by Cecil Barr Currey

Snake Pilot

Flying the Cobra Attack Helicopter in Vietnam

Randy R. Zahn

Potomac Books, Inc.
Washington, D.C.

Library of Congress Cataloging-in-Publication Data

Zahn, Randy R.
  Snake pilot : flying the cobra attack helicopter in Vietnam / Randy R. Zahn.— 1st ed.
    p. cm.
Includes bibliographical references and index.
  ISBN 978-1-57488-565-1 (hardcover : alk. paper)
  1. Vietnamese Conflict, 1961–1975—Aerial operations, American. 2. Vietnamese Conflict, 1961–1975—Personal narratives, American. 3. Military helicopters—Vietnam. 4. Zahn, Randy R. I. Title.

DS558.8.Z35 2003
959.704′148′092—dc21

2002156005

Hardcover ISBN 978-1-57488-565-1
Softcover ISBN 978-1-57488-611-5

Printed in the United States of America on acid-free paper that meets the American National Standards Institute Z39-48 Standard.

Potomac Books, Inc.
22841 Quicksilver Drive
Dulles, Virginia 20166

First Edition

10 9 8 7 6 5 4 3 2

Contents

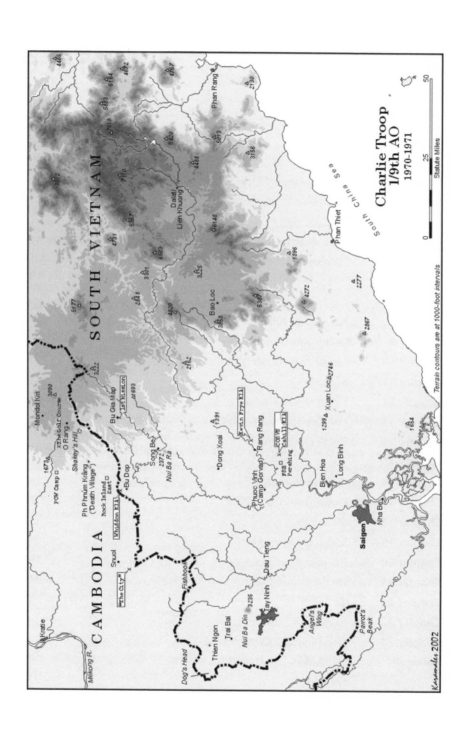

CAMBODIA

SOUTH VIETNAM

Kratie

Mekong R.

Mondol Kiri

POW Camp   1673

Ph Phnum Kriang
("Death Village")
Rock Island
East

Snuol

"The City"

Whitehorn KIA

3090
xThe Golf Course
O Rang

Shakey's Hill

Bu Dop

Fishhook

Dog's Head

Thien Ngon

Trai Bai

Nui Ba Din   3235

Tay Ninh

Dau Tieng

Anger's
Wing

Parrot's
Beak

Bu Gia Map

Let KIA

Song Be

Nui Ba Ra
2372

Dong Xoai

Rang Rang

FSB
(Camp Gorvad)
Pershing

Phuoc Vinh

Kevin Frye KIA

FCE VC
Cahill KIA

Bien Hoa

Long Binh

Xuan Loc

Saigon

Nha Be

Bao Loc

Dalat/
Lien Khuong

Phan Rang

Phan Thiet

South China Sea

Charlie Troop
1/9th AO
1970-1971

Kononovas 2002

Terrain contours are at 1000-foot intervals

0   25   50
Statute Miles

Preface

This story is mainly about my experiences while serving in the United States Army in the Republic of Vietnam.

It is only through my parents' foresight that I am able to reconstruct what happened that year. Communication from servicemen to loved ones in the States was accomplished not only by written communication, but by voice, made possible through cassette tapes. Not only was Vietnam the "first helicopter war," it was also the "first cassette war."

My parents saved, and presented to me in 1981, all of the audio cassettes and letters that I had sent them. The collection contained communications from Vietnam, as well as from basic combat training and flight school.

It took me nineteen years to overcome the ghosts of the past and finally sit down to read the correspondence and listen to my voice recorded so long ago in that far-off place called "Nam." Going through the letters and the tapes took my wife and me close to three months. At times, I was transported back to Vietnam. Something in a letter or on one of the tapes triggered something that allowed me to be there once again. I was able to visualize the people whom I spoke about; I could hear the sounds of the artillery and the aircraft; I could see our base camp; and I could smell the smells and feel the ever-present perspiration.

It brought back many memories, led to many sleepless nights, and turned on the faucet of tears that I thought had run dry many years ago. The dialogue, events, and chronology are as close as my memory allows them to be. Some names have been forgotten or, more likely, I never knew them.

Two names I will never forget. The names of two men, one living and one dead, who are so much a part of me that their stories must be told out of my respect and love for them.

Larry B. Edeal, who has been my best friend for all these years, and Kevin Mark Frye, whom I loved like a brother. May he rest in peace.

So it has come full circle. This book was made possible by my parents, who for whatever reason, hung on to a box of old letters and tapes. It has become a reality because my wife, Kim, has been so compassionate and so very supportive in this effort.

And finally, it is made necessary because I want my sons, Brent and Kyle, to be able to read about and understand what I, and my brothers-in-arms were made to endure with the hope that they shall never have to endure the same.

To all that I have mentioned and to all that served in the First of the Ninth Cavalry, I dedicate this book to you.

Introduction

I had known from an early age that I would serve in the military. Not that it was expected of me, but it was a tradition in my family that I wanted to follow.

My grandfather, born in Hungary, immigrated to the United States at the turn of the twentieth century. He showed his gratitude for the opportunity to live in a free country, by exercising his "privilege" to serve in the military and became a decorated member of Teddy Roosevelt's Rough Riders in the Spanish-American War. My father served during World War II, as did my uncle, who was wounded in action and decorated at Guadalcanal.

The tradition had been established and fortunately, or unfortunately, the United States was involved in a "limited war" when it was my time to serve.

I had a love for aviation from the time I was five, but no one else in my family had flown . . . nor would I for another twelve years.

Thinking back to school days, I remember the kids who wanted to become doctors, lawyers, policemen, firemen, and even the President of the United States. Respectable aspirations, but I always wanted to be a pilot in the military. Like other would-be aviators, I had my heart set on fighters.

Shortly after my enrollment in college I realized that I wouldn't last the four years required to obtain the bachelor's degree necessary to be considered for any of the flight programs that included fighters. The Army was pushing their "high school to flight school" Warrant Officer Candidate (WOC) program, but all they were offering was helicopters, and who the hell wanted to fly those? I had never been in one and didn't understand the aerodynamics that allowed them to fly.

At the time, I was attending Glendale Community College, California, which had an excellent aviation curriculum. One day between classes I was driving down Brand Boulevard and saw a poster in the window of the local Army recruiter's office. It depicted one of the most interesting aircraft that I had ever seen, the Lockheed AH-56A Cheyenne.

It sparked my interest enough to make me stop to talk with the recruiter about "opportunities" in the Army. He knew very little about the Cheyenne, or any of the aircraft in the Army inventory, for that matter. He suggested that I could find out all about them by enlisting for the WOC program. If I passed the written exams, physical, oral boards, and so forth, then I would be given a guarantee, in writing, that I could attend flight school. Making it through flight school would be up to me; the washout rate was running at about sixty percent.

I left uncommitted, but deep in thought. As fate would have it, that night on the news I was treated to a sixty-second segment on the fielding of the Army's newest helicopter, the Bell AH-1G Cobra, which was billed as the world's first "attack" helicopter. My mind was made up.

Having passed all the tests and the physical examination, the last hurdle before acceptance was the oral board. I remember the last question asked. A major asked, "You realize that *if* you complete flight school, you'll be sent to Vietnam, do you not?"

Vietnam was third- or fourth-page news when I went for my oral board. I can't recall reading or studying anything about the country or the conflict in school, and quite frankly, I didn't even know where it was located on the map.

"Oh, yes, sir!" I replied, thinking to myself, "He's so full of shit. It'll be over long before then."

One year later, in March 1970, as my flight departed Travis Air Force Base, California, for the Republic of Vietnam, I remember looking out the window of the chartered Boeing 707 at the Golden Gate Bridge. My face was literally stuck to the window until the bridge was no longer in sight. With tears rolling down my cheeks, I wondered whether or not I would ever see that bridge again . . . or my parents or my home for that matter. Would my next view of U.S. soil be looking down from the aircraft on my return in one year, or looking up from my grave? At nineteen years of age, it became an overwhelming question to ponder.

Chapter 1

A Man Named Larry

The autumn of 1955 was like the other autumns that I could remember in my short life. So were the things we did as a family. Standing on the front seat of my mother's 1946 Pontiac, we drove to the Valley Plaza to do our weekly shopping. It had become a ritual to go to the Plaza. One would have thought there was no place else to do your grocery shopping on a Saturday afternoon.

As we passed one of the runways at the then–Lockheed Airport, a small aircraft took off and flew almost directly over the car. I excitedly asked my mother, "What is that?"

Her response was an exasperated, "It's an airplane," as if I was supposed to know that at five years of age. For several months I went on believing that these hunks of metal called "airplanes" soared through the skies unaided and alone, like birds.

In the summer of 1956, my aunt came to visit from New York. We went to the airport to pick her up, and I was astonished to see her alight from the bowels of an airplane. Till now, I had not understood that airplanes carried people! I asked, "Daddy, how did the airplane know how to get here from New York?" He explained that an airplane was sort of like a bus in the sky. As a bus had a driver, an airplane had a pilot. A smile appeared on my face as I proudly announced to my parents that I, too, would be a pilot when I grew up.

As the years passed, I was preoccupied with all of the things that preoccupy most adolescent boys: school, sports, cars, and girls. I had always done well at school, and my junior year was no exception. Life was wonderful and I thought this would be the perfect time to ask my parents if I could begin to take flying lessons. As we sat down to dinner one evening, I thought about how I was going to ask them.

"Mom, Dad, what do you think about me taking flying lessons?"

I wasn't prepared for their reaction.

"Are you out of your goddamned mind?" my father asked.

Mom was a little subtler. "Oh, honey, it must be awfully expensive and it's so dangerous."

"So is crossing the street or driving to work every day," I retorted.

1

I spent the rest of the meal listening to various lectures. It ended with Mom's final question of the evening, "Besides, why would you want to take flying lessons? You're going to be a doctor!"

I thought, "Right! And tomorrow the sun is going to rise in the west."

Several days passed before I brought it up again. This time Dad had the last word. "We've already discussed it and I don't want to hear about it again. EVER."

It took a few days to formulate a new plan. While working at Tona's Mobil station, I met lots of customers. One guy was a sport parachutist, and I had queried him about learning to skydive. I thought that if I learned how to skydive, I could use that as a bargaining chip to get my parents to let me fly. I would simply give up skydiving for flying lessons!

He suggested that I call his jumpmaster, Larry Perlman, who would be able to answer all my questions. I called that evening and the jumpmaster patiently, and enthusiastically, explained all about the sport and invited me to go through a three-day ground school.

Upon completion of the ground school he handed me a piece of paper. As I began to read it, he said, "Since you're under eighteen, you'll have to have your parent's signature before I can allow you to make your first jump." My heart sank. If they wouldn't approve of my learning to fly an airplane, they damn sure weren't going to sign a piece of paper giving me their blessing to jump out of one!

The next morning I told my mother that I needed a note for school, making up some reason. When she wrote it out I simply placed the document over it and forged her signature. It was a little drastic, but it was, I hoped, the means to an end.

When I returned the signed form, the jumpmaster told me to be at Taft Airport at 7:00 A.M. Saturday morning for my first static line jumps. I don't recall the story I told to get out of the house at 5:00 A.M. that morning, but it worked.

One of the beauties of growing up in Southern California was its natural geography. From my house I could drive ten minutes to the east and be in the San Gabriel Mountains. An hour west was the Pacific Ocean and the beach, and an hour north would put me in the San Joaquin Valley; arid and desert-like in the south; rich and fertile to the north.

As I motored my way the hundred-plus miles toward Taft, I began to question the rationality of this move. After all, it would be awful difficult to learn to fly wearing a body cast!

Larry greeted me as I pulled into the parking lot that morning. The sun was just beginning to peek over the horizon far to our east. Walking toward the ready room I noticed an airplane, with a large section of fuselage ripped out just behind the passenger door, sitting very close to the building. It appeared that something had exploded in it.

I asked Larry, "What in the hell happened to that?"

He rather nonchalantly replied, "Oh, last week one of the guys was getting ready to jump and his chute opened prematurely."

"Okay, continue," I requested.

"Well, it was real premature," he continued, "the chute actually opened inside the airplane. He caught the ripcord on the seat and deployed the chute."

"And?"

"And the wind caught the chute. He tried to get to the door, but wasn't quick enough."

"And?" I asked.

"And it pulled him through the side of the aircraft!"

I stopped dead in my tracks. "You must be joking?" I asked.

He wasn't. I reluctantly asked what had happened to the guy. I wasn't sure I wanted to know, but my curiosity got the best of me.

Larry said, "It wasn't too serious considering what might have happened. It just ripped off his right foot."

"JUST ripped off his foot!" I gulped.

Here I was trying to get my folks to let me fly, getting ready to go up in an airplane for the very first time in my life, a perfectly good airplane, and I, in my infinite wisdom was about to make it a one-way ride!

As I donned my parachute and began to buckle it Larry warned, "Make sure you don't get your nuts caught in the crotch straps. It would be a real uncomfortable ride once the chute opened."

As we boarded the airplane, the controls and instrumentation of the aircraft amazed me. It was a Cessna 172, a rather simple airplane I later found out, but now it was just a maze of buttons, instruments, switches, and other unfamiliar controls.

Once we were cleared onto the runway and given clearance to take off, my face lit up with a smile. Through the space where the door had been removed, the wind began to rush past us, and before I knew it, for the first time in my life, I was flying.

We ascended over the drop zone and I was amazed at how small everything appeared. Cars seemed like toys; houses like little matchboxes far below as we continued our spiraling ascent. With all the new and wonderful things I was experiencing, I still had the presence of mind to check my crotch straps!

We leveled off at ninety-five hundred feet above sea level and I heard Larry yell, "Go!" Jolted back from my wonder, I watched as one of my fellow students plunged toward the earth.

Larry said, "Okay tiger, your turn."

I looked around to see whom he was talking to. Certainly not me! I mean, hey, he didn't really want me to fling myself out of this airplane, did he?

He did.

I maneuvered my way to the door, one hand covering my ripcord, and the other furiously checking the crotch straps. As I sat in the doorway, the wind blowing my legs toward the back of the airplane, Larry leaned down and yelled so he could be heard above the roar of the wind.

"When I tap you on the helmet and say go, you jump out as far away from the airplane as you can, okay?"

I looked at Larry and meekly replied, "You're shitting me, right? You don't really want me to jump?"

He laughed. "You've come this far, you may as well go the rest of the way. Besides, you didn't buy a round-trip ticket!" His sense of humor evaded me.

I sensed the airplane slowing, I felt a tap, heard a "Go," felt a shove, and a massive blast of air caught my whole body. I looked up to see the airplane getting smaller and smaller and thought to myself, *Shit!*

I felt a jolt when the chute opened as I reached the end of the static line. As the parachute blossomed above me, I remember thinking, "Oh thank God!" I had cleared the airplane . . . and my nuts were clear of the crotch straps.

The descent was incredible. Everything was quiet except for the wind, and I was floating; floating on a big cushion of air. First I laughed, and then I began to talk to myself as I watched the hustle and bustle of activity as the world awoke beneath my feet. I didn't want it to end.

"Okay, I'm getting close to the ground now. Don't look down. Whatever you do, don't look down." I had no idea whether or not this was going to hurt, but the sudden stop at the end of this ride was not one I was looking forward to. My instructions were to keep my eyes on the horizon, and as it moved up, reach up real high on the risers. Next, point my toes downward and as soon as I felt them touch, pull the risers down as hard as I could to absorb the shock.

Touch. Pull! Tumble. All of a sudden all movement had ceased, and I lay motionless on the desert floor. After Larry landed, he ran over when he noticed that I hadn't budged. As he approached, I heard him yell, "Are you alright?"

"I don't know," I answered. "Am I bleeding anywhere?" I asked.

"Not that I can see," said Larry.

"Any bones sticking out anywhere?"

Another negative response.

"Good," I said, "I was afraid to look for myself."

"You asshole! Get off your ass and on your feet," he said.

I gathered up my chute and on the way back to the recovery van Larry queried, "Well, tiger, what do you think?"

I smiled and replied, "Let's go do that again."

After several days I once again worked up enough nerve to bring up the subject of flying lessons at the dinner table. The timing had to be perfect and both Mom and Dad had to be in good moods.

One evening everyone seemed to be in a pretty jovial mood and I thought, *It's now or never.* I looked at my father, then at my mother, "Uh, Mom, Dad, I'd like to discuss flying lessons with you again."

My dad didn't miss a bite. He finished what he had in his mouth and smiled. "Your mother and I discussed it after our last conversation. We've changed our minds. If this is something that you really want to do, it's okay with us."

Mom followed, "It'll be expensive and since it's not really something we're thrilled about, don't come to us for money if you haven't got enough for a lesson."

I was ecstatic, but couldn't help thinking, "Right! I forged your signature on a legal document to learn to skydive; I broke the law to coerce you to let me fly. I could go to jail for forgery; I might have been killed jumping out of a perfectly good airplane, had a foot ripped off, or worse yet, I could have got my nuts caught in the crotch straps. And now you change your minds! Shit! Parents!"

Larry was right. I was an asshole.

Twenty-four hours later I presented myself at San Fernando Airport with all of the money I had saved up from working at Tona's Mobil station. I was there for my five dollar Cessna "Ticket to Adventure"—Cessna Aircraft was sponsoring a program that for five dollars you could get your first flying lesson. Once they had the hook in, they waited till you were back on the ground before they set it.

"Well, what do you think? For five hundred dollars you can get your private pilot's license and then you'll be up and flying," said my instructor.

Actually, I wouldn't have cared if it cost five million dollars. I was going to be a pilot.

San Fernando Airport was a small airport at the north end of the San Fernando Valley hugging the San Gabriel Mountains. The single runway was 2,700 feet long and about 40 feet wide. You could just about get a DC3 in, but once it landed it would be there to stay. Los Angeles International, it was not!

It wasn't the closest airport to our house at the northeast corner of the vast San Fernando Valley, but it had a lot of positive things going for it. It was small, had no control tower, and had a flight school with a very good reputation. A former naval aviator owned Glendale School of Aeronautics. Tom Ryan had been a captain when he had retired, but I suppose his biggest claim to fame was the fact that he was the brother-in-law of one of the then-presidential candidates, a man by the name of Richard Nixon.

My instructor was a tall, lanky fellow from Oklahoma. His name was Bill Nye, and Bill was a gentleman in every sense of the word.

I had reported at the agreed upon time for my first lesson, which included an introduction to aerodynamics, a review of the aircraft operator's manual, an explanation about airport traffic patterns, and filling out all the necessary documents before and after the flight.

After what seemed like hours, but was actually only thirty minutes, we walked out to the aircraft, a shiny little blue and white Cessna 150. Bill proceeded to take me through an extensive pre-flight inspection. Once completed, we proceeded to strap ourselves into the tiny aircraft. We progressed through the checklist, and soon it was time to start the engine. I turned on the master switch, switched on the magnetos, pushed in the throttle, and turned the key. The little engine sputtered to life. Bill explained the flight controls and instructed me in how to taxi the aircraft. Much to my surprise the control wheel does very little on the ground; taxiing is all done with throttle and the feet.

He went on, "To get the aircraft to move forward, we add throttle. Once the airplane begins to move, you can back off on the throttle a bit. To turn right, press the right pedal. To turn left, press the left pedal. To stop, pull back the throttle and press on the top of the rudder pedals, that's where the brakes are, okay?"

I nodded in acknowledgment.

Bill taxied the aircraft onto the taxiway from the tie-down where it had been parked, and asked me if I wanted to try it.

"Sure," I responded, realizing that my dream was about to come true. I was at the controls of one of those flying masses of metal.

I made a few uncommanded jaunts on the way to the run-up area, but by and large it wasn't too bad. Arriving at the run-up area, Bill took the controls back and began to explain the run-up checks: run the engine up to full throttle and check the magnetos. It is prudent to find a problem, if one exists, prior to getting airborne. At this point, I had regained control of my adrenaline flow, and my bladder, and listened intently as he went through the run-up. Once completed, Bill taxied in a 360-degree circle to ensure that there were no other airplanes in the traffic pattern or on final approach. Back on our original heading, Bill seemed happy and said, "Okay, you have the controls back. Let's go!"

I looked at him with a puzzled look and said, "What do you mean, let's go?"

"Let's go," he replied, "Take off."

I countered, "Bill, maybe you didn't understand. This is my first lesson. I don't know how to take off."

Bill smiled, "Maybe you don't understand. In order to learn to fly, you have to be in the air. In order to get into the air, you have to take off. I know how to take off, and you're paying me to teach you how, isn't that right?"

"Yes," I replied meekly.

"Then let's go," he said.

By some stroke of luck, and a bit of help from Bill, we managed to become airborne. Once we had safely departed the traffic pattern, I looked at Bill and literally yelled, "I'm flying, Bill, I'm really flying!"

And in his wonderful old Oklahoman drawl, he responded, "Yep son, that you are."

On October 19, 1968, I became a licensed pilot. It was my mother's birthday. I was eighteen. I think she was proud of me, but I'm not sure she saw my accomplishment as the perfect birthday present. I had opened the door to an exciting new life. What I didn't know was how exciting it was about to become; I'm certain if my mom had known where it was to lead me, she would have been far less pleased.

Chapter 2

"Welcome to the Army"

My actual date of enlistment was November 24, 1968. I had enlisted in the delayed entry program so I could attend my brother's December wedding in Newport News, Virginia. On January 7, 1969, I reported to the Armed Forces Examining and Entrance Station in Los Angeles. My parents took the day off to drive me down and spend what time they could with me. The day was spent filling out forms, getting identification cards, and various and sundry other things that only the military could come up with.

At 4:00 P.M. we were ushered into a room where we were handed tickets and briefed on the arrangements that had been made for our travel to Fort Polk, Louisiana. All Warrant Officer Candidates completed basic training at Polk, probably because it was the closest basic training center to Fort Wolters in Mineral Wells, Texas, the Army's primary helicopter center and school.

Transport to Los Angeles International (LAX) would be by military transport, which turned out to be a chartered Los Angeles Rapid Transit Authority bus.

I asked whether I could ride with my folks and was told, "Son, you're in the Army now. You go when the Army tells you, where the Army tells you, and how the Army tells you. You got that?"

Our itinerary included an ordinary scheduled flight to Houston's Hobby Airport on a Continental Airlines red-eye special, connecting to a Trans Texas Airways (TTA) vintage Douglas DC3 to Lake Charles, Louisiana, where we would once again be met by military transport for the trip to Fort Polk.

My folks followed the bus down the Santa Monica Freeway to the San Diego Freeway, and ultimately to LAX. At ten o'clock, they decided that they should start the hour-plus drive home.

My father looked very proud as I hugged and kissed my mother. He knew what I was about to encounter, and he respected my decision to enlist. Dad shook my hand and pulled me toward him. He hugged me very tight, kissed me, and, choking back the tears, whispered, "I love you, babe. Don't volunteer for anything."

"I love you too, Dad," I told him and smiled at his last bit of fatherly advice.

After Mom and Dad departed, I rejoined the other ten WOCs and we made our way to the gate. The flight was scheduled to depart at 12:40 A.M. The gate area was dark and void of human life. We sat and talked, trying to get to know one another, while we waited for someone to show up to check us in.

About midnight an agent came along. We were all pretty tired by now. We had reported in at 7:00 A.M. that morning and it was now approaching midnight. Most of us had been up since before five o'clock; it had made for a very long day.

The airline agent told us at check-in that it would be free seating. We could choose any seat we wanted once we got on the airplane.

Once on the airplane, we all chose window seats in different rows, so we could either stretch out or look out the windows. Besides the eleven of us, there were only a few other passengers on the airplane.

After landing in Houston we entered the second deserted terminal that we had been in that day, made our way to the TTA counter, and learned that our flight didn't depart until 7:30 A.M. Two hours to kill. We parked ourselves on the closest benches we could find and promptly fell asleep.

Awakened by the arrival of hundreds of travelers, we realized we had slept through the first and second calls for our flight. Still half-asleep, we made our way to an old DC3 just as the number two engine belched itself to life. The smoke from the burning oil drifted over the top of the airplane and meshed with the same as the pilot started number one. I had barely sat down as we began to taxi toward the runway, and was asleep again before we reached it.

Dean Scanlon, our travel group leader, awoke me as the aircraft came to a halt on the ramp at Lake Charles.

A big sign greeted us as we entered the terminal, "All military personnel proceeding to Fort Polk, check in at the Military Affairs Desk."

A black sergeant sat at the desk reading a *Playboy* through mirrored sunglasses. He jumped up as we approached, covering the magazine with a big manila envelope, and asked, "You guys aren't going to Puke, are ya?"

"Pardon me?" Dean responded.

"Puke. Are you guys going to Puke?"

Dean gave us a puzzled look before answering. "No, sir, none of us are sick. Just a little tired."

The sergeant laughed. "Don't call me 'sir,' asswipe. Polk. Are you going to Fort Polk?"

When Dean responded that we were indeed going to Fort Polk, the sergeant launched into a tirade, "Fuckin' A man. Why don't them cocksuckers up on post ever tell me a motherfuckin' thing? Son of a bitch. Shit guys, I'm sorry, but the van just left for post. You'll have to wait till I can call him and get him back down here."

"How long will that be?" we asked.

"Well, let's see," said the sergeant, "He only left ten minutes ago. It'll take him another hour and five to get there, twenty minutes fiddle fuckin' around, get gas, and then back to the office. If them bastards will answer their fucking phone, I could probably have him back here in, say, three hours."

"Three hours! What the hell are we supposed to do for three hours," we asked.

"Hey guys, I don't run the fucking Army. I just work here," replied the sergeant defensively. "You guys should probably go kiss the ground till he gets back. I mean, hey, you just survived a flight on Tree Top Airways! Yep, I'd go kiss the ground."

"Can we go get something to eat?" Dean asked.

"Sure man. As long as you got some bread to pay for it," came the sarcastic response.

"We don't," answered Dean, obviously annoyed.

"Tough shit," smiled the sergeant.

Turning to leave, the sergeant laughed, "Oh, by the way, welcome to the Army."

Fort Polk is an immense piece of real estate in southwestern Louisiana and was one of the primary basic combat training (BCT) centers.

When we arrived, we were taken to the reception center, where we remained for several days before being assigned to a BCT company. During our stay there, we were given our first military haircut and were issued uniforms and dog tags. We filled out insurance and other forms, and were given our first shots. Beyond that, we were free to do pretty much as we pleased so long as we did not leave the confines of the area.

Soon the day arrived when I was assigned to C-4-1: Charlie Company, Fourth Battalion, First Basic Combat Training Brigade. We fell into formation outside the billets and were confronted by a group of drill sergeants. They divided us up into platoons and our drill sergeant, a guy by the name of Anthony Albritton, introduced himself with a very sinister looking smile.

"Welcome to C-4-1 troops," he hollered. "You are now nothing but a bunch of pussies. I have been given the task of turning you girls into soldiers and I have eight weeks in which to accomplish that task. That means we are going to work long and hard, and ladies, you have not yet learned the definition of those words."

He stared holes through each and every one of us before screaming, "Let's get started, ladies! Ten-hut! Left face! Forward March!"

He marched our gaggle to the company area on South Fort where we were met by the company commander (CO), 1st Lt. James A. FitzRoy, 1st Sgt. (TOP) Jimmy Peacock, and Senior Drill Sergeant Henry Strong. We stood for an hour or so listening to announcements before the CO announced, "Okay Troops, I need four volunteers." Remembering my dad's advice I stood still and kept my mouth shut. Once the requisite number of volunteers stepped forward, the CO told us, "Now I suppose before you left your mommies and daddies they told you not to volunteer for anything, didn't they? Well, these four brave gentlemen will be driving the aid vehicles while the rest of you dogs march for the next eight weeks."

Basic training meant getting up at 4:00 A.M. and going non-stop until 9:00 P.M. The day normally started out with the bitch box, a speaker system on each floor of each billet throughout the company area, announcing "Formation. Formation."

The first week of basic was nothing but orientations, classes, and lots of physical training (PT). We had classes on military justice, military courtesy, history of the Army, traditions and achievements, safety, and dozens of other subjects. We also received six shots administered with an air gun, simultaneously, and they hurt like hell. We donated a pint of blood and tried to acclimatize to the cold, icy winds.

We were getting to know Sergeant Albritton pretty well by this time. He was a nice guy until you pissed him off. By the end of the first week of training, we were already hearing rumors about pushing us through training because Fort Polk's capacity wasn't big enough to accommodate the number of incoming trainees.

Subsisting on Army chow became a struggle. The chow was pretty good, but the quantities they gave us were barely adequate for our appetites, and we had a whole five minutes in which to eat what little we had. A typical breakfast consisted of a bowl of oatmeal, two slices of French toast, two eggs, corn beef hash on toast (the famous "shit on a shingle"), an orange, and two glasses of milk. It sounds like a lot, but we were usually hungry an hour after we ate. In retrospect I guess I wasn't starving, because I gained fifteen pounds the first three weeks I was there!

By the end of January, I was getting to like BCT more each day; perhaps because it was getting a bit easier as we fell into a routine.

I maintained a positive attitude as I adjusted to military life. I wrote to my folks *"I know that I'm here to do a job and I'm going to do it the best way I can. There were millions of others who wore the same uniform I'm wearing today, including you. Men laughed, cried, fought, and died in it, and you'd better believe that I'm damn proud to be wearing it. I just hope that I can do it as much justice as those who wore it before me."* At that point I had even contemplated making the military my career.

On February 3 those of us who were destined for flight school were released from training to go for our Class One flight physicals, the last major hurdle between us and flight school. There was plenty of anxiety that morning. A no-go on any portion of the physical meant that we were unfit to fly and when we returned to the company area we would be presented with a list of alternatives that did not include flying.

The physical lasted for most of the day, and they examined and tested virtually every major system in the human body. We went from station to station where they took our height and weight, our temperature and blood pressure, and checked our pulse. We had blood tests, x-rays, dental checks, urine studies, EKGs, EEGs, and eye exams of every type imaginable.

Throughout the whole examination almost nothing was said. I listened to every sigh and watched every raise of the eyebrow, desperate for a sign or signal of some sort. But nothing . . .

At the last station, they dilated my eyes. The light was blinding. When the doctor had finished with the eye exam I asked, "When will I know?"

"Know what?" he asked.

"If I passed or not."

"Hasn't anybody said anything to you?" he asked.

"No, nothing. Not a word from anybody," I told him.

"It'll be a few days until you get word officially. There is some lab work that has to be completed but if nobody has said anything you've probably passed."

Graduation was still a rumored event by this time. The word was that they were trying to accelerate our training in order to graduate us early.

I kept pretty good tabs on what was happening at home. Homesickness was one of the new and unpleasant feelings that I was experiencing for the first time in my life. My parents wrote often, probably in their effort to keep from missing me so much, and my friends wrote to tell me about college life, who they were balling, and life in general.

I called home every Sunday morning from one of the pay phones near the company area. Sometimes the queues were so long we had to take turns running back to the billets to regain some of the body heat that the wind had robbed.

One night after the training day was over, the bitch box crackled to life, "Private Zahn, Private Zahn. Report to the orderly room immediately, IMMEDI-ATELY!" I stood looking at the box high up on the wall above the stairs, wondering what I could have done to warrant such an invitation.

Recovering from my bewilderment, I grabbed my hat and double-timed it down the road to the orderly room. To say I was surprised when I entered would be the ultimate understatement. Pacing around the floor was not only Sergeant Albritton, but also the company commander, Lieutenant FitzRoy, and the battalion commander, Lt. Col. George W. Barnitt. Lieutenant FitzRoy kept looking out the window and muttering, "Nope!"

I asked Sergeant Albritton what was going on and he told me that I wasn't in trouble but the brigade commander, Col. A. Lemberes, was on his way over to speak to me.

The brigade commander! I was scared shitless! I had never even seen a real colonel, much less spoken to one.

When Colonel Lemberes arrived, he was directed to Lieutenant FitzRoy's office and asked me to step inside. "Private Zahn reporting as ordered, sir!" I saluted. Returning my salute the colonel offered me a seat. He told me that the post commander, Maj. Gen. Charles M. Mount, had asked him to come down and speak to me. For about thirty minutes he commended me on my outstanding attitude toward the Army.

After we were assigned to a BCT company, a form letter went out to all families telling them which company we had been assigned to and included emergency numbers, and other information. All of them had the post commander's signature on them, although I'm sure he never saw them. My dad responded to the letter and wrote to General Mount. In his letter he included the previous excerpt from the letter that I had written my folks. Because of this, General Mount sent the colonel down to see me.

We talked and both asked and answered many questions. When he had finished praising me for my attitude and patriotism, he asked whether I had any complaints about my training. Talk about opening up Pandora's box!

"Well, sir," I replied, "the only complaint I have is that I don't think we are given an adequate amount to eat at meals, and what we do get, we don't get enough time to eat!"

Colonel Lemberes asked for an explanation, and I told him that we were given only five minutes from the time we entered the mess hall until we had to be out the back door. He responded that he would see to it, shook my hand, and before he departed said, "Private Zahn, if there is anything I can do for you, anything at all, during your stay at Fort Polk, please do not hesitate to get in touch with me."

I thanked him, saluted, and he disappeared out the door.

As I left the CO's office, Lieutenant FitzRoy asked, "Private Zahn. What in the hell was that all about?"

I replied, "Not much, sir. Colonel Lemberes just stopped by to see how I was doing and say hello."

"Is that so?" Lieutenant FitzRoy responded. "Was that all?"

"Yes, sir. Goodnight, sir," I said, saluting.

The next morning at breakfast there was a noticeable difference in the pace of the line. While waiting to enter the mess hall, I was tapped on the shoulder. Looking around, I came to attention. It was Lieutenant FitzRoy.

"Private Zahn, may I have a word with you please?"

"Yes, sir," I responded as I left my place in line.

"Private Zahn, may I ask that in the future if you have a complaint you bring it to me before you go see the brigade commander?"

"Excuse me, sir," I corrected, "but I didn't go see the brigade commander. He came to see me."

Not altogether happy with my response, Lieutenant FitzRoy asked, "Is there anything else I need to know about your conversation last night?"

I replied emphatically, "Only that if I had any problems with anything here at Fort Polk that I was to get in touch with him immediately. If that will be all, sir, may I be excused for breakfast?"

"Dismissed, Private" Lieutenant FitzRoy saluted. "You smart ass!"

When the rest of the company was made aware that due to my conversation with the brigade commander, our portions were increased and sufficient time would be allowed to eat, a seemingly impossible coup, they gave me a nickname that would stay with me throughout Vietnam: "Superjew!"

Within a few days we were on our way to bivouac, the last major training objective of basic. It was a field exercise where we lived in tents, and during the night the drill sergeants and other members of the cadre took on the role of insurgents and attacked us. During these attacks, tear gas, grenades (with fuses only), smoke bombs, artillery simulators, blanks in our M14s, and flares added to the reality of the combat.

Usually these war games turned out to be quite a lot of fun. It was like playing John Wayne; but one night one of the flares started a forest fire. We had to run a quarter of a mile through the woods and swamp, in the pitch-black night, to get to it. It took the entire company of 225 men four hours to extinguish the blaze.

When we awoke the next morning, an announcement was made that we would be graduating on March 14. We had less than two weeks to go.

Preparing for graduation was an exciting time, but I had mixed emotions. I was happy it was over, but at the same time I hated to see it end. I enjoyed BCT and I had learned an awful lot about myself in those two months.

Some of the guys counted classes, some counted PT sessions, and one even kept track of every push-up he had done during basic. I kept track of something else. We were graduating with twenty-one injections.

The day before the event, the KP roster was posted and much to my dismay I was on it. I would not be able to participate in the graduation ceremonies. After all of the work we did to arrive at this milestone, the thought of washing dishes made my blood boil. I asked to speak to Sergeant Albritton and told him that he was free to court-martial me or give me an Article 15 (non-judicial punishment), but I refused to do KP that day.

Sergeant Albritton told me that graduation was no big deal. "All they're going to do is march around the parade field as you've done so many times before," he said trying to cheer me up.

I said, "I don't care. I worked my butt off with my friends to make it through BCT, and I plan to be on the parade field with them tomorrow." I was.

Chapter 3

Sir Candidate

Greyhound provided military transportation for the trip to Fort Wolters. The buses departed Polk early on Monday, March 18, for the six-hour drive across western Louisiana and eastern Texas.

We stopped somewhere east of Dallas and were provided a contract lunch at a Holiday Inn. It was a vast improvement over what we had become used to at Polk. Two hours after lunch, we turned off U.S. Highway 180 under the arch that marked our entrance to Fort Wolters, Texas, and the U.S. Army Primary Helicopter Center in Mineral Wells.

Wolters began life in 1921 as a training camp for the Fifty-sixth Cavalry Brigade of the Texas National Guard. In October of 1940, the seventy-five hundred-acre camp was leased to the War Department and became an Infantry Replacement Training Center.

The camp was officially turned over to the Army on March 22, 1941, and became the largest Infantry Replacement Training Center in the nation. Following the end of World War II, the flag was lowered for the last time on August 15, 1946.

After the war, Wolters was purchased by a group of local businessmen and converted into a thriving industrial center. For the next five years it operated as Camp Wolters Enterprises, Inc.

Early in 1951, the Air Force was looking for a home base for the aviation engineers and the camp was reactivated as Wolters Air Force Base. In March of 1956 the Secretary of the Army, Wilbur M. Bruckner, visited the base with a group of Defense Department and Army officials for an inspection of the facilities. The wheels were in motion and on July 1, 1956, control of the base was transferred to the Army to embark on its new mission: training helicopter pilots.

On September 26 of that year, the Primary Helicopter School became an official U.S. Army School and the first class reported for training on November 26. There were thirty-five students, all warrant officers. They graduated on April 27, 1957.

In 1957, the center had a fleet of 125 helicopters to meet its training requirements.

On June 1, 1963, the installation was redesignated as Fort Wolters, thus becoming a permanent military installation. Soon after, it was designated the U.S. Army Primary Helicopter Center.

To meet the growing demand for pilots necessitated by our involvement in Vietnam, several expansion programs took place and besides the main heliport on the fort, Downing Army Heliport was built adjacent to the Mineral Wells Airport. Downing had parking space for three hundred helicopters, but still the demand outgrew the facilities.

In January of 1968, Dempsey Army Heliport was constructed on a plateau west of Mineral Wells. It accommodated a further five hundred aircraft bringing the total training fleet to more than eleven hundred helicopters.

The twenty-week curriculum that I was going to follow was that of the Warrant Officer Rotary Wing Aviator Course (WORWAC). Originally, the curriculum was set up so that the first four weeks were the WOC Indoctrination Training Course, or Officer Development classes. As the Army became more comfortable with the entire curriculum, the first four weeks became known as pre-flight; primary helicopter training without a helicopter!

For a week after arriving at Wolters, I was what was known as a "snowbird." Snowbirds came in various forms. Some were candidates who had either not started flight school yet or had graduated and were awaiting transport to one of the advanced flight training schools. Others had washed out and were awaiting reassignment. Still more were setbacks in need of additional training.

The liberties we were afforded compared with Polk were a real culture shock. We could actually leave the company area to go to the Post Exchange or WOC Club almost at will.

One of my first visits was to the bookstore to buy some stationery with the school crest and a picture of a helicopter on it. I couldn't wait to write home.

Wolters used three different types of helicopters: the Hughes TH-55A Osage, the Hiller TH-23 Raven, and the Bell TH-13 Sioux. Which one you flew depended upon one thing . . . how tall you were.

I knew so much about helicopters upon my arrival, I bought stationery with a TH-23 on it and told my folks it was a TH-55!

It wasn't until two weeks after our arrival at Wolters that we were assigned to training companies. On April 2, I was assigned to Headquarters and First Warrant Officer Candidate Company (First WOC), red hats, "The Big Red One."

We were bussed from the snowbird billets up the hill to First WOC with all of our gear. As the buses came to a halt alongside the billets, a tac officer approached. He was quite tall and had red hair and a face full of freckles from the Texas sun. He stood menacingly at the exit in his starched khaki uniform, highly polished gloss black helmet, and mirrored sunglasses.

Screaming at the top of his lungs, he ordered us "OFF THE BUS, OFF THE BUS. MOVE, MOVE, MOVE!" All the time while he was yelling at us he slapped a swagger stick against his right knee with a loud crack.

As I disembarked from the bus, the tac yelled in my face, "You better get a move on, Candidate!"

"Yes, sir," I replied.

"WHAT DID YOU SAY, CANDIDATE?" he screamed.

I stopped dead in my tracks. "Yes, sir," I repeated, confused.

"Candidate, you're in flight school now," he yelled from about one inch in front of my face, "and in flight school the first two words out of your mouth had better be sir, candidate. DO YOU UNDERSTAND?"

"Yes, sir," I yelled.

"WHAT DID YOU SAY?" he screamed again.

"SIR, CANDIDATE. YES, SIR!" I replied.

"SIR, CANDIDATE WHAT? What is your name, scum?" the tac officer asked.

I was beginning to get the picture. "Sir, Candidate Zahn, ZAHN SIR!"

The tac officer backed away and smiled. "Candidate Zahn, huh?" he inquired.

Relieved a bit that he had got out of my face, I replied, "Yes, sir."

"YES, SIR!" he screamed. "Drop down and knock out twenty-five push-ups, you miserable slime. SIR, CANDIDATE, SIR, CANDIDATE, SIR, CANDI-DATE," he repeated. "DO YOU UNDERSTAND?"

As I was doing my push-ups I had finally got the message. "Sir, Candidate Zahn. Yes, sir. I understand, sir."

"Good," said the tac officer. "Now get on your feet, grab your gear, and get into formation."

"Sir, Candidate Zahn. Yes, sir."

The tac officer snickered, "Very good, Candidate Zahn, very good. I have your name now slime ball and we'll meet again. Now get."

Without a response, I grabbed my gear and joined the formation. I had just been introduced to stress training.

Our days in pre-flight began at 4:30 A.M. and went straight through until lights-out at 10:00 P.M. Throughout the day we had classes, physical training, more classes, and finally a mandatory study hall from 7:00 until 8:30 P.M.

During our four weeks of pre-flight, we studied aircraft systems, aerodynamics, meteorology, flight rules and regulations, radio procedures, and various other aviation-related topics. These were interspersed with Officer Development (OD) classes that were essential to our development as officers.

The officer students who formed part of our class had been to an Officer Candidate School (OCS), so they were attending flight school, living in government quarters, and drawing twenty-five dollars per day Temporary Duty allowance (TDY) along with their regular pay. We, on the other hand, were in effect doing our OCS simultaneously with our flight training. Inspections were the routine and we operated on the merit/demerit system, mostly demerits! Underwear and T-shirts had to be rolled with no creases and were to be rolled six inches long—no longer and no shorter. Socks had to be rolled into small rectangular frames that we constructed from cardboard; the top drawer had to be pulled out six inches and the bottom drawer twelve inches, exactly. The doors to our closets had to be opened to ninety degrees from the wall. There had to be even space between each and every hanger in the closet, and all of the sleeves of our shirts and jackets had to be turned out so that the patches could be seen.

Beds were made so a quarter could be bounced off of them; shoes lined up parallel with the long line of the bed and spit-shined so your name could be read in them in a bent-over position. Laundry bags were to be hung at the end of the bed, and the drawstrings wrapped around the frame evenly, with no twists in the string, and tied in a prescribed manner. Razor blades were to be free of hair, shaving cream, and water spots—the sink free of the same—towels hung free of wrinkles, and the concrete floor was to be spit-shined as well. This was accomplished using buffers, wax, ripped up old Army blankets, and alcohol.

If anything was out of order, dirty, wrinkled, out of alignment, or not as otherwise prescribed, demerits were awarded. The rooms were inspected daily after we had left for class, and sometimes again after we had returned from lunch and were off to the afternoon classes.

If a certain amount of demerits were issued, you kissed your post privileges or weekend pass good-bye.

Reveille was fifteen minutes before formation and at first, there just wasn't sufficient time to shit, shower, shave, and prepare the room for inspection prior to formation. Rooms were to be ready for inspection anytime we were not in them.

When we first arrived, we used to sneak around with flashlights making beds and attending to other matters. By the end of the first few weeks we had established a routine and we could be ready, with five minutes to spare. If we had spare time, we were urged to help our roommates. Teamwork was stressed to the maximum. We could do anything we wanted basically, as long as we all did it together. If any one candidate didn't participate, everybody but him got in trouble. The reasoning was that obviously that particular candidate didn't understand the necessity to operate as a team, and we had failed to get the message to him. Combat aviation is no place for loners.

Progress reports came out at the end of the pre-flight phase of training to let us know how we were progressing and to rank us against our fellow candidates. We saw our first washouts in the first few weeks of training. Some couldn't handle the academic workload, some couldn't cope with the regimen, and others just stressed out. I completed pre-flight with an overall average of 93.1 percent. I was in the top 5 percent of the class.

At Wolters, whenever we had a dance or social evening, girls used to be bused in from some of the surrounding colleges to accompany those candidates who were unmarried or didn't have a girlfriend. Denton College for Women was a favorite.

We would be in formation, and as the girls came off the bus we would be paired with whoever emerged from the bus as we proceeded to the door row by row. There was no way to know whom you would end up with or what she would look like. It was typical for the guys to throw five dollars in a kitty before the bus arrived. The one who ended up with the ugliest girl got all the money: "the pig pot." I'm sure the girls had a similar arrangement.

Chapter 4

"You Want to Kill Yourself?"

Primary flight training was broken into two phases, Primary One and Primary Two. Primary One was a basic introduction to the helicopter. It lasted for eight weeks and included fifty hours of actual flight time. During these fifty hours we were expected to learn how to hover, fly a traffic pattern, and learn all of the basic maneuvers and emergency procedures.

I was assigned to a TH-55A flight. The Aircraft Division of Hughes Tool Company designed the TH-55. Known as the Hughes 269 in the civilian market, it was a small, almost tiny aircraft powered by a 180-hp Lycoming piston engine. The cockpit sat two, side by side, and occupied most of the fuselage. The tail boom looked like a broomstick sticking out the back. The rotors were powered by seven fan belts, big rubber bands instead of the traditional transmission. It was small and sleek with a twenty-five-foot rotor diameter and a maximum speed of eighty-six miles per hour at sea level. It sounded like an angry hornet and those of us who flew this great little machine affectionately dubbed it the "Mattel Messer-schmitt."

Our instructors were civilian contract employees who worked for Southern Airways. We were to be flying out of Downing Army Heliport.

As we approached the heliport for the first time, a certain amount of anxiety and excitement was evident in the bus.

Each flight-training period began with a briefing in the classroom. During the briefing, our flight commander, Don Walgammott, would brief us on the weather, assign us aircraft, and tell which stagefield we would be operating from. The area around Fort Wolters was dotted with stagefields with Vietnamese names: An Khe, Chu Lai, Phu Loi. The stagefields consisted of three parallel runways or lanes, a parking area, and a control tower. Each runway had three helispots, and depending upon which maneuver or procedure you were practicing, the tower would assign a lane to you and a spot to land on. It was quite common to have twenty helicopters or more operating out of a stagefield at any given time.

The pace of Primary One was fast and furious, and we soon found out that the stress training carried over into the cockpit. I wish I had a dime for every time I got smacked over the helmet with a pointer.

19

Flying a helicopter is no easy task. It takes a lot of time and even more coordination to master. The helicopter has three basic controls. The cyclic stick, which sits between the pilot's legs, controls the rotor disc through three hundred and sixty degrees of travel. It is most often referred to as the control that allows movement fore and aft or right and left. The collective pitch is a lever to the left of the pilot, and this is raised or lowered to either increase or decrease the pitch in the rotor blades. In other words, it controls the rate of climb or descent. There are also two foot pedals, which control the anti-torque tail rotor at the rear of the helicopter.

Sir Isaac Newton deduced that for every action, there is an equal and opposite reaction; hence, without the tail rotor, while the rotor blades are turning in a counterclockwise direction, the fuselage would spin beneath them equally as fast in the opposite, or clockwise direction. To complicate matters, whenever the collective is raised, the blades tend to slow down due to the increased drag placed upon them by the increased pitch. To combat this, a twist grip–type throttle is placed on the end of the collective to compensate by adding or decreasing engine power, once again depending upon whether the pilot wishes to climb or descend. When power is added or the rotor RPM increased, the pedals must be moved in a coordinated fashion to keep the fuselage in line with the path of flight.

At the end of the collective, forward of the throttle, is a small control box, which, depending upon the type of aircraft, has several buttons, switches, or Chinese hats used to control the searchlight and its direction.

On the top of the cyclic is a grip that has one button for the intercom, another for the radio. It may have several other buttons for external cargo hooks or trim releases.

It is quite conceivable that while the feet are controlling the pedals, the right hand and right arm and the left hand and left arm might be working independently of one another but in coordination to control the aircraft.

We were given slightly less time than the average civilian helicopter student pilot to solo, but as my instructor, Hamilton Burtness, once told me, "We ain't got time to screw around with you kids!"

One of my two roommates washed out in the pre-solo stage. I returned to the room as he was clearing out his closet, tears streaming down his face. His disappointment was too great for him to hide.

I began to worry about myself at that point. I thought I was progressing quite well, but about a fourth of the class had soloed by now, and nothing had been said to indicate that I was ready, or even close to being ready.

During my next flight period, Mr. Burtness asked me to pick the aircraft up to a hover and set it back down. I did so . . . not as smoothly as I would have liked to, but what did he expect for seven hours of helicopter time?

CRACK! The pointer smacked my helmet as Mr. Burtness screamed into the intercom system, "GEEZUS CEERIST! Haven't you learned anything these past two weeks? You can't even put this machine back on the ground without giving me a whiplash!"

I was devastated to say the least. The thought of my roommate packing his gear was beginning to come too close to home. Mr. Burtness's sudden outburst had caught me totally off guard. He had never yelled at me like that before and I certainly was doing no worse than on my previous flight. Perhaps the problem was that I was doing no better either!

"Take me to the hover pattern," he instructed.

The hover pattern was a series of old car tires laid out in a pattern connected by white lines. The idea was to progress around the pattern with the aircraft moving frontward, backward, or sideways to the right or left, as instructed. The tires marked the spots where turns were to be made in order to keep the lines in sight. At all times we were to maintain a constant height, speed, alignment, and rotor RPM. Turns were to be made in a prescribed manner, either around the nose of the aircraft, the tail, or the mast.

After flying the pattern sideways to the right, I was ordered over to the parking lane. This was not a good sign so early in the period and I began to sweat.

Landing the little TH-55, Mr. Burtness looked at me and said, "You know what the Z in your name stands for, Candidate? Zero! You're a fucking zero." He continued, "You are going to kill somebody the way you fly and it ain't going to be me."

He unfastened his shoulder harness/seat belt combination and began to climb out of the aircraft. "You want to kill yourself? Kill yourself. I'll watch from the tower."

After his confidence-building performance I was supposed to go solo? My self-esteem was gone, but his tactic worked. I was so scared that I might really crash, at the same time determined to prove him wrong, that I didn't even know he wasn't in the aircraft with me, that's how focused I was.

After the first circuit, I landed and looked around but Mr. Burtness was nowhere in sight.

I sat on the spot for a short period of time when the radio crackled to life.

"Do it again," said Mr. Burtness.

I called for takeoff clearance and made two more circuits of the traffic pattern before I was told to park the aircraft and shut down. Mr. Burtness came out as the rotor blades stopped turning. He had a smile on his face and greeted me with a firm handshake. "Good job, Candidate Zahn, good job," he said while nodding his approval. My self-esteem had returned and I was thrilled that I had got past that hurdle.

After we left the heliport that evening to return to post, we made the obligatory stop at the Mineral Wells Holiday Inn. Tradition had it that when you soloed you were carried through an arch made from crossed rotor blades and were thrown into the pool, flight suit and all.

From the blades hung a sign that said "Through these rotor blades pass the best helicopter students in the world." It is still there.

After soloing, we were authorized to wear an orange disc under the WOC brass on our hats and an orange shoulder board on our uniforms. Our flight caps displayed a cloth set of wings with the letter "S" in their center. I was overcome with pride.

With the solo behind me, it was back to work mastering the aircraft. It goes without saying that the less you have to think about flying the helicopter, the more brain capacity you have to be aware of your surroundings and what is going on around you.

In Primary Two, we would have to be very aware of our surroundings, for this was the phase that made us put the aircraft to work.

We would soon be applying the basic skills we had learned to landing in unimproved sites called "confined areas," on pinnacles and slopes, flying in formation, night flying, and air navigation.

There were three types of confined areas that ranged from multiple-aircraft-sized fields to holes in the trees barely big enough to fit the rotor blades down through. The areas were designated by an old car tire placed in the landing area and painted white, orange, or red. White-tire areas were large and we were authorized to land in them while flying solo or with our stick buddies (i.e., other students who shared the same instructor). Orange-tire areas were somewhat smaller in size and we could use them for practice but only after we had been into the area with an instructor. Red-tire areas were there for instruction only.

The area surrounding Mineral Wells was literally covered with these tired areas, courtesy of local landowners.

Slopes were practiced to accommodate landing on a hillside or uneven ground and pinnacles to teach us the principles involved in landing the aircraft on high ground with barely enough area to accommodate the landing gear. Sometimes we had to balance on one skid, because the area was too small for both of them.

"Formation flight" is a maneuver that taught us precision flying. The leader must maintain his height, heading, and speed because the rest of the flight takes all of their cues from the lead aircraft.

Navigation was quite primitive. All we had were the basics . . . needle, ball, and airspeed, and to arrive at a given destination at a given time was calculated by flying time and distance. Fortunately most of the rural Texas towns have a big water tower with the name of the town painted on it. I don't know if this was done intentionally for the benefit of the student pilots, but it was not an uncommon sight to see helicopters hovering around water towers until the trainee pilot found himself on the map.

On July 17 after returning from our morning's flying, we had gathered in our classroom at the heliport for our daily de-briefing. At first the instructors were nowhere to be seen, but finally they came into the room with the flight commander. A hush fell across the room as the flight commander stood.

"Gentlemen, I have just been advised that there has been a crash and the aircraft may have been assigned to our flight. Is anybody missing?"

A big lump formed in my throat as I looked around the room. "St. Andre. Where's Mike?" someone asked.

One of the candidates asked the flight commander how bad the crash was. I will never forget the tears rolling down the commander's face as he announced very compassionately "Gentlemen, Candidate St. Andre is dead."

Michael St. Andre was the first of my classmates to be killed in a crash. He would not be the last.

Primary Two lasted eight weeks and provided us with an additional sixty hours of flying time. Graduation from the U.S. Army Primary Helicopter Center was a milestone for many, and a stepping-stone for most.

Four weeks prior to graduation, I found out that I wouldn't be going to Fort Rucker, Alabama, the U.S. Army Aviation School (USAAVNS), but to Hunter Army Airfield in Savannah, Georgia, where there was a USAAVNS Element to handle the overflow that Rucker could not accommodate.

At 2:00 P.M. on Friday afternoon, August 15, 1969, as a Red Hat of Warrant Officer Rotary Wing Aviator Course class 69-41, I had overcome my first hurdle on the way to receiving the silver wings of an Army aviator.

Chapter 5

"Where Are You Going?"

After six days I arrived at Hunter and signed in on Thursday morning, August 21. Hunter is a very picturesque installation with large trees full of Spanish moss. Apart from the airfield itself, the post reminded me of a college campus.

Hunter began as an unimproved "flying field" in 1928. In 1940, it was named after a young World War I ace, Lt. Col. Frank O'D Hunter, a native of Savannah. The field was acquired by the Army in 1941 and was the final staging ground for B-17 crews on their deployment to Europe. It was returned to the city after the war until the Air Force came back in 1949 after swapping Hunter for Chatham Air Force Base, the county's military airfield, which had proved insufficient for military use.

The Strategic Air Command (SAC) occupied the field until April 1963 when command was handed over to the Military Air Transport Service (MATS). When the Air Force announced they were moving out of Hunter in 1967, the field was scheduled to be deactivated, but that decision was reversed when the Army once again took command to establish the United States Army Aviation School Element Headquarters.

After signing in to Warrant Officer Candidate Company D, I was assigned a room and told to be in formation at 2:00 P.M. sharp.

At Wolters we had all heard horror stories about Hunter. The tacs had told us that Savannah was a nice place to be stationed and for the privilege that we were being afforded, we would pay for it! Standards were said to be higher than Rucker's and the washout rate was twice as high.

As we assembled in formation, our tac officer approached us along with a tac sergeant. A tac sergeant was new to all of us. Both were dressed like the tacs at Wolters, in immaculately starched khakis with their signature gloss black helmets. The tac officer brought us to attention. "Gentlemen, welcome to Hunter Army Airfield and Warrant Officer Candidate Company D. Prepare your rooms for inspection as you did at Wolters. I will make corrections as I see fit. There will be no demerits for the first three days. If there are no questions, I'll see you in formation Monday morning at zero four thirty. Have a nice weekend!"

The two of them turned and walked away as we all stood in shock. Was this the same Army that we had left in Texas?

Hunter not only looked like a college campus, but it was very much like one. Aside from our flying, we had classes, homework, and tests, but when we were done for the day we took off for Savannah Beach.

Our first four weeks of flight training at Hunter was the basic instruments (BI) phase. We would be flying the Bell TH-13T, a helicopter with a great big Plexiglas bubble and an open tail. My instructor was a German exchange pilot named Wolfred Neubauer.

BI was all about learning to fly without visual reference. The student's side of the bubble was whited out to prohibit seeing out of the aircraft to the front or the right, and a screen was placed between the student pilot and the instructor in the left seat. To ensure that the student couldn't see out, a hood was worn on the helmet visors that restricted the field of view to the instrument panel only.

The aircraft was equipped with instruments to tell whether the helicopter was straight and level, in a turn, climbing or descending, the airspeed, altitude, heading, and all of the pertinent instruments to monitor engine and rotor parameters.

The only thing we were never taught about this aircraft was how to start it! Mr. Neubauer started the aircraft, did all of the checks, hovered out to our takeoff pad, and then handed the controls over to me to perform an instrument takeoff (ITO).

BI was just that, basic. Mastering the helicopter was quite an ordeal, and just when I thought I had reached a certain level of competence, I was once again made to feel inept and my self-esteem and confidence quickly eroded.

Within two weeks of beginning BI, some of the candidates began to disappear again. Some were set back in classes for additional training and some washed out.

Instrument flying is not like flying visually. A pilot has to ignore the senses and believe the instruments. Actually, that's good advice generally, whether you can see or not. After coming to grips with the general handling of the aircraft under instrument conditions, the next four-week phase, advanced instruments (AI), would be to once again put the basic skills into practical use and learn how to fly instrument approaches and navigate by instruments.

The instrument airways and stagefields were, like Wolters, named after airfields in Vietnam, and the airway adopted the name of the main instrument corridor in South Vietnam, Blue Two.

Just prior to takeoff, Air Traffic Control would issue a clearance telling us what altitude to climb to, what routing we would take, and so forth.

About midway through AI, I was given a clearance to "Maintain runway heading until climbing through five hundred feet. Turn left radar heading one zero zero, climb and maintain two thousand feet to Skidaway Intersection. Blue Two to An Khe."

This was a fairly straightforward clearance and one I had been given before. I read it back to the controller for confirmation.

The takeoff was fine and I climbed to five hundred feet before turning to a heading of one hundred degrees. I continued climbing to two thousand feet and leveled off waiting for the needle on my navigation instrument to center indicating I had arrived at Skidaway. Everything was going fine, Skidaway was identified, and I made the mandatory position report. It was all downhill from there.

I continued to fly cheerfully enough, until Mr. Neubauer asked, "Where are you going?"

"Up Blue Two," I responded. A leading question like this most always indicated that something wasn't right.

I began to scan my instruments more closely and noticed an abnormal indication on my main navigation instrument. It should have been indicating a centralized needle, but it was deflected all the way to the left.

Again the question came, "Where are you going?"

I began to get quite uncomfortable because I didn't have a clue where I was or how I got there.

Mr. Neubauer asked, "Where's Blue Two?"

I immediately responded, "I'm on it."

"Look at your instruments," Mr. Neubauer coached before repeating, "Where's Blue Two?"

I was becoming very confused and flustered at this point and asked him to take control of the aircraft while I tried to find myself. He took the controls maintaining our heading and altitude as I continued in total confusion.

After several minutes I finally had to admit defeat. "I'm lost, sir," I said.

"Okay, take off your hood and look outside," authorized Mr. Neubauer.

I did as he said and looked out my window. Blue, nothing but blue, but it wasn't the sky! We were a mile or two out over the Atlantic Ocean heading east.

Mr. Neubauer smiled and said, "I appreciate your wanting to take me home, but we haven't got enough fuel to make the other side. I suggest we turn around."

The funny thing was that at this point I still had no idea how I had screwed things up so badly. We shouldn't have been anywhere near the coast.

During the post-flight de-brief Mr. Neubauer explained. "Your takeoff was splendid. You climbed to five hundred feet as instructed and turned onto your assigned heading for the intercept. Your instrument scan was fine and you were right on the money when you identified Skidaway."

"Then how did we get over the Atlantic?" I queried, still puzzled.

"Your identification was fine, Candidate Zahn," continued Mr. Neubauer, "but once you got there, you forgot to turn to track up Blue Two, you dumb shit!" It was said in a manner that was meant to be funny but I failed to see the humor. It goes without saying that this was not one of my better performances. I was given a failure report for the day's flight.

The ability to fly on instruments was not only required, but also essential to longevity. I appreciated that point, but that appreciation gave me no love of doing it. October 15 was my final instrument check-ride. The long, tough, rough road was finally over and I was awarded my Tactical Instrument rating.

Upon completion of instrument training, we were once again given progress reports that indicated our standing in the class. I was in the top ten percent, which in most cases meant that I would be offered advanced schooling upon graduation. Which school it would be depended on allocations at graduation time.

Instrument training marked the end of the worries about washing out. Once we had progressed through instruments, one really had to screw up to get thrown out. By this time, the bottom line was that Uncle Sam had too much time and far too much money invested in us to allow us to depart.

We were now senior candidates and were treated like officers. No more "Sir, Candidate" and the candidates junior to us had to salute and call us "sir."

Contact training began the following Monday. This is what we had all been looking forward to for all these months. It meant that there would be no more going back to the bottom and looking up. It seemed every time we had completed a phase of training, and were at a peak, we fell back to the bottom of the valley and had to begin the long hard climb all over again. Contact was our introduction to the infamous Bell UH-1 Iroquois family of helicopter, the "Huey."

The Huey was the first turbine-powered helicopter that we had encountered, and I'm sure I speak for all who have ever flown this aircraft when I say I developed an immediate love affair with the Huey.

It was big and powerful and had a wonderful feel to it. The sound of a Huey will always be indelibly etched into my brain. The WHOP WHOP WHOP of the blades is better than a symphony.

Contact was a four-week phase of training. Everything we had learned up to this point was now honed to perfection in the Huey. All that we learned in the eight weeks of Primary One, in the TH-55, was relearned in a week in the Huey. The next three weeks were spent doing all of the Primary Two maneuvers in the Huey, with the addition of training in hauling internal loads and carrying external loads beneath the aircraft. Because this was the aircraft that most of us would be flying in Vietnam, we became very intimate with it.

The final weeks of flight school were broken into two phases, Tactics and Tac-X. Tactics was a two-week phase that, as its name implied, taught us the art of employing the Huey in tactical roles.

Tac-X, on the other hand, was a weeklong field exercise. We would be operating as an "Assault Helicopter Company" somewhere on Fort Stewart, Hunter's neighbor installation. There was an air of excitement as we prepared for the week. We would be living in the field, away from the barracks, with no more worries about demerits and inspections.

Unfortunately, Tac-X didn't get off to a stellar beginning. One of the aircraft from our officer class went into the trees inverted, killing Capt. Daniel H. Plemmons and his instructor, Capt. Stanley B. Albert. The other student, Lt. William A. Warren, was in serious condition with first-degree burns over sixty-five percent of his body. Lieutenant Warren died a few days later. This was a grim reminder to all of us that although we were now having lots of fun, tactical aviation was no game.

Our week in the field was great. Each day we were assigned a different mission enabling us to employ the aircraft in different combat roles. One day we flew troops around and inserted them in a landing zone (LZ), picking them up later in a different area, a pickup zone (PZ). The next we might be assigned ash and trash missions (logistics), command and control, medevac, or even the role of a gunship. Each day was different and exciting. Thursday was our last flying day as student pilots.

Friday was spent in open-air classrooms and the subject was "escape and evasion" (E&E). Funny how they saved this for last! The classes we attended addressed the terms of the Geneva Convention, the identification of booby traps, what plants and animals we might like to consider eating in a survival situation and how to prepare them, a review of land navigation, and how to conceal ourselves from an enemy.

We were grouped into teams of four, two officer students and two WOCs. Around five o'clock in the evening we were given either a live rabbit or a live chicken and some fresh garden vegetables. We got a chicken and some carrots! With them came the greeting, "Here's dinner gentlemen. Enjoy it!" Talk about fending for yourselves.

After dinner (and I use the term loosely) we sat in our teams as the E&E instructor went over our instructions for the remainder of the training. There was one starting point and four finish points. Each team had to negotiate their way from the starting point along one of several different routes to their assigned finish points. Each member of the team was given an individual piece of equipment; one had the map, one a flashlight, one a compass, and one a canteen full of water. The object was to negotiate our way through the course.

Against us was the cold. December 7 in southern Georgia is anything but warm. The temperature averaged about forty degrees Fahrenheit. The distance between the start point and the finish point was five kilometers and we would be anything from knee-deep to chest-deep in swamps. There were mosquitoes, snakes, and alligators in the swamps, and a ranger company from Fort Stewart that was acting as the aggressors. Their mission was to try to stop us from reaching our objective; the exercise was to begin thirty minutes after official sunset.

Let it be said that it was one of the coldest, most miserable nights I have ever spent in my life. My team arrived at our objective a little after two in the morning. We had evaded capture, were soaking wet, covered in mud, tired, hungry, freezing cold, and absolutely elated!

We were given some sandwiches and hot soup and the buses were running with the heat going full-blast. As soon as a bus full of candidate/officers had arrived, we were taken back to Hunter, arriving there about 5:00 A.M.

We spent most of the weekend packing up our belongings. We would be moving off-post into hotels for no other reason than we were allowed to.

There is a policy in the Army that one must be an officer before one can be an aviator. On Monday, December 15, we graduated from the Warrant Officer Candidate course and were awarded our bars and warrants as Reserve Warrant Officer, grade one (WO1) of the Army under Title 10, United States Code, Section 591 and Section 597. A formal graduation party was held that night at the Officer's Club. We did look sharp in our dress-blue uniforms.

Tuesday, December 16, 1969, 9:00 A.M., Warrant Officer Rotary Wing Aviator Course Class 69-41 became the last graduating class of the year and the decade. My father pinned on my silver wings and I had never felt a greater sense of accomplishment and pride in my life. I had made it.

Chapter 6

Deadeye Dickhead

Having graduated in the top ten percent of my flight school class, I was offered advanced training . . . for a price. Depending on the number of allocations I could select from Chinooks, Medevac, or Cobras. All I had to do was sign a contract agreeing to change my status to Voluntary Indefinite (Vol Indef) in exchange for the additional training.

I flew in a Chinook up to Fort Sill, Oklahoma, while in training at Wolters and wasn't real impressed. Besides that, they make a damn big target. Medevac was given serious thought, but the glory of saving lives didn't override my nineteen-year-old desire to stay alive myself. The Cobra, on the other hand, was the aircraft that made me enlist for flight school in the first place.

The Bell 209, or AH-1G Huey Cobra, as the Army designated it, was the first attack helicopter in the world.

The concept of the armed helicopter was first investigated in 1963 with the OH-13X, the Sioux Scout. This was a highly modified tandem-seat version of the OH-13, the observation model of the TH-13 that I had flown in instrument training. With Vietnam escalating, the armed variant was urgently required, and in the interim, the HU-1 was modified to carry two machine guns and sixteen air-to-surface rockets. HU-1 was the designation given the Iroquois and it was this designation that began the popular nickname of Huey.

Thirteen HU-1As were modified and flown in combat by the Army Utility Tactical Transport Helicopter Company.

It wasn't until 1962, under a tri-service designation scheme, that these aircraft were redesignated the UH-1A and UH-1B, respectively. Even after the redesignation, however, the name "Huey" stuck. While the UH-1s were proving themselves in Vietnam, the Army forged ahead with the advanced aerial fire support system (AAFSS), which gave birth to Lockheed's AH-56A Cheyenne. The Cheyenne was a hybrid aircraft, big, powerful, agile, and very costly.

The Cobra evolved from the Huey family of aircraft. It had the wide-chord rotor blades of the UH-1C, along with its transmission system and the more powerful fourteen hundred horsepower Lycoming T-53-L-13 turbine engine.

Unlike the Huey, the Cobra has a very narrow, sleek fuselage. The widest point of the fuselage is only three feet two inches. I say unlike the Huey, but in many ways they were alike; eighty percent of their components were interchangeable.

The Cobra could carry a wide array of weapons systems on its stubby wings, and has a turret under the nose of the aircraft. The turret could deflect 107.5 degrees right and left of center, could shoot down at an angle of 50 degrees, and the upward deflection varied from 10.6 to 18 degrees depending on where you were shooting. This variance prevented the co-pilot from shooting off his own rotor blades.

Besides the ability to shoot back, the Cobra could dive 90 degrees and bank 135 degrees, making it a very maneuverable aircraft.

Someone once told me that shooting at a Cobra with small arms was like shooting at a pencil with a BB gun from fifty yards.

After the obligatory signature on the dotted line, I received orders to report back to Hunter for transition into the Cobra, beginning on February 6. The big difference between flight school and Cobra school was that I was now an officer living off-post and drawing twenty-five dollars per day temporary duty allowance besides my normal pay.

The Cobra transition was a four-week course. Classes were held at Cobra Hall and the flight training was conducted in the tactical flight area with a good deal of time spent on the ranges. The academic portion of the course was heavy on armament, weapons systems, and ballistics, as one would expect flying a gunship.

The other major area of attention and instruction was maintenance. Because of their configuration and crew complement, Cobras didn't carry a crew chief like most of the other aircraft in the inventory. The bottom line was "if you have a problem in the field, you either sort it out or sit in the jungle and wait!"

Flight training would be pretty straightforward once we got there, but before that we had to endure the obligatory dollar ride in the front seat. The dollar ride consisted of the instructor pilot (IP) doing his utmost to get the student to spill his guts all over the cockpit. Steep banks weren't too bad, but when he put the machine into a ninety-degree dive and we saw the ground rushing toward us, even the most macho among us were weakened. The G-force encountered in the pullout was one thing we had never experienced either and it took some getting used to.

The rotor system on the Cobra was designed around two fundamental aerodynamic phenomenons that were not incorporated into the design of other helicopters: pitch cone coupling and transient torque.

Pitch cone coupling was the inherent ability of the rotor system to unload itself during high G maneuvers and transient torque allowed you to go into very abrupt banking maneuvers without overtorqueing or unloading the system so that you encountered negative Gs, a fatal maneuver in a helicopter.

The Cobra differed from the Huey in three important respect. Forward visibility from the aircraft commander's seat (the backseat) was very restricted. Also, the aircraft sits much higher than a Huey so its center of gravity is higher, making it that much easier to roll over on the ground. And it's a lot faster. The Cobra had a maximum speed of 190 knots, or 219 mph. Things happened much more quickly; therefore, reaction time had to be that much snappier! Fundamentally, the maneuvers were the same, but the Cobra's idiosyncrasies were quickly brought to light by the IPs.

The front seat of the AH-1 has space capsule controls. The cyclic that normally rests between the legs is mounted on a small side console on the right side of the cockpit. The controls have a 4:1 ratio so they are four times harder to move than the standard controls that are in the backseat. Learning to fly the aircraft from the front seat was a new challenge.

The biggest portion of the training was dedicated to the ranges and weaponry. Three days were spent in the front seat learning the ins and the outs of the turret-mounted weapons, as well as the sighting system. The standard armament contained in the XM-28A1 turret system was a 7.62mm M-134 machine gun and a 40mm M-129 grenade launcher.

The M-134 is an electrically driven, automatic, air-cooled six-barreled gun. Depending on the trigger detent engaged by the pilot, this minigun is capable of shooting a six-second burst at either two thousand or four thousand rounds per minute. After six seconds, the shooter must release the trigger and then pull it again to fire it. Without the interruption, the barrels would melt. For the uninitiated, it is very much like an electric Gatling gun. You don't want to be on the receiving end of it.

The M-129 is an electrically driven, rapid-firing, air-cooled weapon as well. It can fire a ten-second burst at four hundred grenades per minute.

The turret is usually controlled by the co-pilot/gunner who occupies the front seat of the Cobra. He has full control of the turret to aim and fire the weapons. Primarily, depending on the role the Cobra is employed in in combat, the turret is invaluable for getting ammo on the ground before the pilot can align the aircraft with a target to engage it with rockets and to cover himself once he breaks off a rocket run. The pilot can also shoot the turret-mounted weapons from the backseat, but only in the stowed position.

The stubby wings on the Cobra are nothing more than hard points to mount more weapons on. They offer nothing in the way of aerodynamics. Wing store configuration varied, again with the mission. The aircraft we flew at Cobra School had an assortment of systems that included XM-18E-1 minigun pods or a combination of nineteen tube or seven tube 2.75-inch folding fin aerial rocket pods.

The XM-18E-1 pod is a self-contained unit, housing a 7.62mm machine gun, its own electrical system, a battery recharging system, and a maximum of fifteen hundred rounds of ammunition.

We would have to become intimate with each and every system, their ballistics and capabilities before we left Cobra School.

On my first day in the backseat we flew out to the range and my IP told me to shoot a pair of rockets at the range markers—big orange triangular signs that delineated on one end of the range when we could start firing and at the other when we would have to go "weapons cold."

His reasoning was that sometimes it was impossible to see the impact on the range, which was a swampy area, but it was almost always possible to see around the range markers because they were mounted in an area of sandy earth with the dust and dirt highly visible.

I rolled in on my first rocket run, punched off one pair, and watched the range marker disappear in a big cloud. I was incredibly impressed with my performance, but my IP got very upset. "I said shoot at it! You ain't supposed to hit the fucking thing! You dickhead," he muttered.

Evidently, if an IP or his students hit a range marker, the IP had to physically replace it.

Flying the Cobra was exhilarating! It was fast and incredibly maneuverable; the visibility flying from the front seat was fantastic and in every sense of the word, it was an attack aircraft.

On March 9, 1970, I graduated from the AH-1 Cobra Transition/Gunnery Course Class number 70-15.

Next stop: Vietnam.

Chapter 7

Anybody but the First of the Ninth

It was 1:30 A.M. when the intercom crackled to life in the American Airlines 707. "Gentlemen, I hate to wake you but I thought you might be interested to know that you're now over the Republic of South Vietnam. We should be landing at Bién Hoa Air Force Base in about thirty minutes' time. The approach angle will be steeper than most of you are accustomed to, but rest assured that it's normal procedure for landing in theater. May I take this opportunity to wish you all God's speed and good luck? I'll be back a year from today to take you home."

There were lots of stretches and yawns throughout the aircraft as we awakened. We had been traveling for almost twenty-one hours including a stop in Honolulu with a further stop at Kadena in Okinawa, and our circadian rhythm was severely disrupted.

I looked out the window until my eyes adjusted to the darkness. As we descended I could catch the odd glimpse of an explosion and what appeared to be fireflies buzzing around. They were tracers.

We touched down at approximately 2:00 A.M. Vietnam time. When the door of the aircraft was opened we were introduced to the smell that was unique to Vietnam: a combination of cordite, burning human feces, jet fuel, smoke, and nuoc nam (a pungent fish sauce). We also got our first encounter with the most oppressive humidity ever imaginable.

A non-commissioned officer (NCO) came up the stairs, commandeered the intercom, and instructed us to disembark and make our way into the terminal area without delay.

I tried to take in the sights and sounds as I made my way to the terminal but I was on sensory overload. My clothes had begun to stick to me as soon as I left the aircraft, artillery was firing in the not-too-far-off distance, and fighter aircraft were taking off and landing with monotonous regularity. When we actually entered the terminal, the jeers of the guys waiting to get on our plane, both officers and enlisted, were overwhelming.

"Hey newbie, you ain't gonna make it. Better get measured for a body bag. Hey man, give me your girlfriend's name and number 'cause she'll need somebody to love her when you get greased!" I couldn't understand why they were saying these things to us.

We waited in the terminal for about an hour receiving instructions, and were then told to get on the buses. We had heard about the bus trips when we were in flight school. The buses had made ripe targets for the Viet Cong (VC) in the past. They would simply wait for one to drive by, throw a grenade through a window, and boom: a dozen dead or seriously wounded GIs.

In their infinite wisdom the Army put chicken wire over the windows so those grenades would bounce off rather than go through the windows. But our Army didn't have a monopoly on brains, because the VC would simply attach a fishhook to the grenade and hook it onto the wire.

We had heard these stories all through our training and figured they were just trying to scare us. It worked. As I walked out to the bus, I was transfixed by the chicken wire. I climbed aboard, stacked my duffel bag up against the window, and kept a very low profile as we left the confines of Bién Hoa Air Force Base under armed escort down Highway 1 to the Ninetieth Replacement Battalion at Long Binh.

The Ninetieth Replacement Battalion was commonly known in-country as the Repo Depot. It was located in Long Binh, between Bién Hoa and Saigon in what was the rear area.

I got very little sleep the first night at the Ninetieth. I was jet lagged, uncomfortable from the heat and humidity, and very anxious about it being my first night in-country. Tanks and self-propelled eight-inch Howitzers rolled by in the night, and finally I just got up and started walking around. It was more comfortable being outside in the wisp of a breeze than lying in my bunk. My thoughts were very far away and the apprehension about the next year was almost unbearable. I rounded the corner of the hooch just as the sun was rising, and froze. There, not ten feet away, was a Vietnamese person crouching close to a water trailer. My first reaction was to sound the alarm, but I was scared to turn my back on him. The thought of getting shot or stabbed in the back my first night in-country wasn't very appealing.

As I stood there frozen, the person rose. Much to my relief my first encounter with the country's indigenous people turned out to be an elderly Vietnamese woman who was filling a water jug. She smiled and bowed slightly as she walked by.

I continued to stand there and look at the spot from where she had just emerged. The scene was incongruous: the water trailer next to the concertina wire, a self-propelled eight-inch Howitzer lumbering down the highway, and the orange glow of one of the most beautiful sunrises I had ever seen. This was truly a land of contrasts.

As the hustle and bustle of the day's activity began, notices were posted telling us where to report and when. After breakfast, we had to report to an admin office to fill out a dream sheet. The dream sheet was a form designed for us, the individual soldier, to tell the Army where we wanted to be stationed and what we wanted to do.

I started asking around about the different units and who needed Cobra pilots. Virtually everyone I asked told me that everybody needed Cobra pilots but to steer well clear of the First Cavalry Division. They were reputed to be a division full of crazy bastards who wanted to win the war single-handedly. I put in for every unit I could think of that had Cobras . . . other than the Cav.

The next order of business was a dental check. This wasn't the ordinary dental checkup that we had endured in our youth. This was a dental check to be recorded so in the event of a dismembering death, they would be able to identify the remains.

On March 19, I was issued with Special Orders Number 78. "Following indiv having been assigned this station/organ is further assigned as indic. No travel involved. For the individual: Reassigned to 15 AG Co Admin APO 96490."

The Fifteenth AG (Adjutant General) Company Admin was the division's replacement company. While the Ninetieth assigned personnel to divisions throughout the country, the Fifteenth AG at APO 96490 assigned personnel to companies and squadrons within the division. I had just been assigned to the First Cavalry Division (Airmobile).

My dream had just turned into a nightmare.

Later the same day, a deuce and a half (an M-35 two-and-a-half-ton cargo truck) arrived and those of us who had been assigned to the Cav threw our belongings in the back and climbed in to begin the journey back north to Cav Rear.

The First Air Cavalry Division (Airmobile) Rear was located just across the runway at Bién Hoa from where I had arrived the day before. Talk about contrasts. The Air Force side had paved streets, air-conditioned billets, banks, movie theaters, and snack bars. Cav Rear had muddy dirt roads, GP medium tents, and a few proper buildings to house administration functions and the REMFs (Rear Echelon Mother Fuckers) who were stationed there.

I was assigned a hooch that was nothing more than a wooden building with a corrugated tin roof. Openings cut about three-quarters of the way up the wall covered with screen mesh. Around the perimeter of the building were fifty-five-gallon drums filled with dirt and covered with a layer of sandbags. The purpose of the drums was to absorb shrapnel from incoming mortar or rocket rounds that impacted close to the building. If the bad guys scored a direct hit then it just wasn't a good day.

There were bunkers between the buildings that were close enough to escape to in the event of incoming. Driven by a mixture of apprehension and curiosity, I reconnoitered the most expeditious route to the bunker and was greatly relieved to see the entrances barred by one of Mother Nature's miracles: a massive array of long-established spider webs.

My first night in the rear was no better than my night at the Repo Depot. While we were still supposedly in the rear the Cav had several artillery batteries stationed there, and until we learned the difference between outgoing and incoming shells, it made for a very restless night. In addition, we were literally right next to the run-way, and the fighters and bombers taking off and landing all night made it difficult to sleep.

In the morning we were formed up for an in-country indoctrination. This lasted for an hour or so and we were given an in-processing form that outlined who we had to go see and where. We had to in-process with medical, supply, finance, and admin, among others.

At the hospital I was quickly signed off after being told that I would get a flight physical once I arrived at my unit of assignment. There were similar stories at supply, nothing more than a signature was required—a mere formality. At finance I had to fill out some insurance forms. Serviceman's Group Life Insur-ance (SGLI) covered us, but the choosing of a beneficiary took on a new signifi-cance. Before I left finance I learned how much money I would be making: $445.44 per month.

I also sent home my U.S. dollars, as they were non-negotiable in-country. The military used Military Payment Certificates (MPC) to prevent black market monop-olies. Everything was rounded off to the nearest five cents. A surprising fact was that since I was an officer I would be expected to pay for my meals in-country. We were charged three cents for breakfast and a nickel for lunch and dinner.

At Admin we were given yet another dream sheet to fill in. It seems the Cav adopted the same concept as the rest of the Army. So once again, I asked ques-tions and once again the answers were the same, "Everybody needs Cobra pilots so no matter what you put down you'll probably get it."

I had learned about the Second of the Twentieth (2/20th) Aerial Rocket Artillery (ARA) and that seemed like quite a good assignment. The 227th and 229th Aviation Battalions (Assault Helicopter) both had attack helicopters, so that was another option.

The one unit I was told to steer well clear of at all cost was the First of the Ninth Cavalry. These guys had a reputation of being real cowboys, too good to call in the troops, and their losses were high. I opted for a bit safer and saner exis-tence so put in for the 229th, the 227th, and the Second of the Twentieth, in that order, anybody but the First of the Ninth. As I handed in the form, I was told ini-tially that I would be going to the 229th Aviation Battalion (Assault Helicopter) at Tay Ninh.

I had seen some of the locals around the base camp and they were very strange to me. I had seen very few men, but the ones I did see were small in stature and minded their own business. The females—known as hooch maids—were employed in the mess halls and cleaned the billets. Some of them were real friendly and many of them were quite attractive. It sure would have been nice to be able to understand what the heck they were talking about, though.

After handing in the dream sheet, the next order of business was filling out Cav Form 44, the Lightly Wounded Personnel, Next of Kin Notification form.

On this form we had to indicate whether or not we wanted our next of kin (NOK) to be notified in the event that we were *LIGHTLY* wounded. There was no definition of what lightly wounded meant. If we chose not to have them notified, we were required by regulations to notify our next of kin of this fact. The next paragraph stated, "Notification will automatically be made in the event you are seriously ill, wounded, killed, or missing in action." Formalities!

The Cav had a four-day in-country indoctrination course called the First Team Academy (FTA) at Bién Hoa. I attended the first day and soon realized that it was geared for the infantry. The day consisted of activities like detection of booby traps, methods to search and destroy hooches, locating bunkers, and the like. Nothing to do with aviation or, more to the point, aviators. At the completion of the day's training we were told that the following day we would be treated to a live fire demonstration of a Cobra gunship. I opted to go to the Air Force side to take in a movie and some air conditioning instead, and that's where I spent the next three days.

On the morning of March 23, I was handed my Special Orders Number 85, "58. TC 209. Following individual having been assigned this station/organization is FURTHER ASSIGNED as indicated. NTI. FOR THE INDIVIDUAL Reassigned to: HHT 1st Sqdn 9th Cav WAGTTOA. Reporting date: 23 MAR 70." So much for "anybody but the First of the Ninth."

The last official order I received at Cav Rear was "Pack your bags. There's a Chinook at the transient pad that's going to Phuoc Vinh. Be on it!"

I checked in at the Transient Pad and was directed to a Chinook whose rotors were turning on the pad. I boarded the giant helicopter through the rear cargo door and grabbed a seat at the rear of the aircraft.

The Chinook was the same model of the tandem-rotor helicopter that I had flown in as a WOC on a trip to Fort Sill. It made an even bigger target than I had remembered as we lifted to the north for the trip to Phuoc Vinh.

I was very nervous as we climbed out over hostile territory. It was only twenty miles north to Phuoc Vinh, but that was twenty miles worth of opportunity for the bad guys to take pot shots at us. I looked out the back of the aircraft, hydraulic fluid dripping on my duffel bag, as Bién Hoa disappeared in the distance.

Before I knew it, we had started our approach to Phuoc Vinh. Its official U.S. name was Camp Gorvad, the headquarters of the First Cavalry Division (Airmobile).

Lt. Col. Peter Gorvad, commander of the Second Battalion of the Twelfth Cavalry, was killed after midnight on March 8, 1969, when intense rocket and mortar fire of the First North Vietnames Army (NVA) Division destroyed his command bunker at Fire Support Base Grant. Two 120 mm rockets hit the bunker in the opening bombardment of the assault, killing Colonel Gorvad and other members of his staff.

We hovered to a pad at the base of the tower as the rear door lowered on its hydraulic jacks. Once on the ground, we grabbed our gear and departed the aircraft. As soon as the last guy was out, the aircraft lifted into a hover, blowing sand and crap all over everybody. Being such a large target for the enemy, the CH-47 tended not to hang around anywhere for too long.

There was nobody there to meet us, so we made our way to the control tower building to ask directions to our respective units of assignment.

"Excuse me, sergeant. Can you tell me where the First of the Ninth are?" I asked.

"Yes, sir, they're down at Pine Ridge," he told me.

"I'm afraid you'll have to be a bit more specific, sarge. I'm new. Where the hell is Pine Ridge?"

"Oh, sorry, sir. Well, there's one in South Dakota but the one you're looking for is down the runway on the same side as we are. The First of the Ninth ramp is called the Pine Ridge Pad. You can't miss it, sir. They have the Cobras with the shark's teeth on them," he told me.

Heaving my duffel bag onto my shoulder again, I headed down the side of the runway. I had only taken about ten steps when the 155mm artillery battery at the northeast end of the base camp opened up and scared the shit out of me. I dropped my duffel bag and dove to the ground right behind it with my heart beating a mile a minute.

A young soldier who was standing close by chuckled and said, "You'll get used to it, sir. It'll help when you're able to tell the difference between incoming and outgoing."

Gathering my gear and my wit, I continued down the runway taking in as much as I could. To the east was what looked like a plantation of some sort, to the west a small lake sat just off the end of the runway. To the north was a refueling point (POL) and beyond that were buildings similar to those I had seen at the rear at Bién Hoa. On the south side was much the same except for a large yellow building that was oriental in appearance and whose purpose I could not fathom.

The smell was typical of what I had experienced since arriving in-country; cordite, shit, and jet fuel is the best description I could come up with.

The temperature was in the nineties and that in itself didn't bother me. Having grown up in southern California, I was used to temperatures of a hundred degrees or more. It was the humidity that was so suffocating. Humidity levels often matched the temperature in Vietnam. One wouldn't think it possible to sweat while taking a cold shower, but it was the norm in Nam.

I continued along the runway until I came to a bunch of L-shaped revetments. In one was a fully armed Cobra painted with shark's teeth as the sergeant had said. It looked awesome.

Coming to a road I turned to the right and the first building I came to was the tactical operations center (TOC) of Charlie Troop, First of the Ninth Cav. A few yards farther and across the street I came to a big white arch with a sign that read, "Through these ranks pass the boldest cavalrymen the world will ever know." Just beyond in the center of a lawn was a rotor blade buried in a concrete memorial-type plinth. The blade was painted in Cav red and white and listed on it from top to bottom were all the campaigns that the First of the Ninth had ever participated in, from the Indian Wars up to and including Vietnam. It was very impressive.

The First Squadron of the Ninth Cavalry was constituted on July 28, 1866, as Company A, Ninth Cavalry. It organized in September of that year at

Greenville, Louisiana. From then until 1883, when Cavalry companies officially were re-designated as troops, the Ninth Cavalry campaigned against the Comanches, Utes, and Pine Ridge Indians and spent four years in New Mexico. They participated in the War with Spain at Santiago, the Philippine Insurrection, World War II, the Korean War, and now Vietnam. The squadron's list of decorations, awards, and citations went on and on.

I followed a sign that led me to squadron headquarters. It was an imposing-looking older building, stuccoed, yellow in color on the east edge of the large lawn with the blade in front of it. On the lawn were all sorts of captured enemy equipment, machine guns, anti-aircraft guns, bicycles, and other things that I didn't recognize.

I walked down the path that ran through the middle of the lawn, around the rotor blade, and entered the orderly room where a Specialist Four Class (Spec4) was seated. I handed him a copy of my orders and took a seat.

Reviewing my orders the Spec4 looked up and said, "Mr. Zahn. Welcome to the First of the Ninth, sir."

"Thank you," was all I could think to say.

"Sir, you're assigned to Charlie Troop. If you'll go and report to the orderly room, your orders will follow you. It's the building just across the lawn. The CO will see you sometime today or first thing in the morning, sir. He likes to formally welcome newbies to the squadron. Till then, if you have any problems check with your orderly room. Real Cav, sir!" he said.

"Real Cav?" I asked puzzled.

"Yes, sir. Real Cav. That's the squadron motto," he explained.

Grabbing my gear once again, I headed back across the lawn to the Charlie Troop orderly room. The building was wooden with screens replacing the windows a la Cav Rear.

Another Spec4 was seated at a desk, naked from the waist up due to the heat. Behind him was a large fan going at full RPM. It did nothing more than move the stifling air around, but at least it created a breeze.

"Good Morning, sir. Can I help you?" he queried.

"Good morning, I'm Mr. Zahn and I've just been assigned to Charlie Troop. I was told to report here," I answered.

"Well, you were told right, sir. If you'll have a seat, Captain T, the XO [executive officer] will see you. The CO is out flying," he told me.

Taking a seat, sweat rolling down my face, I stopped to reflect on the last week and to take in my new surroundings. I was tired, probably still jet lagged, and sat with my eyes closed.

"Mr. Zahn!" boomed a voice from a back room.

"Sir!" I answered.

"Please come in."

I got up and tried to straighten out my uniform as I walked through the doorway. To my right was a man wearing an olive drab sweat-soaked T-shirt seated at a desk. On the desk was his nameplate, "Captain Enn Tietenberg, Executive Officer."

Captain Tietenberg was blond and stocky and I wondered about the strange name. He was born in Tallinn, Estonia, on January 22, 1936. I faced him, came to attention, and saluted. "Good morning, sir. WO1 Randy Zahn reporting as ordered."

Returning my salute, Captain Tietenberg put me at ease so I could relax and look at him as we spoke. I handed him a copy of the orders assigning me to Headquarters and Headquarters Company, First Squadron, Ninth Cavalry, and told him that the squadron orderly room clerk said my orders assigning me to Charlie Troop would follow.

Captain Tietenberg offered his hand and said, "Welcome to Charlie Troop, Randy. I'm Enn Tietenberg, the XO. Most of the guys just call me Captain T. Where you from?"

"Sunland, sir. Sunland, California," I answered.

"You don't say," Captain Tietenberg smiled. "I used to live in Van Nuys."

"Really, sir?" I asked.

"I see you've graduated from Cobra Hall," he stated.

"Yes, sir," I responded proudly.

"Too bad," he said.

"Too bad, sir? Why too bad?" I asked.

"I'll tell you why Mr. Zahn, because we need scout pilots. We need people to fly OH-6s, Loaches. So, regardless of your qualifications, we are short of scout pilots!" he stated.

"You still are, sir!" I said before I even realized the words had come out of my mouth.

Looking up across the bridge of his nose, he glared at me and said, "Pardon me."

"I said you still are, sir. I am not going to fly scouts."

"And why is that Warrant Officer Zahn? Are you too good to fly scouts?" he demanded.

"No, sir," I answered. "I am not too good, but I enlisted to fly Cobras. I busted my butt in flight school to get Cobras and now that I am a qualified Cobra pilot, that is what I want to fly."

"Oh is it, Warrant Officer Zahn," he stated rather than asked.

"Yes, sir. I guess an Article 15 or a court-martial wouldn't get me off to a great start here, but that's what it'll take to get me to fly scouts," I retorted matter of factly.

"Go to the red hooch and find yourself a bunk," he ordered in disgust.

It was probably not the most auspicious start to my combat career, but I was determined to fly Cobras.

Leaving the orderly room, I headed off looking for a red hooch and wondered about its significance. I also wondered why I had gone from Randy to Mister to Warrant Officer in the course of about three minutes. I think I knew the answer. I had not made a good first impression.

Chapter 8

Know Your Enemy

The squadron TOC was across what looked like a parade field with the crossed sabers of the Cavalry painted on a perforated steel planked (PSP) outer wall. To the right was another yellow stuccoed building with a large screened-in veranda and continuing on to the right a non-descript building.

I walked to the middle of the parade ground, looking in all directions for a red hooch but there was none to be found. Confused, I left my gear by the closest building and returned to the orderly room to ask directions.

"Can I help, sir?" the Spec4 asked.

"Yeah, you can. I can't seem to find a red hooch anywhere," I explained.

Breaking out in a smile the specialist told me "Sir, the hooch isn't painted red. We call it the red hooch because that's where all the weapons platoon pilots live. The Red platoon. Snake pilots!"

I mouthed my thanks as I retreated from the office. Snake pilots! I was going to fly Cobras.

As I walked around the building I heard Captain T laughing. "Fucking new guys," he said. "And he wants to fly Cobras. God help us!"

I retrieved my gear for what seemed the hundredth time that day and found the red hooch. It was directly across the parade ground from the squadron TOC and, fortuitously, was the building next to which I had left my gear.

The hooch was a long, narrow wooden structure built on a slab of concrete. Like the vast majority of the buildings I had seen, it was three quarter walled with screens around the top quarter. Unlike the others I had seen, the parade ground–facing screens, the east side, were mostly covered with plastic.

I opened the side door and entered a long narrow corridor that ran the length of the building. Plywood sheets were nailed up on each side to form the outer walls of the rooms. The place was as quiet as a morgue.

I slowly made my way down the hall until I came to an open door and saw somebody asleep. I knocked and the person woke up with a big stretch. He sat on the side of the cot rubbing his eyes and said, "Hi! I'm Kevin Frye!"

"Hi, Kevin! Randy Zahn."

Shaking hands, Kevin asked, "You just get here?"

"Yeah, just came up from Biên Hoa. I've been assigned to Charlie Troop and the XO told me to find a bunk in the red hooch," I told him.

"Hallelujah," Kevin said with a big smile. "I'm not the FNG anymore!"

"What the hell is an FNG?" I asked.

"You are!" he said, "the Fucking New Guy!"

There were no spare bunks available in the hooch so I temporarily parked myself in a bunker adjoining the red hooch. About a quarter of the way down the corridor, a small cross-corridor led off to the right and immediately outside the side door was the entrance to the bunker.

The architects of the bunker didn't give much thought to aesthetics! The ever-present fifty-five-gallon drums filled with sand surrounded the bunker. Sandbags had been placed on top of the drums two deep up to the roof. The roof was covered with more sandbags and a layer of PSP. Standing upright on the PSP were more drums, another layer of PSP, and another double layer of sandbags. The air gap created by the drums was purposely built to counter time-delayed fused rockets or mortars. The theory was that the round would arm on contact with the sandbags and the explosion would occur in the air gap prior to penetrating the sandbagged roof or even worse, the ceiling of the bunker.

The bunker was entered through an L-shaped entrance, again to prevent shrapnel from penetrating the interior.

The interior itself was far more than I had expected. The guy that lived in it on a regular basis, CW3 Dave Lawley, was on rest and recuperation (R&R) somewhere, so although it was temporary I was going to make the most of it. A single bunk was inside, electric lighting, a TV, toaster, a table with six chairs, and a wet bar. A stocked wet bar at that!

I unpacked what I needed for a few days and Kevin came over, "Hey Randy, let's go have a drink."

Kevin Mark Frye hailed from Newport, Rhode Island. A military brat, his father, Warren, was a CWO4 in the Navy based at Cecil Field in Florida. Seven months older than myself, Kevin had been a long-time member of the Civil Air Patrol.

The non-descript building that I had seen earlier in the day was the Officers' Club. The interior was relatively Spartan but was clean and air conditioned. Approaching the bar, Kevin asked me what I would like.

"A nice cold coke would be fine, thanks," I told him.

"A coke! Don't you want a beer or something?" he asked.

"A beer? Kevin, I'm not twenty-one," I told him somewhat embarrassed. Kevin just laughed and said, "They're not going to card you, newbie. Have whatever you want."

"A coke will be fine, thanks," I answered.

We chose two bar stools close to the air conditioner and Kevin started telling me about Charlie Troop.

"We fly hunter-killer teams, or pink teams," he began.

"Pink teams? Sounds like a bunch of fucking pansies. Why do we call them pink teams?" I asked.

"Easy," Kevin continued, "The gun platoon is the red platoon. The scouts are the White platoon. Send a hunter, the scout, and a killer, the Cobra, and you have one red and one white. Red and white? Pink. The Lift platoon is the Blue platoon so if a lift bird goes out with us, we become a Purple team. Simple ideas for simple people!"

We sat in the club for a while and Kevin continued to brief me on hooch maids, R&R policy, and other things until the club started to fill up with guys coming back from flying, or commissioned officers who staffed the TOC.

As dinnertime approached, Kevin showed me the way to the mess hall. The mess hall was a massive building that was separated by a wall down the middle. The wall separated the enlisted from the officers. The building itself looked very new compared with the other buildings in the area. I asked Kevin if it was recently built. Kevin told me that just before he had arrived in the troop there had been nothing there but a burned out building. I immediately surmised that it had been hit in an attack and burned down. Kevin straightened me out.

"Evidently the food used to be really bad," he explained. "The troops got pissed off and told the mess sergeant that if it didn't improve they were going to burn down his mess hall."

"So what happened?" I asked.

"They burned the fucking place down! Now we got a new mess hall, a new mess sergeant, and decent chow," he finished.

"What happened to the guys that did it?" I wondered.

"Nothing," Kevin said. "You can get away with all kinds of shit in a combat zone!"

I never was able to substantiate that story.

That night I attended my first Red Platoon meeting, in the bunker where I was living, and met the rest of the guys. The platoon leader was a lanky captain with reddish-blond hair and a big bushy mustache by the name of Gary Jacobson; call sign "Red." The aircraft commanders (ACs) were CW2 Ed McDerby (26), CW2 Mike "Felix" Poindexter (27), CW2 Hubert Kuykendall (28), CW2 Grover Wright (24), and CW2 Myron "Monty" Lamont (23). CW3 Dave Lawley, whose bunker I was occupying, was away on R&R and not present.

I was introduced to them all and to the rest of my fellow front-seaters; besides Kevin there was WO1 Steve Beene (Beeny), WO1 Danny Rager (Rags), WO1 Vaughn Caine, and WO1 David Zimmerman (Zeke).

Each AC had his own call sign that he kept throughout his tour of duty. The "White," or scout platoon leaders' call sign was White and the pilots' call signs ran from one-zero to two-zero. Red call signs were two one to two nine, and the lift platoon had call signs from three-zero up to four whatever.

The front-seaters in the Cobras or the co-pilots in the Hueys were simply known as X-rays, so if I were flying with Red, my call sign for the day would be "Red X-ray."

The meeting covered items from the day's missions to aircraft in maintenance, crew assignments for the next day, any relevant intelligence data for the next day, and areas of interest to conduct visual reconnaissance (VR).

After the meeting Red took me back to the TOC for a short briefing. He explained the tactical map that was posted and showed me the locations of friendly troops, suspected enemy areas of concentration, fire support bases (FSBs), and areas of responsibility of the different brigades.

Charlie Troop's mission was to support the First Cav's First Brigade in Phuoc Long and Long Khanh Provinces, which were known as War Zone C.

The area was criss-crossed with trail systems that were given the names of the COs of the units that had discovered them. The two that we had to concentrate on were the Adams Trail and the Jolley Trail, both sub-systems of the famed Ho Chi Minh Trail.

After the brief, Red told me that the next day I would be meeting the squadron commander, LTC Clark Burnett and the troop commander, Maj Galen Rosher. After that I would be going back down to Bién Hoa to get my flight gear issued. At least this time I wouldn't have to lug all my gear with me. When I returned I was to report back to the TOC for my aviator orientation by the operations officer, Capt. Mike Martin.

The orientation lasted a couple of hours and covered many different subjects. They included command relationship between aviation unit and support commanders; mission and organization of habitually supported units; supported unit standard operating procedures (SOP), aviation unit SOP, signal operating instructions (SOI), and crew duties; responsibility and authority of the pilot in command and senior passengers; weather briefings; and rules of engagement.

I was then invited to get my maps put together, laminated, and posted with all of the pertinent information before the brief continued. Once I had finished the map, Captain Martin continued with map orientation; preferred flight routes and border restrictions; areas of known or suspected enemy activity in our local area of operations (AO), capabilities and limitations of enemy weapons; flight following and artillery warnings; plus a host of other subjects.

I made my way back to the bunker in the dark and noticed that the whole place took on an eerie appearance. As hot as it was, I got chills.

I ran in to one of the guys coming back from the club and asked where the showers were. He pointed me in the right direction so I quickly changed out of my clothes and headed for a welcome shower. I wanted to wash the sweat and dirt off before I went to bed.

The shower room was a small, corrugated tin building at the south edge of the troop area. On the roof four 55-gallon drums were filled each day by a water bowser. Out of the bottom of each drum a length of hose carried the water into the building. Each hose had a small tap on it that, when turned on, allowed water to come straight down in a stream. I went in and turned the first tap I came to, nothing. The second tap dribbled a bit before running dry and the third and fourth were already wide open and bone dry.

Somebody emerged from the shitter next door and I asked him if there were any other showers. He told me that if you want a shower, you had to get there early, before all the water had been used up. I was hot, sweaty, exhausted, and just to add to it I was now pissed off as well. This wouldn't be the last miserable night in Vietnam, but I managed to fall asleep as soon as my head hit the pillow.

Hours later I awoke to the sound of turbine engines and rotor blades as the teams cranked up to head out for the day's flying. It was 5:00 A.M.

I fell back asleep but woke back up about 7:00 A.M. and headed to the mess hall. I went through the line and got my chow before being told that Major Rosher would like me to join him for breakfast.

Major Rosher was a career officer who was highly respected by the troops. He offered me a chair at his table and proceeded to welcome me as we ate. I choked a little when he asked why I had chosen Charlie Troop. I couldn't muster up the nerve to tell him that I hadn't chosen Charlie Troop; Charlie Troop chose my young ass. He proceeded to tell me that I wouldn't be sorry. Charlie Troop had recently been honored by the general's staff as the best unit in Vietnam, and he was certain that once I had been there for a few weeks I would decide that there was no place in-country I would rather be. He did succeed in making me feel welcome and told me that I would be officially welcomed at the "hail and farewell" on the twenty-sixth. Colonel Burnett joined us shortly thereafter and offered his welcome and pep talk at the same time.

After breakfast I went back to the TOC to find out when and where to catch a ride back south to Bién Hoa. As I approached the TOC I noticed the troop motto "Fight 'em where we find 'em!"

"The family car will be leaving at ten hundred hours," I was told.

"Car?" I asked.

"Yeah, that's what we call the Huey that does all our logistics runs and ash and trash missions," said Captain Martin. "It'll be out on the assault strip about 9:55 A.M."

The flight to Bién Hoa was much more pleasant in the Huey than in the Chinook. The sliding cabin doors were pinned back, and the cool air flowing through the aircraft was refreshing.

Shutting down at the transient pad, the crew gave me directions to the flight gear issue point and told me they would wait for me. It didn't take long to conduct my business and as soon as I returned we cranked up and headed back north.

After lunch Captain Martin briefed me on the AO and helped me to post my map. Each day the location of known friendly elements had to be "posted" to avoid any friendly fire incidents. When I had finished my map I made my way back to the club to enjoy the air conditioning and on the way passed several local women. These were the hooch maids I had been told about. Hooch maids cost $10 per month. They cleaned the rooms, did the laundry, ironed, made the beds, and polished boots for the price. Any other favors were to be negotiated on an individual basis but were officially frowned upon.

I went back to the bunker and was startled as I opened the door. Two hooch maids were inside chattering away and moving the dust from one place to the other. The older woman was about five-foot-one-inch with her long black hair pinned up behind her head. She wore black silk pajama bottoms and a silk blouse. Her face was wrinkled and her teeth were badly stained from chewing betel nut.* She smiled as I walked in and curtsied ever so slightly. "Hallo. Mamasan," she said patting her chest with her hand.

"Mamasan?" I questioned.

"Ya, Mamasan," she confirmed. "This my babysan, Kim," she said pointing to the other girl.

I looked at the other girl for the first time and noticed that she was much younger, in her teens, and very pretty. Kim was slightly taller than her mother and also wore her long silky hair pinned up. She had a roundish face and a lovely smile. Unlike Mamasan, Kim had pearly white teeth. As she turned to face me she reached up to unpin her hair. It was beautiful. It cascaded around her face and about three-quarters of the way down her back. Kim looked at me and said, "I Kim, what you name?"

"Randy," I answered.

"Landy," she tried and both she and her mother broke into giggles.

"No, not Landy. Randy," I said emphasizing the R.

"Landy," she tried again and the two of them continued to laugh and converse in their native language.

Mamasan was obviously the businesswoman of the two. She stopped laughing and asked, "You want Mamasan be hooch maid?"

Somewhat hesitantly I asked, "How much?"

She said "Fipfteen dolla!"

"Fifteen." I said. "I thought hooch maids get paid ten dollars!"

"Ya," she responded drawing out the a, "but we two. Ten dolla Mamasan and fipf dolla Babysan!"

She was a very astute old woman. I was standing there making googoo eyes at her daughter and she took on a stern look. "Ah, you numbah ten GI," she said. "No look Babysan like dat!"

"What?" I asked somewhat embarrassed.

"Mamasan see you looking. Don't be numba ten. You just babysan youself," she said.

I agreed to the fifteen dollars for the two servants and wondered what I had got myself into.

At the platoon meeting that night I sat through the summary of the day's activities and when the crew assignments were announced I was excited to learn that I would be flying my first combat mission the next day. I would be flying in the front seat with Red once I had had my local area orientation flight in a UH-1 with Captain Martin.

The troop motto said a lot about what we did. As the eyes of the division, we often found bad guys in areas where there were no friendly troops. If we didn't

---

* betel nuts are palm nuts from the areca tree, which resembles a thin coconut palm. They stain the teeth dark red.

fight them then and there, they would be half way back to North Vietnam by the time we could organize support.

The role of the front-seater in the Cobra was varied and intense. His primary mission was to keep his eye on the "scout."

The scouts flew a light observation helicopter (LOH), the Hughes OH-6A Cayuse. The "loach," as it was affectionately known, was a fast, agile, and very powerful little aircraft. It was shaped like a pregnant egg lying on its side and had four rotor blades. Not only was it known for its speed and power, but also because their pilots loved them because they were very crashworthy.

The scouts' job was to fly their aircraft at tree-top level and conduct visual reconnaissance. This often meant bringing the aircraft to a hover using the down-wash from the rotors to blow the trees apart so the crew could see what was on the jungle floor. More often than not this didn't find favor with the bad guys and they would do their utmost to blow the Loach out of the sky. The job seemed almost suicidal and the scout pilots were the bravest of the brave.

Charlie Troop Loaches flew with the pilot in the right seat, an observer in the left, and the crew chief (CE) in the back. The observer normally carried an M-16 or Colt automatic rifle, CAR-15, and some smoke grenades, while the CE had an M-60 machine gun, fragmentation grenades, incendiary grenades, white phosphorus grenades, and any other kind of ordnance he could lay his hands on. The observer's mission was not only to observe but also to get a smoke grenade out if they came under fire.

When the "taking fire" call came, the scout pilot did his best to get them out of harm's way while the front-seater in the Cobra would use the turret to get rounds on the ground to keep the bad guys' heads down. The Cobra had to be physically aimed at the target to shoot rockets, so the aircraft had to be maneuvered into a steep turn and dive to start a rocket run. The smoke was the only thing that the Cobra had to aim at, because trees in a jungle were no use for navigation.

In the Cobra, the sole purpose of having an x-ray in the front seat was to protect the scout. If he lost visual contact at any time it had to be announced so that the aircraft commander could locate the Loach for him. If they both lost the Loach, the Loach crew would either have to throw a smoke out for identification or the Loach pilot would be asked to climb back to altitude until visual contact could be made again. The scout pilots enjoyed neither scenario. Throwing ordnance out depleted their supply and bringing them up to altitude cost time, and in some cases, targets. The cardinal rule for the guns was "If you can't see the Loach, you can't protect him," and keeping the scout alive was why we existed.

Another important aspect of the job was map reading. The Loach crew didn't carry a map and the x-ray had to become expert at map reading. Jungles don't afford a lot of geographical features so we had to map read by even the most insignificant terrain features.

The importance of map reading and obtaining accurate six-digit grid references could not be overemphasized. If the Loach got shot down, we had to be able to tell operations where he was and right now. If we had to put in artillery or an air strike, we had to give them the coordinates of the target. Ordnance is expensive, and besides that, if you gave an inaccurate grid reference, people could die in the time it took to adjust the fire.

Spot reports also had to be accurate. The scout would tell us on a discrete frequency what he was seeing and we would relay that information back to Ops to pass on to higher authority. If we needed the Blues, a medevac, an aerial rocket artillery strike, to put in a combat assault or any number of other things, we had to be accurate. Map reading became second nature to us.

More important, the Cobra AC was the mission commander, and he had to have his shit together. What started out as a Pink team could end up involving dozens of aircraft and hundreds of people.

There was a very steep learning curve at the beginning of the tour; lots to learn and lots to assimilate. It was a bit like the chicken-and-the-egg syndrome. You had to have the experience to gain the knowledge you needed to do the job, but if you didn't have the knowledge you might not live long enough to gain the experience.

I met Red in the TOC at 4:30 A.M. on the morning of the twenty-sixth. We were going to support a long-range patrol (LRP) (pronounced lerp) that day. Originally known as "long-range reconnaissance patrol" (LRRP) (still pronounced lerp) until late 1967, that name stuck with them. The LRRPs consisted of experienced combat veterans who were chosen from grunts among the divisions and brigades. They were usually chosen for the skills they had acquired in the bush, their ability to patrol without making a leaf flutter, and their bravery and willingness to place themselves in harm's way.

The LRRPs usually operated in teams of four men: a point guard, a team leader, a radio operator, and a rearguard, who was commonly referred to as the tail gunner. Sometimes there were six. Our boys were assigned to Company H, Seventy-fifth Infantry (Ranger) who could trace their roots back to Merrill's Marauders, the famed deep penetration unit from World War II. The Seventy-fifth was designated as the parent unit of all LRRPs, now known as Ranger Infantry Companies.

The LRRPs were to avoid enemy contact as much as possible. Their main mission was intelligence gathering. They normally patrolled until they found a trail and then set up an ambush using fields of cross fire and Claymore mines. When they struck, they had to be quick and hit very hard. They didn't want to leave any enemy soldiers alive for fear that they themselves would be hunted down or that a larger element could be alerted.

When the LRRPs came across something too big to take on by themselves they would call in a pink team to further exploit the target or pursue the bad guys. If contact was imminent, they didn't hesitate to call for artillery, an airstrike, or gunships.

We were going to check out a bunker complex that the LRRP had come across the previous night. It is hard to describe how I felt that morning. I was a mixed bag of exhilaration, excitement, intensity, and fear. I was exhilarated at the thought of finally getting out to do what I had been training for during the last year, and excited about getting to play John Wayne for real. I was intense because I needed to know what was going on and be an effective member of the team, and scared that I would be too frightened to perform well.

After the brief I went out to pre-flight the aircraft while Red finished up his paperwork and got the signal operating instructions.

I walked out to the aircraft in the pitch blackness, stumbling a few times over unseen obstacles. Flashlights were not conducive to longevity. They made a great target in the dark!

Arriving at the aircraft I opened the front canopy and threw my helmet and maps into the front seat. The crew chief had all the panels open and as I proceeded around the aircraft checking for leaks, loose wires or hoses, bearing wear, end play and oil levels, he followed behind me, securing everything back in place.

Red arrived and we both climbed in, he in the back and me in the front. As he went through the start sequence the engine began to whine and the blades began to turn. I took a deep breath and let it out slowly as he lifted into the hover. I was off on my first combat mission.

One good thing about taking off so early was that it was still relatively cool and the aircraft would actually hover. We usually took off with the aircraft well over its maximum certificated gross weight. If we didn't, we either wouldn't have enough fuel to get where we needed to go and remain on station or we wouldn't have enough ordnance to be of any use when we got there.

Taking off, we headed north toward Song Be with our little bird, the Loach, safely tucked up under our wing. Song Be was an old French resort town on the Song Be River about thirty-five miles north of Phuoc Vinh. Also known as Fire Support Base Buttons, it was a large forward area base camp with a runway long enough for resupply aircraft to come into, or for battle-damaged fighters to use as an emergency landing strip. We used it as a refuel and re-arming area and had a small forward TOC located here.

The flight up to Song Be was uneventful and the orange rays of the sun rising in the east were just beginning to streak over the horizon. Just to the south and east of Song Be was a large mountain called Nui Ba Ra. It stood 2,372 feet above sea level and more than one aircraft had flown into the side of it in the blackness of a moonless jungle night. Once the pilot acquired the lights of the base camp and the neighboring city, he made sure they remained east of his track and that nothing obscured them until he arrived.

After landing, both the little bird and us refueled before repositioning to the revetments to shut down. Red went into the TOC for an up-to-date pre-mission brief and the rest of us headed to the mess tent to grab a quick bite to eat. Red joined us in the mess tent and briefed us while he ate breakfast.

"Okay, the LRRP has a bunker complex. There are no signs of any recent use, but it is too large for them to scope out on their own. They want us to have a look-see and see what kind of trouble we can stir up. Any questions?" Red asked. There were none, so we headed back to the aircraft.

On the way Red briefed me more about what to expect. "Randy, your whole purpose in life is to keep the little bird in sight at all times. If you lose him, even for a second, let me know. I'll give you the center of mass of the area we're going to be working, so that should help you find it on the map. Before we let the little bird descend from altitude we have to ID the LRRP's position. We don't want him descending on top of them. It's easy to make mistakes in the dawn."

"Why don't we wait till the sun comes up?" I asked naïvely.

"Because the night belongs to Charlie," Red explained. "During the day, they tend to go underground. First light is the best time to catch them. They've usually been humping all night, they're tired, and they make mistakes."

"Next," he continued, "once we get a positive ID on the LRRP team, we'll get a free fire clearance and you'll test the turret, both the minigun and the chunker. No sense in sending the little bird down if we can't protect him!"

We cranked up again and got a commo check with the scout pilot on our discrete UHF (ultrahigh frequency) radio. The UHF channel assigned to a pink team was sacrosanct and nobody was to interfere without invitation.

Before we took off Red instructed me to call and get an artillery clearance. "Be a bit difficult to explain getting blown out of the sky by our own artillery," he said.

After we took off again, the little bird safely in-tow, Red continued his brief. "Okay, if the little bird yells "Taking fire," I want you to get rounds on the ground to keep the dinks' heads down until I can get rockets on the way. You'll have to brace yourself because I'll just slam the pedal to get us turning and follow through with the cyclic. If you see any tracers coming our way, you yell and tell me which way to break. You got that?"

"Yes, sir," I answered with a renewed sense of fear. "How can you tell if they're shooting at us though?" I asked.

"Oh you'll know, pal. You won't usually get tracers out of AKs, so if you see any you'll either see a red line which'll probably be from a 30-caliber machine gun or you'll see 51-caliber shells," he told me, "and knock off that sir shit! Everyone calls me Jake."

"Right Jake, what do 51-cal look like?"

"You can't miss them," he replied. "They look like big green golf balls."

We made contact with the LRRP radio operator on the FM (frequency-modulation) radio on the second attempt and Red told him there was a hunter-killer team en route and asked for a sit-rep (situation report).

The radioman was barely audible as he whispered into his mic, "Right Red, we've been following a trail that shows moderate recent use. It runs southwest to northeast. About ten yards from our present position our point can make out some bunkers. We'd like you to VR it and tell us what you've got."

Red responded, "Glad to help out. Give me a vector to your house and a bingo when we pass over."

After a few small changes of direction we received a bingo and marked the position on the map. I listened as Red briefed the scout, keeping him at altitude for the time being.

Red changed frequencies on the FM radio and made another call, "This is Cavalier Red. We're on station. We have a solid ID on our boys. Are there any other friendlies in the area?" he asked.

"Red," they replied, "there are no other friendlies in the area, I repeat, no other friendlies. You are cleared to arm and fire," said the radioman at Brigade.

I told the Scout that we were cleared to shoot while Red switched back to the LRRP frequency and told them that we would be testing our weapons and not to get excited. Red switched the weapons selector that supplied power to the turret from safe to arm. I lifted the sight, looked through the reticle, and squeezed the action bar, causing the turret to slew and the trigger to fire the minigun, which came to life with a sound not unlike a deep-throated burp. A solid line of tracers raced to the ground. Releasing the trigger, I popped off a few rounds from the 40 mm.

"The turret is fully serviceable," I announced.

"Okay," Red responded, "but don't screw with the sight. Just pull the trigger and walk it in visually."

We told the little bird that he was cleared in and the ballet began. Scouts were like dancers. They all had their own unique moves and after flying with the same scout for a number of times, communication became less and less because I got to the point that I knew exactly what he was doing. The speed of the aircraft, the shape and size of the pirouettes he flew, and the paces he put the Loach through spoke volumes about his pucker factor.

Normally the scout would keep his speed up and fly large clockwise turns when he first got down on the trees. If they didn't draw any fire and as he became more comfortable with the area, he would slow the aircraft and the radius of the turns got smaller and smaller, until finally he brought the aircraft to a slow hover to take best advantage of the rotorwash.

The Cobra would remain at fifteen hundred feet and fly counterclockwise in circles the size of which would allow us to keep the little bird in view and inside of our turn. Fifteen hundred feet kept us just out of small arms range and when we did have to roll in on a rocket run it gave us lots of time on target. We would normally vary our speed as we covered the little bird, but the cardinal rule was never to fly at ninety knots. That's the speed the VC had been trained to lead an aircraft for when they shot at them.

With a refuel, we remained on-station for almost five hours. The scout counted twenty-five bunkers that were all abandoned and some badly damaged. The LRRPs found numerous weapons as they followed the scout through the complex, but day one produced no contact with the enemy.

Shutting down back at Phuoc Vinh, I had logged 5.8 hours of combat time and found myself very exhausted. The adrenaline rush was subsiding and fatigue was setting in.

I headed back to the bunker, turned on the fan, and fell asleep.

After dinner we headed to the club for my first Hail and Farewell. This was the traditional welcome to the squadron for us new guys and the chance for everybody to say good-bye to the guys who had made it and were going home. I sat with Kevin, Steve Beene, and Danny Rager. We x-rays tended to stick together and the four of us had become inseparable.

Alpha and Bravo Troops had flown in from their respective bases at Tay Ninh and Lai Khe. The wine and beer were flowing freely and the roasts had begun. Each table had several bottles of wine, so the rule of the night was share and share alike.

Our Blue platoon leader, Lt. John Mackel Jr., was on his way home and feeling no pain. The wine on his table had been depleted so he reached across to the next table to grab another bottle when a captain from Bravo Troop slapped his hand away and told him, "This is our wine!"

Blue said, "Excuse me, sir, but the wine belongs to everybody. I need some for the toasts."

The captain was unrelenting and the words started flying. Before I knew what was going on they were both on their feet, chairs bowled over, and the verbal abuse was about to become physical.

About that time Maj Chuck Jolley, the Bravo Troop commander, intervened and had words with his captain. Shortly thereafter, he ordered, "Okay, Bravo Troop, let's saddle up and go home."

Among lots of moans and groans, Bravo Troop got up and left, knocking over tables, chairs, and bottles on the way.

"Holy shit!" I exclaimed, "Is this normal for Hail and Farewells?"

Steve started to tell me that this was the first time he had ever experienced any type of altercation at a Hail and Farewell when Major Jolley came back in. He stood by the steps that led to the bar and waited until there was almost dead silence. "Charlie Troop" he challenged, "Bravo Troop awaits you."

Almost immediately, everybody was on their feet and heading for the door. I followed the rest of the guys. Outside Bravo Troop was lined up along both sides of the path leading to the club, gauntlet style, and at the end were Major Jolley and the captain.

Major Jolley called Blue and Major Rosher over. Looking straight at Major Rosher he said, "Galen, I think we ought to let these two settle this like men. My guys are just here to make sure nobody interferes."

After reaching a mutual agreement the captain began to take off his shirt. Just about the time he had it almost off with both arms occupied, Blue attacked. He cold-cocked the captain, knocking him on his ass and proceeded to beat the shit out of him.

Before it had progressed too far, Major Jolley once again intervened, pulling Blue off of his captain and threatened, "That's it, Lieutenant. Your ass is mine. I'm going to court-martial you for striking a superior officer!"

"Goddamn it, Chuck," interrupted Major Rosher, "You're not going to court-martial anybody! You made the rules and your boy lost fair and square."

"Galen," Major Jolley shot back, "Charlie Troop is the sorriest fucking outfit in the country."

Major Rosher normally had a cigar in his mouth and a smile on his face. He took the cigar out and threw it on the ground before glaring at Major Jolley. "Chuck," he said, "you take that back and apologize to my troop or I'll kick your ass, and you damn sure won't court-martial me!"

Major Jolley knew that he had overstepped his bounds and complied with Major Rosher's demand. Apologizing to us all, he said in a much more subdued voice, "Okay, Bravo Troop, let's go home."

They headed for the flight line where their Hueys were parked and most of Charlie Troop returned to the club. I stood there in the black of the night trying to make sense of all that had just taken place. Were we here to fight the Viet Cong and the NVA, or each other?

Major Rosher was one of the last to enter the club and I noticed, that in my eyes at least, he was about a foot taller.

Chapter 9

Going after Them

I began my first full month in-country with a 5:00 A.M. wake-up and a six o'clock takeoff. The normal routine was to fly up to Song Be and this morning would be no different. Our missions were many and varied that first day of April. Being tasked to cover two different medevacs proved that nobody was fooling around.

Steve had just been promoted to aircraft commander and I was flying with him on my first bomb damage assessment (BDA). Very often the Air Force would put in air strikes using any number or assortment of fast jets or bombers up to and including the Boeing B-52 Stratofortress. The Air Force called them BUFFs (big ugly fat fellers). The Army called them BUFFs too (big ugly fat fuckers). I liked our version better.

After an air strike went in, we would be called upon to assess the damage the bombs had done. At times it would be frustrating to find that they had missed the target completely or there was no target there to begin with. As crazy as it sounds, targets for B-52 strikes were chosen by personnel thousands of miles away in Hawaii. On other occasions there would be damaged or destroyed hooches, caved-in bunkers, exposed munitions or other war materials, and dead or wounded bad guys.

The shock and concussion caused by the detonation of the bombs could literally gel one's brain. It was not uncommon to find bad guys walking around dragging their weapons behind them in a zombie-like state. Killing them was an act of mercy.

On the way back to Phuoc Vinh, ops called us to tell us that a convoy had been ambushed at the Mary crossroads east of Song Be. The intersection got its name because of its proximity to Fire Support Base (FSB) Mary. We headed over to the area and found a deuce and a half on fire and troops shooting into the tree line. As Beeny was occupied on the radios trying to find out what was going on, I noticed muzzle flashes off to the left front of the aircraft. I yelled to Steve, "Break right!" There was no response so again I yelled, "Break right, Steve!"

After my second warning and not getting any reaction I grabbed the controls and rolled the aircraft onto its right side as green golf ball–sized shells passed down the left side of the aircraft, 51-caliber anti-aircraft shells. My actions somewhat startled Steve and as he looked up he also saw the rounds passing.

"Holy fuck," he yelled as he grabbed the controls.

"Didn't you hear me?" I asked.

"Yeah, but you're just a newbie so I didn't pay attention," he said.

"Steve" I answered, "I may be a newbie, but I haven't got a death wish."

We expended what munitions we had left on the area from where the muzzle flashes came before returning to Phuoc Vinh. The contact had been broken and, as usual, Charlie had disappeared back into the jungle. We didn't let the little bird go back down to see whether we had actually hit anything because we had no rockets to protect him had he taken fire.

The sun had set by the time we shut down in the revetments back at Pine Ridge. Steve filled out the logbook as I did a walk-around inspection of the aircraft. This was standard operating procedure. We didn't very often come back after taking hits and not know about it. A round impacting the aircraft sounded like somebody smacking the side of a car with a hammer, but in the heat of a fire fight and as focused as we became, it was possible. Rounds going through the rotor blades also could not be heard from the cockpit. The aircraft was okay.

Steve and I walked back to the TOC and I asked him what we did for the day. His response was "ten hours fifteen." It had been a long day.

The next day was another long one. More than thirteen hours in the air yielded a huge enemy base camp–sized area. The little bird nosed around as best as he could from his aerial vantage point and estimated that there were over five hundred hooches and bunkers in the area connected by trails, roads, and bridges. We also found six VC who no longer graced the earth with their presence by the end of the day. We called in spot report after spot report and requested ground troops to exploit the area, but our request fell on deaf ears. We couldn't so much as muster an air strike that day. There were other priorities we were told. I began to wonder at this very early stage of my tour if the United States really and truly wanted to win this damn "war."

A letter from Mom and Dad arrived at mail call that day. Mom was upset that I hadn't been writing every day as I had promised and she was upset that I wasn't answering many of the questions that I was asked.

It was difficult to know how much to tell them. I wasn't writing every day because after a full day of flying and an adrenaline ebb, all I wanted to do was go to sleep. Some things I decided not to mention for fear it would worry them sick, others simply because I hadn't rationalized them myself and couldn't verbalize how and what I was feeling.

Our Pink teams took on a new element over the next few days. An Air Force OV-10 Bronco Forward Air Controller (FAC) began to accompany our teams into the AO. They knew that if there was anything to be found, we would find it and they wanted to be in on it.

The OV-10 was a purpose-built machine derived from Department of Defense studies carried out in the early sixties. It was one of several designs submitted to meet the Marine Corps' LARA (Light Armed Recon Aircraft) specification.

The Bronco was chosen for its superb all-round vision cockpit, short takeoff and landing (STOL), and rough field performance. The Air Force procured 157 of these robust aircraft for use in the FAC role to replace the older Cessna 01s and 02s. Unlike the previous FAC aircraft, the OV-10 had four machine guns fitted for self-defense in addition to its marking rockets.

The Bronco orbited well above us as we worked our areas, and it was comforting to know that we had access to almost instant air strikes should they be required. Too bad they hadn't been around a few days earlier.

On April 6 I flew with Red. We were working the area well to the north of Song Be. This was the closest I had been to the Cambodian border. Our mission for the day was to VR around Bu Gia Map. Bu Gia Map had been one of the last North Vietnamese strongholds in III Corp.

This area of northern III Corp was one of the largest virgin jungles in Vietnam. The enemy haven was a triangular piece of mountainous terrain near an abandoned airstrip originally constructed by the French Army in the early fifties. Sometime in 1965, a small group of Special Forces–advised troops had been decimated there. The area had been seldom reconned by any Allied troops after that and the base had been abandoned in early 1966.

The NVA had moved in shortly after it had been vacated by our troops and rumor had it that the Communists used it as an R&R center for their troops.

Aside from a few forays by Special Forces units and a longer sweep by the 101st Airborne Division in 1966, the NVA had been left virtually untouched there until the Cav moved into the AO.

On March 22, the First of the Twelfth Cav had closed FSB Jewel and opened FSB Snuffy at the south end of the Bu Gia Map airstrip. We didn't know why, but for some reason there was a lot of renewed interest in the area. At the time we didn't realize that Snuffy was to become one of the fire support bases that would support our incursion into Cambodia the following month.

The area had shown signs of heavy recent use and one of the teams had received ground-to-air fire on several occasions the previous month while finding bunkers and fighting positions, military structures, and trenchlines. We didn't make any contact during the day although the signs of recent use were still evident. Red told me about an arc light that took place on March 19. A B-52 strike, commonly referred to as an "arc light," is a devastating bombardment that does incredible damage. The Air Force had sent in a photo reconnaissance aircraft immediately after the strike to verify the hit. Photos showed that the bombs were "walked" along the entire length of the dirt runway, rendering it useless. A direct hit.

When they sent another photo recon flight up the next day to see whether they could find any bodies, they were amazed to find all of the bomb craters filled in and the runway back in service. A LRRP had reported seeing Russian-built helicopters going in and out as well.

At the end of what proved to be an uneventful day we headed back toward Song Be as the family fox came to life, "Red, this is Eight-zero."

"Eight-zero, Red, go."

"Red, Eight-zero, have you got enough fuel to return to your target area? We have friendlies in contact, they're in bad need of some assistance," forward ops officer, Capt. Steve Leischner, advised. This was what was known as a last light mission.

"Eight-zero, Red, roger that, give me a grid."

"Roger Red, they're about three clicks (kilometers) east of the airstrip. They have two men down."

"Roger that," Red responded.

Red instructed me to tell the little bird to head back to Song Be as it was going to be too dark for him to be of use and we wouldn't have adequate fuel to remain on-station once we shot for these guys. I did as I was told as Red attempted to make contact with the LRRP.

I damn near jumped out of my seat when they finally answered the radio. The crescendo of small arms fire and mortar rounds was overwhelming. The voice at the other end of the radio sounded terrified. "Red, please hurry. We're in deep shit. My radio op is dead and I have another man down. We can't get to him. They're all over us."

Red tried to calm the voice. "Okay, we're on the way. Do you have a grid for me?" he asked.

"Shit Red, hurry," he yelled as the audibility of the small arms became louder and louder. "We're about three k's east of the airstrip . . . hurry, Red. Please hurry."

I was, at the same time, mesmerized by the surrealistic sounds of what was happening over the radio, and terrified by it as well.

"Just keep your heads down for a few more minutes and we'll be there to help," Red told him as he pulled more power.

"Red, I've got four men down. They're on us. Oh shit, it's no use. Thanks for trying but we're goners."

"No, damn it," Red yelled, "pop smoke, I say again, pop smoke!"

There was no reply.

I sat there staring ahead, at nothing, as the tears welled up in my eyes. "Why couldn't they have held out for just another minute," I asked.

The only response I got from Jake was "Cotton picker!" In frustration, he rolled in on an area approximately three clicks east of Bu Gia Map and expended all of our rockets.

The feelings of helplessness, sadness, and frustration were emotions I had never experienced all jumbled together like this. It overwhelmed me and I had tears in my eyes all the way back to Phuoc Vinh.

Mail call that day made up somewhat for what I was feeling. During my school years I was like a big brother to a girl a few years behind me in school, Cyndy McGinnis. Cyndy was stunning with long black hair, freckles, and beautiful green eyes. These were only the dressing for this lady with a super smile and wonderful personality. Today's mail included a package from Cyndy. The long letter bringing me up-to-date on all that was going on at my alma mater was nice, but the real prize was the five-by-seven school photo that she had sent me. I put it up on the shelf in my room and was immediately threatened with an Article 15 for harassing the troops!

The other letter on that day was one of reprimand from Mom for not writing just a few lines every day so they knew I was all right. I wrote back, *"It's not hard to put an envelope in the mail each day, but I'll tell you why I don't. A lot of things happen around here that I will not tell you about. Sometimes I get very depressed and sometimes I get very lonely and I just don't feel up to it. I know how hard it must be on you and Dad having me over here, but please try to keep your mind off of it. Bear with me and have faith."*

Dad wrote that he wished he were there with me to take care of me. I remember thinking what an incredibly stupid thing to say. I would not understand his feelings until I had children of my own.

On the morning after the incident at Bu Gia Map, I received orders for my first Air Medal for distinguishing myself by meritorious achievement, while participating in sustained aerial flight, in support of combat ground forces in the Republic of Vietnam. In other words, I had twenty-five hours of combat flight time.

I flew every day for the next eighteen days and in a letter to my Dad a sense of frustration was already creeping in. *"Yes, Dad, I'm beginning to see what war is all about and believe me, it's nothing like what you read about at home. To be honest, what you read there is nothing but pure bullshit. I really have serious doubts as to whether or not the U.S. wants to win this war. It is really asinine to go out and put your life on the line and you have to call for clearance to shoot at somebody who is shooting at you, and believe it or not, we have to. Yes, war is really bad, especially when it is fought as a game."*

The days dragged on and started to meld together. From one day to the next I would be doing good if I could tell you what day it was. Weekends meant nothing because war and warriors take no time-outs. All I knew was that one day was hotter, lonelier, and more depressing than the other. I finally had to ask my mom to send me a calendar so I could keep track of the time.

The Army tried to provide us with some entertainment. We usually had a movie or a floor show at the club in the evenings, but so many of us went to bed so early that the audiences were limited.

Every now and again I would get a copy of the *Record Ledger,* my hometown newspaper. Some of the others got their respective hometown papers, too. There was the inevitable notice of somebody's death in combat in Vietnam and article after article about the protests and moratoriums. They had an incredibly detrimental effect on our morale.

"You know, you both say keep your chin up and do a good job. We do our best," I would write home, *"really, but I'll tell you what the biggest depression factor for the GI over here is. It's the fact that people in the United States couldn't give a bigger shit about us. You would not believe how low morale gets when we hear about the moratoriums and protests going on there. We're putting our lives*

on the line for those sorry people. Granted, a lot of us don't want to be here, but we are here and we try to do our best. Why can't people understand how we feel? We didn't start this damned war. Are they that blind?"

For the first time, I began to realize the unpopularity of Vietnam.

"As for myself," I continued, *"I am just fine, but very tired. I try to keep myself occupied as much as possible when I'm not flying. I usually find myself lying in my bed nine thousand miles from home and end up getting very depressed. I've tried the movies, to no avail. I watch them and for a few minutes I get happy. Then they end, you walk out the door, and you're slapped in the face by reality and you find yourself even more depressed. Oh well, I can endure."*

The next day, I got some great news. One of the guys had DEROSed and that made one of the bedrooms available in the red hooch. Kevin and I grabbed it and became roommates in name only because the room was, for all intents and purposes, uninhabitable at the time.

We installed a sink with running water. (Actually an ammo can that we sunk into a cabinet was what we chose to call a sink.) Placing a fifty-five-gallon drum on the roof that collected rainwater provided the running water. We cut a hole in the side about two inches up from the bottom and stuck a hose in it that ran down through our wall into a tap at the sink. Spartan, but it worked.

The previous owners of the room had built in some closets and Kevin and I finished paneling the walls with wood that we salvaged from rocket boxes. We even used our Yankee ingenuity to make some stain. The rockets came packaged in a tarpaper barrier and dropping a few of these into a pail of jet fuel made a lovely mahogany-looking stain. Flammable as hell, but it served the purpose.

Flying as much as we were, it was difficult to get the room done, but on the twenty-first I was presented with a solution to the problem. I was summoned to the Aid Station by our flight surgeon, Joseph Eckhert, and was unceremoniously grounded for three days due to fatigue. AR 600-107, paragraph 4a(4) allowed us to fly a maximum of 140 hours in any given thirty-day period. Doc Eckhert told me that I had flown 148.3 hours in the last twenty-one days.

To finish off the room we got a double burner electric hob and I went down to Bién Hoa on that first day off and bought an eight-cubic-foot refrigerator for eighty-two dollars. While I was there I went to the O Club on the Air Force side of the base and had a big T-bone steak. This was a real treat, because by the time we came back from flying, our meal was usually cold leftovers.

The room was very comfortable and proved to be a more than adequate home away from home for Kevin and me. On that same day, we became roommates for real.

On my second day off I made my next purchase from the PX, a nineteen dollar portable cassette player. Kevin and I went to the club to watch *Romeo and Juliet* that night and I came back to the room to make my first tape to the folks. At first I was very apprehensive and self-conscious. It seemed really weird talking into the microphone, so I would normally record when I was alone or whisper into it under my blanket at night.

The first thing I asked Mom and Dad was to get some of my friends over to talk on the tapes that they would be sending me. I hungered for familiar voices and the news of what was going on and who was scoring with whom. Even the process of making tapes would depress me. It made me think more about home and its significance in my life. The inability to go there in person was heartbreaking because in my thoughts I was there every day.

My first day back in the air we worked the area north of Song Be again. On the way up that day we were assigned a mission to cover a convoy on its journey from Phuoc Vinh to Song Be as a result of the Mary crossroads ambush earlier in the month.

Normal rules of engagement would not allow us to shoot at anything within a click either side of the road, the reason being that there could be friendly recon platoons sweeping up on either side of the convoy. Convoy cover was one of the most incredibly boring missions we could draw. A convoy averaged about thirty miles per hour and all we did was fly circles around it all the way to its destination.

Just north of Dong Xoai, a little less than half way to Song Be, the little bird started taking ground fire from a VC in a spider-hole next to the road. The usual procedure then was to call the element that controlled the AO that that particular segment of road (redball) belonged to in order to get clearance to fire.

While we were doing that, the little bird high-tailed it, so the VC started shooting at us. The radio operator took forever, which was not unusual, so while we waited for him to get back to us, we rolled in and blew the VC away.

The radio operator finally came back to us and denied us clearance to fire. We complied by adjusting the grid where we just killed this guy outside the thousand-meter buffer zone and called in one VC killed by helicopter (KBH). Hell of a way to fight a war.

When our LRRP was in the AO we usually kept a Cobra at Song Be at night as a ready reaction aircraft in case they got in trouble during the night. This night would be my turn to spend the night and I wasn't looking forward to it.

Leaving the relative comfort of our room and the relative security of a big base like Camp Gorvad for a sleeping bag in a GP medium tent at Song Be was not in the least bit appealing. Also, Song Be was much closer to the bad guys and much more prone to get hit by rockets and mortars at night.

We secured the aircraft in a revetment and made our way to our forward TOC. After a short brief by Captain Leischner, we found the mess tent and sat down to an incredibly good meal.

There were open-air movies for the troops at Song Be, but I headed back to our assigned tent to get some shut-eye. Sleep didn't come easy because of the unfamiliarity of the area and the ever-present sounds of outgoing artillery fire.

I finally fell asleep but awoke to the sound of something moving around. I did my best to see what I could in the limited light of the night without moving. I didn't know whether the enemy was probing us and there was a VC in the tent or what.

I laid for another minute or so before something jumped on my chest. I about jumped out of my skin! I grabbed my flashlight and shone the light into the beady eyes of a rat that was about a foot long. It looked at me in indignation and scurried out the door. My skin was crawling as I grabbed my belongings. I headed back to the aircraft on the flight line, opened the ammo bay door, and spent the rest of the night there under the stars.

On the twenty-sixth I was grounded for the day to get my hours down again. I wasn't the only one who was high on hours. Division wanted as many Pink teams as they could get in the AO every day and it was having a devastating effect on not only the pilots' hours but the maintenance program as well.

An operations order was issued that day that limited us to flying only half the day, six hours max. We were simply flying too much. To prove the point, I was again grounded on the thirtieth. Even having been grounded for five days of the month, I still had managed to log 173 hours.

"I have seen many things to prove the ugliness of war. Some things happen and all you can do is ask yourself why. I only hope that somebody somewhere has the answer. As for me, I can only try to understand. A verse sticks in my mind, 'Ours is not to reason why, ours is but to do or die.' I know how true that is now."

What I didn't know at the time was just how ugly the war would become. Things were abuzz that day, and I didn't know why. That evening we were all ordered to a Commander's Call at the TOC at 8:00 P.M. To my knowledge this was the first time this had ever been done. We piled into the TOC somewhat puzzled, asking questions; when Major Rosher came in, it got very quiet. He told us that during the conflict that we knew as Vietnam, we were at a disadvantage. Up until that day, from the time the first U.S. troops arrived on the beaches of Vietnam, the North Vietnamese freely occupied parts of South Vietnam's two neutral neighbors, Laos and Cambodia. The Ho Chi Minh Trail and its adjoining network ran through both countries and served as a major infiltration and reinforcement route, as well as a supply route to build up massive amounts of war materials and set up division staging areas.

The Allied Command (MACV) were restricted from crossing into either one of these neutral neighbors thus allowing the North Vietnamese to continue to build up, develop, and retreat into the ever-more-sophisticated sanctuaries they had been allowed to occupy without fear of our intervention. This fact had frustrated us to no end knowing that the NVA could cross into the South, attack us, and then retreat with impunity across the border.

The Communist buildup was getting so blatant and so threatening that President Richard M. Nixon had made the politically sensitive decision to conduct an offensive against these sanctuaries, and on March 27 the planning for the offensive had begun.

The main assault would initially take place on the Fishhook area of Cambodia and would be code-named "Toan Thang," or Rockcrusher 43. Brig. Gen. Robert M. Shoemaker was given command and control of the Fishhook assault and the gathering force was named "Task Force Shoemaker."

The division had received notice that we had to prepare to launch the assault within seventy-two hours of notification. On the twenty-eighth this had been cut to forty-eight hours after permission had been granted to include the Brigades in the planning stages.

On April 30, the thumbs up for the operation had been given.

"Gentlemen," Major Rosher said, "Tomorrow we're going after the enemy. We're going to Cambodia."

The whole place erupted in a loud cheer. For the first time we didn't have to wait for them to come to us. We were going after the bastards and we were going to hurt them bad.

Chapter 10

Death at the Border

"I ain't going to fucking Cambodia," said double-ace Tommy Whiddon.

"Come on, Tom, for fuck sake. This is our chance to hit them where they sleep," we told him.

"No, goddamn it, I don't want to die in Cambodia," Tom protested. "I came here to fight in Vietnam. Not fucking Cambodia. I am not going to die in Cambodia!"

"Who the hell said anything about dying?" I asked him.

Cambodia had remained neutral in the eyes of its government. By allowing the North to continue to use its length for the Ho Chi Minh Trail and its border regions as sanctuaries, our definition of neutrality did not match theirs.

"I can't believe it," I said in exasperation, "we get to go into Cambodia and I'm grounded!"

The early morning hours of May 1 saw the usual mist plumes rising above the jungle canopy. Thirteen thousand miles away in Washington, it was still April 30 and President Nixon was addressing the nation: *"In cooperation with the Armed Forces of South Vietnam, attacks are being launched this week to clean out major enemy sanctuaries on the Cambodia-Vietnam border. Tonight American and South Vietnamese units will attack the headquarters of the entire military operation in South Vietnam. The possibility of winning a just peace in Vietnam and in the Pacific is at stake."*

The main thrust of Toan Thang 43 was aimed at the Fishhook area of Cambodia east of Quan Loi and north of Tay Ninh. Thus it was that Alpha Troop, based in Tay Ninh, and Bravo Troop, based in Quan Loi, were the first elements of the First of the Ninth to cross the border.

The invasion began in the wee hours of the morning when six B-52s let rip in the dark of night. Their mission was to loosen up the jungle that the grunts would soon be humping through. The bombs had just stopped exploding when a massive artillery prep commenced at 6:00 A.M. For the next six hours ninety-four heavy artillery pieces fired almost twenty-five hundred shells at targets that had been pre-selected by aerial recon photos and intelligence reports.

Fighter-bombers streaked across the border on their way to deliver 185 tactical airstrikes while South Vietnamese airborne battalions were airlifted into LZ

East and LZ Center, two fire support bases that had been carved out of the jungle by Daisycutters. These fifteen thousand-pound bombs explode seven feet above the ground so as not to make a crater.

Alpha and Bravo Troops were also the first elements of the division to cross the border into Cambodia. Charlie Troop supported Alpha and Bravo Troops in the first days of the incursion, as we were to be part of the thrust called Toan Thang 45 that didn't launch until May 5 in the area north of Bu Dop. We dominated the air as our "hunter-killer" teams found lots of panicky NVA running around and trying to hide.

Missing that first day because of some stupid regulation really pissed me off, but at least I would be off grounding status by the fifth. I decided to make the most of it. I hopped on the "family car" and went to Long Binh. George Phillips, my good friend from BCT, flight school, and Cobra school had arrived in-country and I went to see him. George was really surprised to see me and we had a nice visit. He wanted to know all about the war and I told him what I knew.

From there I hitched a ride down to Saigon. It was an impressive city with lots of beautiful old buildings, but a coat of paint wouldn't have gone amiss. If I tried real hard, I could almost forget I was in a combat zone. I went to the USO where I made a telephone call home; $16.50 for three minutes, but it was worth it. I found out from Dad that Congress had just authorized a pay raise for the military. I was now making $622.82 per month.

On May 3, Jim Cyrus, a Bravo Troop scout, found one of the largest NVA military installations of the war. Almost by accident, Cyrus discovered what was to become known as "the City."

The City was a massive supply complex three kilometers long and one and a half miles wide. It contained more than three hundred buildings with all weather bamboo walkways that were stacked with arms, ammunition, clothes, food, and medical supplies. Charlie Company, First of the Fifth Cav had the honor of exploiting the City on the ground, while our hunter-killer teams provided the air cover. The City was nothing less than a startling discovery and its loss hurt the NVA terribly. Besides the complex itself, the initial count turned up seven hundred new SKS rifles and four 12.7 mm dual-purpose heavy machine guns.

On day two, Delta Company First of the Twelfth was inserted and came up with additional discoveries of their own. They found 1,123 individual weapons, ninety-two crew-served weapons, sixty-two anti-tank mines, and over 500,000 rounds of small arms ammo. The odd trophies of their find were 359 British Enfield rifles, three small WWII machine guns of Russian manufacture, and even some good old homegrown Remington and M-1 carbines. While we hurt the enemy by locating and eliminating them, the ground pounders hurt them equally by finding cache after cache of weapons, supplies, and ammunition.

The Officer's Club was pretty raucous those first few nights of the invasion. Spirits were high and a renewed life seemed to be prevalent in all of us.

Meanwhile back in the States insanity reigned. The word we got through the *Stars and Stripes* and AFVN was that protests against the war were gaining in strength day by day, and at Kent State University in Ohio students were occupying the faculty buildings. Then on May 4 troops from the Ohio National Guard opened fire on the protesters, killing four and wounding eleven others. Within a few days 450 colleges across the United States closed in protest. What in the hell was going on, we wondered?

Fires had been set in buildings at Berkeley, Yale, and Stanford Universities and the President of the United States was publicly referring to these students as "bums."

Mom and Dad sent me a newspaper article from the *LA Times* and it only served to reinforce my opinion that the media were conducting a campaign of misinformation. One article was about "the troops" in Vietnam, us, who were supposedly defying senior officers and disobeying orders. They even used the word mutiny. The article insinuated that none of us wanted to go into "neutral" Cambodia and many were refusing to do so. What bullshit! At Phuoc Vinh we almost fought one another for the available seats in the aircraft and were absolutely ecstatic that we finally got to go after the bad guys rather than waiting for them to come to us.

The only one who wasn't happy was Tommy.

Tommy Leon Whiddon was shorter than average. With short black hair and a wisp of a mustache, he was a master of the language of the day. Everything was "groovy" and Tommy could "dig it" with the best of us. Born in Florida on February 16, 1949, Tommy had graduated from flight school at Fort Rucker and deployed to Vietnam on March 3, 1970. He arrived in-country two weeks before me.

On Charlie Troop's first official day in Cambodia, I was flying with CW2 Myron Lamont (23). WO1 Chuck Frazier, whose call sign was one-six, was flying our little bird. He was running a road toward the northeast when we came upon a complex of structures. The maps indicated that this was a forest reservation office. We didn't buy it. The main building looked like some sort of headquarters building. It had a flagpole and a parade ground in the front with trenches and fighting positions around it. Two long rectangular buildings sat to its rear and along a treeline. Across the dirt road that we had followed into the area were some hooches, one with a number of antennas attached to its corrugated tin roof. That was the first target. One-six's crew shot the place up and set it on fire with an incendiary grenade.

Having set the communications hooch on fire, we upset the hornet's nest. One-six began taking ground-to-air fire from back across the road at the headquarters building. We rolled in and put three or four pair of seventeen-pound rockets through the roof.

One-six headed back to the rectangular buildings and found numerous uniforms and other military paraphernalia. These were barracks buildings. We engaged but not before most of the NVA troops had made their way out of the buildings into the surrounding jungle.

Throughout most of the morning we had intermittent contact in the area so we ended up calling in ARA and an airstrike. The barracks had been burned to the ground and the main building was badly damaged. The final insult was when

Chuck and his crew stole their flag. Chuck hovered up next to the flagpole while his crew chief unclipped it and they trailed the flag out the door of the aircraft almost all the way back home.

That night the weather was too bad to get back to Phuoc Vinh so we headed to Quan Loi. We landed at Bravo Troops' pad and shut down in their revetments. After securing the aircraft I went to look up my old flight school buddy Bob James. We visited a while before he invited me to spend the night there. We talked well into the night.

While we had teams in Cambodia, we also continued to work our normal AO, albeit much closer to the border. A lot of the NVA and VC were high-tailing it across the border into the now-safer Vietnam. We were waiting for them. Other elements would launch desperate attacks on our bases in Vietnam. Quan Loi, home of Bravo Troop, got hit by seven 122mm rockets on the night of the fifth. Two U.S. soldiers were killed and seven were wounded. The 122 was a terrifying weapon. It was classified as an individual heavy rocket and was fired from a light, easily portable launching stand. It was about four feet long and had a range of ten miles. Fortunately for us, it wasn't terribly accurate.

The NVA had a goal in mind by launching these rocket attacks, ground probes, and making other scattered contacts. They had already learned that they couldn't match our might. One radio call and the whole world would cave in on them—hunter-killer teams to find them; ARA, artillery, air strikes, and infantry to destroy them. But if they could divert our attention and make us pull troops and assets out of the field to reinforce the base camps, their compatriots could concentrate their efforts on evacuating the much needed supplies that we were finding, exploiting and destroying.

Cambodia was like a turkey shoot. There were enemy soldiers everywhere and some so green that when the LOH hovered over them they just stood there gawking at it. Most of them didn't live long enough to decide whether they should shoot or run. In the first two days of the operation, units of the Cav eliminated 562 NVA.

The sixth started out as any normal day, whatever normal was. Steve Beene and Danny "Rags" Rager were flying together as high bird for Whiddon (11).

Steve, being the Cobra AC, was the mission commander, and vectored Tommy around open areas. From his higher vantage point, the high bird usually does all of the navigating while keeping the scout out of harm's way as much as possible and vectoring him into areas of opportunity.

While our hunter-killer teams were working in Cambodia, I was back at Phuoc Vinh oblivious to what was going on out in the AO. I had already flown several missions into Cambodia after President Nixon announced our incursion into the supposedly neutral country. Today was no different from the others except that Rags decided to bring along a tape recorder to see whether he could pick up the sounds of the radios and the cockpit.

"Groovy and our turrets fully operational," announced Aircraft Commander WO1 Steve Beene. "Oh man a village. Wow!"

Tommy didn't want to be in Cambodia. He was adamant that he was sent to fight in Vietnam, not in a neutral country that we held no apparent hostilities against. Today Tommy was in Cambodia. "Okay, I got a gook down here hiding in that trench!" he reported to Steve.

"Ah, roger, make sure he's an enemy type. He may be just a friendly," Steve warned.

(This exchange clearly shows the thoroughness in ensuring the safety of innocent civilians, contrary to what the media was reporting.)

"He's right by the hooch with the green fatigues hanging in it," Tommy continued.

"If you think he's military . . . he's yours."

"Yeah, my observer and my crew chief think he's definitely a gook." The scout crew continued to observe the individual as they hovered over his head.

Steve responded, "If he thinks he's a gook, he's yours."

A short time passed with more conversation before Tommy yelled, "TAKING FIRE! We took a round, we got oil leaking! Two-four, Two-four, I got oil pressure going down. I've got a transmission oil warning light on. I'm heading to the south."

A large field south of the village provided a location to put the aircraft on the ground. While the scouts avoided open areas in flight, when a problem arose it was an ideal place to put down. The Snake had good fields of fire in all directions and could shoot into the tree lines to keep the bad guys' heads down until a lift ship could get in and pull out the crew.

Steve called in a spot report to Operations as Rags vectored the scout ship back toward the Vietnamese border. The ops officer responded by asking for a grid coordinate. "Two-four, Eight-zero, if you'll pass a grid we'll get a couple of teams over there."

"Two-four, Two-seven. Fox," called CW2 Mike "Felix" Poindexter.

"Uh, Two-seven, this is Two-four. Go."

"Man, I'M GOING DOWN, I'M GOING DOWN!" Tommy yelled.

"DOWN BIRD, DOWN BIRD!" Steve cried.

"Eight-zero, this is Two-nine. Crank the blue birds, the little bird is going down," ordered Major Rosher.

"Goddamn it!"

"Have you got him?" Rags queried.

"No!"

"Blue, this is Two-nine."

"Get us a grid right now!"

"Say again. There he is! Over there, over there, over there. I think he's on fire!" Rags yelled.

"Roger, we do have a down bird. We do have a down bird. I think he's on fire at this time. We're en route to his area. I'm up guard and I'll be staying up guard in case he made it out."

"I don't think he did," Rags added. "Get down, I'm going to go out."

"Okay, stay off the mic," Steve told him.

"Eight-zero, this is Two-four. It's just north of Bu Dop. Just north of the strip. He didn't quite make it. It's in the bamboo and the aircraft is on fire and I can't establish commo with him yet. Oh, God!" Steve exclaimed with despair in his voice. "Oh, man!"

"Come on!" Rags said wishfully.

"We've just been bounced off of Song Be," called Medevac One, "Understand you have a little bird down here. We should be out to your house in about ten. Can we get a readout on the crew?"

"So far, we have one individual lying beside the aircraft. He's hurt real bad," Steve responded. "We can't even tell who it is. That's how bad he's messed up, and he moves to wave once in a while, but that's all. I don't know if the, uh, anybody else got out of it or not. We just have to assume they're still inside the aircraft."

Tommy Whiddon and his crew chief, Gary McKiddy, died that day. I heard them die in the privacy of my room. Staring at the cassette player I began to wonder how I came to be in this place called Vietnam and I pondered my own mortality.

The official report was listed as Item 52 of the "Daily Staff Journal or Duty Officer's Log" from Camp Gorvad. It stated

> IN: 1000, FR: 1ACD, TO: TT43 (Toan Thang 43), 3/C/1/9 inserted to SEC a downed OH-6A at XU975334, complete 0915H. OH-6A rec'd GAF, crashed and burned resulting in 2x US KIA, 1x US WIA. UH1H rec'd GAF while inserting 3/CC/1-9. Res: 3x US KIA, fm 3/C/1-9.

While this report conflicts with what we know to be the truth, a further extract from the "Operational Report for Quarterly Period Ending 31 July 1970" further muddled the facts.

> (e) 6 May 1970—At 0900 hours an OH-6A and UH-1H from Troop C at XU956427 received heavy ground-to-air fire from a village. Results were two (2) US KIA, four (4) US WIA and two (2) aircraft destroyed.

Aircraft Commander Capt. Rhett Lewis was flying the Huey that went in. His co-pilot, WO1 Chuck Orr, had only been in-country for two weeks. Rhett was one of the most experienced lift ACs in the troop and an exceptional pilot.

The Huey did not take fire. There were many factors that led to their crash. The aircraft they were flying had just had two 50-caliber machine guns mounted on it. The guns, and the ammo required for them, added lots of weight to the aircraft. They also had a squad of Blues and had just re-fuelled when they got bounced for the downed LOH. Unfortunately, the crash site was less than a five-minute flight from Bu Dop, which didn't allow for any fuel to be burned off.

It was very hot when they arrived on station and Rhett's aircraft was very heavy. As he brought his aircraft to a hover over the trees, there simply wasn't enough power to maintain the rotor rpm, and having bled off those precious rpms, he began to settle. He attempted to lower the nose to get flying speed again, as training dictated, but the rpm loss continued and he went into the trees.

There are a lot of questions that to this day go unanswered. Was it Tommy's loathing for the war in Cambodia that wouldn't allow him to land? Did his Charlie Echo and Oscar influence him? What? Why?

When all of the oil in the main gearbox ran out, everything overheated to the point that gears started to melt and eventually welded themselves together causing the gearbox to cease. When the gearbox ceases, the rotors stop turning and the aircraft tumbles out of the sky like a not-so-graceful rock.

Crew Chief Gary McKiddy was flying as observer that day to give his roommate and best friend, Jim Skaggs, a chance at the gunner's position. Gary was thrown from the aircraft on impact and reportedly wasn't too badly injured. Realizing the danger his crewmates were in, he returned to the burning aircraft to pull out Skaggs. Skaggs was badly injured and Gary pulled him clear of the aircraft before returning to get Tommy out.

When he returned to the aircraft, either the main fuel or the munitions blew up. Gary was killed trying to rescue his pilot and friend, Tommy Whiddon, who didn't want to land in Cambodia. Instead he died in Vietnam, by a few hundred meters.

The whole fiasco was so unnecessary that the loss of two aircraft, two KIAs, and several WIAs can hardly be justified.

One thing I learned about flying in combat though is never to second-guess the decision of an aircraft commander. If you're not in the machine and you don't have all of the facts, then you have no right to ask, "What if?" or say, "I would have." You just don't know.

Had Jim Skaggs been conscious or had anybody else witnessed Gary's act of heroism, he no doubt would have received the Medal of Honor. The fact that he didn't is another tragedy of war.

Tommy Whiddon was the first of my close friends to be killed in action. He wouldn't be the last.

On Friday, August 5, 1999, a barracks and a day room at the Charlie Company, First of the Ninth's area at Fort Hood, Texas, were dedicated to Sgt. Gary Lee McKiddy. Jim Skaggs spoke, and more than one hundred former Ninth Cavalry and family members were on hand to show support and honor one of our own.

We were all tired from flying so much but the targets were moving and we wanted to get to them before they got out of range.

On 7 May, One-six, Chuck Frazier, was doing a routine recon near FSB Myron when he noticed a road running out of a small village. Chuck was curious about this road because it showed some very heavy recent use by trucks. Running the road out of the village, One-six and his crew spotted pallets stacked off to one side. Chuck recalled that the overhead jungle canopy was so thick that they couldn't see very far down into the jungle.

The next day "two of the pallets we'd seen previously were gone and there were truck tracks leading to the spot. We followed them and saw three two-and-a-half ton trucks loaded with troops in complete NVA field uniforms," One-six continued.

"They heard us and tried to dismount the trucks and hide. We engaged and killed twenty-three of them and destroyed their vehicles."

The team continued to exploit the area and made additional finds. As word filtered back to higher headquarters through our spot reports, LTC Francis Ianni, commander of the Second of the Twelfth, sent his Delta Company to make a combat assault into the area.

Delta Company landed about five hundred meters north of the site and moved south. Two platoons swept the area and fifty meters after crossing the road they came into contact with about forty to sixty NVA soldiers. While breaking the ambush, one of the Cobras hit a hidden cache, blowing it up and revealing the complex.

Although smaller in area than the City, this new complex proved to be the biggest ammo site captured during the Vietnam War. Named after an arsenal in Illinois, "Rock Island East" yielded more than fifty individual camouflaged caches. Each one was stacked six feet high on twenty-by-fifteen pallets about twenty to thirty meters apart on alternating sides of the road.

Rock Island East was approximately twenty-two miles northwest of FSB Buttons at Song Be. The NVA didn't give it up without a fight. We had Pink teams over the site for several days until all resistance had died and the ground troops were able to move about freely.

In all, 326 tons of ammo and weapons were found at Rock Island East, over six and a half million rounds of .51-caliber anti-aircraft ammo alone. Official figures credited the First of the Ninth with 498 of the 868 NVA killed during the week of May 3 through May 9.

Back at Phuoc Vinh the only thing we really looked forward to was a shower after being in the aircraft for up to twelve hours. More often than not, having flown last light missions, we got back to find empty water tanks.

The mood was jovial in the evenings and we gathered in one or another of the hooches to gloat over the day's accomplishments. To the outsider we would have seemed like a bunch of teenagers celebrating the victory of a football game over our archrivals. Some of us *were* still teenagers!

Kevin and I always enjoyed company in our room. It had a homey "stateside" atmosphere and we were renowned for keeping our fridge well stocked with cold drinks. The other thing we were always good for was Kraft macaroni and cheese dinners. Both of our parents sent them in care packages along with Kool Aid and other things we couldn't get in-country.

Cyndy's picture was on my desk right in front of the door and it was always the first thing I would look at as I entered the room. It always made me stop and think for just a minute. I looked at her smile and was grateful for making it through another day.

After the guys left in the evening, Kevin and I would usually have a deep conversation about one subject or another until one of us dozed off.

I often got very lonely and melancholy at night just thinking about home and where I would like to be. Vietnam was a place I didn't want to live in, and I certainly didn't want to die there either.

What was life like during those days people have asked? What did you do? *"You fight the war and when you got done you went home. Well, not home, but back to the hooch to think about home! A typical day consisted of an early wake up, usually before sunrise; a quick breakfast; flying all day; and then when you got back you showered; if there was water left in the tanks! Then you ate; if the mess hall was still open or the O Club hadn't run out of food, and then you fell into your bunk to get some sleep."*

While ground action continued to be heavy, our war, the air war, continued to hurt the NVA. Having said that, it was one-sided at best.

On the eleventh, Kevin was flying with Dave Lawley and one-six was their little bird. They were assigned a BDA mission for an airstrike that had gone in earlier in the day. Chuck was flying low over dense jungle late in the afternoon. They were about thirty miles north of Song Be. Chuck saw the largest mess hall he had ever seen. It had been partially destroyed by the blast. As he continued to "snoop and poop," they began taking fire from NVA who were wearing green uniforms. Chuck's charlie echo opened up and killed twelve of the NVA. Lawley rolled in and scored twenty-five more kills.

Documents captured from the enemy were an invaluable source of intelligence. They often included unit designations, locations, troop strength, and reports of their activities. One thing the NVA and VC were very good at was hiding their casualties. We would often get into contact and see them fall but when we went back in to assess the situation after the contact had been broken, all we would find were blood trails—sometimes nothing at all.

This made it difficult to assess how much damage was actually inflicted on them and they reckoned it was having a morale effect on us, too, because we were expending much ordnance, getting shot at, and seeing no result.

The rest of the week produced many more small contacts, and we were able to confirm the demise of about forty more NVA troops.

Our missions continued to be fairly routine, except when fate, irony, or the bad guys interrupted that routine.

One such *routine* had to be changed as a result of the first few weeks of fighting in Cambodia. Up until now we crewed the aircraft with two crews each day. The first crew would fly what we called "first light." This was a 6:15 A.M. takeoff and they would fly until 12:30 P.M. Then one of the troop's UH-1s would fly the relief crews, up to where the aircraft were, drop off the last light crews, and take the first light crews back to base. The last light crews would fly from 12:30 until after the sun had set.

Because of the amount of flying we were doing and the level of activity, we could no longer afford to break away a UH-1 to act as a taxi. The aircraft were all flying so much that the crew chiefs had little time to maintain them; spares were hard to come by, and we were, if the truth were known, having a difficult time fielding enough aircraft.

We were also short of personnel and were running out of crews to continue this two-crew pattern. We were simply flying too many hours, so it had to be changed. We began to field three teams a day and the same crew would fly all day. This often meant a fourteen- or fifteen-hour day in the cockpit. The benefit of this new plan was that it gave those who weren't flying a day off and an opportunity to get their cumulative hours down.

The level of activity in the Cambodian area of operation was actually starting to taper off a bit by now. The major cache sites had been discovered and were being exploited and destroyed, and the largest concentrations of enemy troops had either been neutralized or disappeared into the jungles. Daily activity was down to the teams finding small pockets of NVA, isolated hooch and bunker complexes, and getting shot at.

One day our little bird was running a trail that had shown some heavy recent use and encountered four NVA carrying a guy on a stretcher. When they heard the helicopter coming they dropped the guy, grabbed their AK-47s, and took off running. The casualty was a double amputee. His face was all bandaged up as well. He was, unfortunately, killed in the ensuing firefight.

On our days off, we hopped rides down to Bién Hoa. It was amazing how differently the Air Force lived in a combat zone from those of us in the Army. Bién Hoa east was First Cav Rear, a tent city with dirt roads and the bare essentials. Bién Hoa west was the U.S. Air Force base complete with paved roads, shuttle buses, air conditioned billets, movie theaters, a Bank of America branch, a huge post exchange, and ice cream stands.

There is a story about the Army going in and building an airfield. When they asked for more funds for the niceties, they were told that they had spent their budget on the airfield and they would have to make do. The Air Force would go in and build theaters, clubs, barracks, leisure facilities, and so forth. When they got done they would say, "Gee, this would be a great place to build an Air Base. Can we have some more money?" Now I know that the story is true.

About this time I received a letter from home as a result of my telling the folks about Whiddon's and McKiddy's deaths. I was less than amused when friends and family members started to write and tell me they knew exactly how it felt to be in the situation I was in.

I wrote back that I didn't think so. *"You don't know exactly how it feels to be sitting around on a quiet night with all your friends and all of a sudden mortars start exploding around you. You don't know what it's like getting your bird shot up and not knowing whether or not you're going to make it back or you're going to crash. And least of all you don't know what it's like covering one of your best friends in a LOH and all of a sudden he gets shot up, and he starts flying back to safety, to civilization, and he crashes. And the only thing you can do up there is sit and watch the aircraft burn and watch him die, and if you know that feeling and you know how it feels to just sit there and watch, and cry because there's nothing else you can do, then fine. Then you can write and tell me that you know what it's like being over here. Until then, I don't want to hear that crap. I want to hear happy things. I want to hear about things that are going on back at home. I don't even want to be reminded that I'm here."*

I copied Rag's tape and sent it home with instructions: listen to this and then tell me you know what I'm going through. I never got another letter like that again.

Mamasan sent me a message through one of the other hooch maids that she wouldn't be at work for a few days. I learned from the other girls that her papasan had been killed. I didn't know if this referred to her father or her husband or whose side he was on, but when she returned to work she was never the same smiling outgoing person I had hired.

As a result of the downturn in activity along the border areas, we started moving farther north into the country. We were briefed that we could fly up to a designated east-west grid line and no farther. We ignored it. As we ventured farther into no man's land, we tended to fly at higher altitudes. Nobody really knew what kind of defenses the NVA had up there and we didn't want to find out by marking our last known position with burning wreckage.

The Cambodian jungle was much the same as Vietnam—dense triple canopy vegetation. As we progressed farther north it was almost as if somebody had drawn a line, with jungle on the south side and on the north just green grass through roughly rolling hills. I nicknamed it the "golf course."

About five miles south of the golf course the topography was very mountainous. The mountains had an average elevation of 2,100 to 2,275 feet. This required careful consideration as to how we would conduct hunter-killer operations. If the LOH was scouting a valley and we maintained our standard 1,500-foot orbit above him that put us well within small arms range. If we flew 1,500 feet above the highest terrain, we wouldn't be able to offer the scout immediate protection and chances were very good that we would have difficulty maintaining visual contact with him.

It was pretty much up to the individual aircraft commanders how to conduct the mission, but most of them started working the scout from the top of the mountain down. If he was satisfied that the areas he had reconned were cold, we would feel a bit more comfortable flying closer to the terrain.

Flying along on one particularly beautiful morning we came upon a lovely little village nestled in the trees on top of a plateau. I was flying with Double-deuce (22) David Zimmerman that day. Zimmerman, or "Zeke," was a thin, wiry character. Of all the aircraft commanders we had, I liked flying with Zeke the least. He didn't instill in me a great sense of confidence and he wasn't, in my opinion, a particularly gifted pilot.

Cambodian Highway 14 ran north through the village, but the road south of the village was very difficult to see. I checked my map and found that we were getting an aerial view of Ph Phnúm Krâng, about eleven and a half miles inside Cambodia. The fact that we were only less than a dozen miles inside Cambodia bears witness to the fact that the NVA had built most of their caches, training centers, hospitals, and respite facilities just across the border from Vietnam. That's where most of our efforts had been concentrated up until now. Another factor was that politicians had limited us to a depth of twenty miles.

The NVA would attack us in Vietnam and then make their way back across the border, where they would sit thumbing their noses at us because they knew that politics and the American media forbade us chasing them back.

Ph Phnúm Krâng was as picturesque a village as one could hope to see. Hooches ran along the tree lines, leaving room for the main road and some shops in the center. Flowers bloomed in the front yards. At the northwest corner of the village was a church. The only thing that it lacked was people. The village appeared to be abandoned. It was eerie.

The little bird flew around and through the village several times at high speed. He didn't see anything suspicious. Feeling pretty secure he began hovering around and looking in the windows of the hooches. As he moved off to the southwest corner I noticed two guys running from some bushes. Just as the little bird was about to go and check them out, he received fire from one of the hooches where he had been snooping. They returned fire killing the guy who was doing the shooting and then headed north to check out my sighting.

As he approached the two individuals, they, too, began firing and ran into the church. This church was unable to provide them with the sanctuary that they so desperately sought. We put a pair of rockets through the front door and then all hell broke loose. Both the little bird and we started taking fire and no matter where we went to get away from the fusillade, it prevailed.

The LOH headed west of the village about a click and was still taking fire; he headed north and then cut back to the east and was still taking fire. We followed as always. Our mission was to protect the scout. The scout was screaming. We headed south; about a thousand meters east of the village yet were still taking fire. It was relentless! At one point it sounded as if somebody had hit the side of the aircraft with a ball peen hammer. BAM! BAM! then I realized that we had been hit. I scanned what few instruments I had in the front seat and nothing looked out of the ordinary. I asked Zeke how things looked and he said that he thought we were okay.

It was a strange feeling knowing that we had been hit by enemy ground fire and not knowing what damage had been done. Was the engine going to quit? Was the transmission going to freeze up? It really focused my attention and I finally understood what "puckering" meant.

Finally when we were about three or four kilometers south of the village the scout reported that the firing had stopped. The little bird had been hit, we were hit, and the area around the village for at least a kilometer in all directions was saturated with NVA troops.

I called in the report and asked for artillery. I was told that there would be no "arty" and we were unable to return fire. I was flabbergasted and asked for an explanation.

"That village is friendly," I was told.

"Yeah, well the friendlies just shot the shit out of us," I argued.

Looking back toward Ph Phnúm Krâng, I could see flames shooting out of some of the burning hooches about two hundred and fifty feet into the air. This had to be the result of secondary explosions because hooches didn't burn like that.

Unable to convince our highers that the friendlies had obviously become hostile and after a continuous refusal to shoot artillery, frustration set in. There were alternatives, so we called our old friends in the OV-10s and requested an air strike. The fighters arrived on station and we went to work on Ph Phnúm Krâng. When the fighters reported taking intense ground-to-air fire, attitudes changed back at brigade.

When we got back to Bu Dop for fuel and armament I noticed that we had taken a round through the hydraulics bay. It went in the left side of the aircraft through the bay and out the right. It had missed all the plumbing and reservoirs.

I had the following day off. I had flown twenty-three and a half hours in the previous two days. It took three days of constant contact, air strikes, artillery, and a B-52 strike along the heavily occupied western edge to finally overcome the resistance and take the village. The NVA had infiltrated Ph Phnúm Krâng one night months before, marched the entire civilian population out into the jungle, and shot them. The village then became a ready-made sanctuary.

Ph Phnúm Krâng was renamed "Death Village." By now it was a memory. It had been blown off the face of the earth. On May 7 Company A of the Seventh Cavalry air assaulted in to establish Fire Support Base Neal. Some anti-aircraft fire met them but that quickly ended. As they began to exploit the area they found increasing amounts of weapons and rice.

Within ten days, the NVA had regrouped and mounted a more intensive defense of the larger cache sites that we knew had to be in the area. On the ninth, Company A were in contact for six hours straight in an effort to take one hill. The NVA defense was very intense and at the end of the battle, Company A found a large hospital complex on the summit.

Having won the battle of Death Village, we continued to move north toward the golf course. I was flying with Two-seven, Mike Poindexter, who we all affectionately called "Felix." Felix was tall and slender with surfer-style hair that he was constantly brushing out of his eyes. One of the more experienced ACs in the platoon, Two-seven was a good man to fly with. He was almost always cool and composed and ever the professional soldier aviator. He was what I aspired to be when I made aircraft commander.

Just where Highway 14 came out of the jungle into the golf course was a small hamlet called "O Rang." A few buildings occupied the south side of the road. One had the most extensive array of antennas that I had seen since I'd been in-country. Trench lines surrounded the building, with fighting positions at the corners, and the entire area was surrounded by concertina wire. Approximately five hundred meters to the east was a large pit where some sort of anti-aircraft weapon had once been. Happily, it was now empty.

To the north a short narrow dirt road twisted along a treeline to a complex of buildings. As was SOP at the time, we went up at altitude out of harm's way. The area produced no ground fire so we continued north. We didn't dare shoot up the place because we weren't really even supposed to be there.

As we flew, our heads were continually on the move looking for tracers, flak, aircraft, or anything else that might be up there. At almost exactly the same time Felix and I noticed a strange-looking black jet flying around at about the same altitude as we were at. I was pretty scared and noticed the crack in Two-seven's voice when he called in the spot report. It turned out to be a B-57 Canberra, probably a recon sortie.

A large city was on the map and we continued north until it came into view. It had an airport with a very long runway. We spotted hardened aircraft bunkers along the runway, with warehouses lining the east side. On a hill to the northwest we saw several anti-aircraft positions and what appeared from the distance to be a radar site. This was Mondol Kiri City.

Having seen the runway and the bunkers we climbed even higher. How high was safe? Knowing we were a lot farther north than we were authorized to be, we took a last look and started to turn back to the south. Out of the corner of my eye I caught some movement on the runway. An airplane was taking off!

We are in deep shit. My heart was pounding.

We had a full load of armament and I was pretty good with the minigun, but what type of aircraft and how well armed it was we wouldn't know until it got within range. The aircraft was slow moving, which was a relief. We deduced that it wasn't a MIG sent up to intercept us. The aircraft continued its slow climb and we descended to meet it. We were still well above it when we identified it as an observation aircraft, much like our 01 Bird Dog. I knew immediately from the shape of the aircraft that it hadn't been built in the west. It was all black with no markings of any kind.

We continued our descent until we were close enough to see the pilot, who now began to turn to the north. Because we were above and behind the aircraft, we had no reason to believe he even knew we were there. He took no evasive action. The pilot was Asian and wore a black helmet with a red star on the side. I called in a spot report and then called Paris Control. This was the call sign of the main air traffic control agency for U.S. fighter aircraft in Vietnam.

I described our location, the sighting of the aircraft, and the color. Next, I described the pilot and the fact that he was now heading north, and asked for permission to engage it. Permission was denied with Paris Control stating "the aircraft is confirmed friendly."

"What?" I asked no one in particular.

"How can it be a friendly aircraft and how can they confirm it so quickly?" Felix asked. It had just taken off from a Cambodian airfield, it's unmarked, the pilot has a red star on his helmet, and he's heading north.

"Friendly to whom?" I asked Paris Control.

Once again we were told to break off contact and to get back south. Reluctantly we turned away and headed toward Bu Dop to refuel. A minute or two after we rolled out of our turn a flight of U.S. Air Force F-4 Phantoms streaked by us. I could only guess what their target was.

One of the oddities of this war presented itself on May 19. It was Ho Chi Minh's birthday and the NVA called a cease-fire until noon. How they managed to get the word to every swinging dick in the jungles of Vietnam that it was Uncle Ho's birthday and they weren't supposed to shoot at each other was a paradox to me. For whatever reason, the cease-fire didn't apply to us. We would have ignored it anyway.

After flying eight and a half hours that day we were anxious to get back to Phuoc Vinh but it was not to be. The monsoons were particularly heavy that evening and we ended up in Song Be for the night. Based on my previous experience there I punched the two releases on the ammo bay door and made myself a bed.

Sunrise brought the steam from the jungle and the discomfort was immediate. My flight suit stuck to my body, another fact of life.

Fortunately, all we had to do was get the aircraft back to Phuoc Vinh to change crews that morning. Good thing as I was duty officer that night. The mortars rained down at 11:45 that evening, so part of my duty was taken up inspecting the aircraft and troop area for damage. There was none.

A routine of flying every other day became the norm. This enabled us to field three teams a day while keeping our hours down to a reasonable level.

I wandered down to the TOC on May 25 to see what was going on and, from the transmissions coming over the family fox, it sounded as if One-six was having another exciting day. A few miles south of FSB Neal, he had found another motor pool. The team engaged the area with organics and called in an airstrike as well. When it ended, the tally was thirteen jeeps destroyed, two deuce and a halves destroyed, four jeeps damaged, five bunkers destroyed, fifteen 55-gallon drums destroyed, and five NVA killed.

War is a funny thing. It affects different people in different ways. One of the scout pilots who had arrived in-country after me had a penchant for crashing, and unfortunately, not as a result of hostile action. The first time it happened it was kind of funny. He was flying around a small clearing south of FSB Buttons. The clearing had a large tree in the middle of it when he straightened up and flew straight into the tree trunk, bouncing off like a bumper pool ball and into a smaller tree, according to Two-seven, who was covering him that day.

The second time, Major Rosher was out in *Good Vibrations,* his UH-1C gunship, and arrived on the scene. "Blue, this is Six, understand he took a round through the compressor?"

"I don't know yet, Six, we haven't arrived at the aircraft yet," replied Mike LaChance, the Blue platoon leader.

A few minutes later, "Blue, this is Six. Understand he took a round through the compressor?"

Sounding exasperated Blue replied, "Six, this is Blue. We still have to hump about another hundred meters until we get to the aircraft."

A few more minutes passed and "Blue, this is Six. I understand that he took a round through the compressor."

And the reply, "Six, this is Blue. We're just about there now."

Two minutes later, "Blue, this is Six. I understand you've arrived at the little bird and he took a round through the compressor."

"We're just checking over the aircraft now. There are no apparent bullet holes and negative on a round through the compressor," LaChance reported.

"Blue, this is Six," Major Rosher came back sounding a bit exasperated. "Put one there, goddamn it!"

He had ordered the Blues to "put a round through the compressor section." The reason he did it was to at least give the appearance that he had been shot down. The pilot was christened with the nickname "Crash."

The third time it happened I was flying with Two-six, Ed McDerby, when the down bird call came. "Down bird, down bird, about three k's southwest of Bu Gia Map."

We headed that way as we verified the position. We overheard on the radio that it was "Crash" and the joking started. But it ended abruptly. The aircraft was burning badly and only one person was observed outside the aircraft when White platoon leader, Lt. Ron Beyer, got over the wreckage.

Here is where the mystery begins. The aircraft, OH-6A 67-16547 was classified as a combat loss; in other words, he was shot down and the crewmembers burned to death in the wreckage. The pilot was burned, too, and was subsequently medevaced to Japan.

In combat, people who serve together tend to stick together and cover for one another. I have no reason to believe or accuse anybody of lying, but certain things just don't add up. Nobody actually recalls a "taking fire" call. Okay, sometimes things happen so fast and an aircraft may get hit in a vulnerable spot so that it goes down before anybody knows what happened, but that was certainly the exception rather than the rule.

Very little ordnance was expended that day—and little, if any, hostile action. There are also no after-action reports or spot reports about the "shoot down" in the archives. Perhaps there was no action to report?

I wish to cast no aspersions on anybody but I still have grave doubts as to the accuracy of the circumstances surrounding this "shoot down." The pieces in this jigsaw didn't fit together properly then, and still don't.

During the morning of May 31 we had flown off a couple of loads of fuel with no real activity. After refueling for the third time we headed back into Cambodia and began running Highway 132 west out of O Rang. We were back into triple canopy but the road was easy to follow. The scout overtook a courier riding a bicycle down the road. His gunner shot the guy and knocked him off his bicycle. He rolled into the underbrush so we rolled in. One of our seventeen-pound rockets must have hit the guy square in the back. When the LOH went back in to see if we had got him he reported, "I think you got him. All I have down here is a leg!"

We continued to follow the road and came upon a small village, Bûy Phlôk. There were a few hooches to the north and a compound on the south side of the road. The compound was completely surrounded with high fences and had guard towers in all four corners. To my surprise, there was also a basketball court—to my knowledge Cambodians didn't play basketball. The little bird didn't venture too close and, realizing that we may have stumbled upon a POW compound, we opted to get the hell out of the area and call for help.

The spot report was called in and we were told to return to Bu Dop immediately for a formal de-briefing. We described what we had seen in great detail and the decision had been made that the following morning all three troops of the squadron would team up in an attempt to liberate any U.S. POWs that we found. It was a delicate operation because if we screwed it up, the NVA could just kill everybody and hightail it. A lot of coordination took place during the night and in the morning we headed north in force.

The command and control (C and C) aircraft with the squadron commander, Lt. Col. Clark Burnett, stayed high at first. They carried a South Vietnamese interpreter on board.

Two LOHs broke the morning's silence as they homed in on the compound. There were no signs of life and the gate was ajar. The scouts hovered over the fence and started a slow and meticulous search of the buildings. Nothing. The compound had been abandoned.

While they were conducting their search, a Cambodian woman emerged from one of the hooches across the street and just stood in the road. The C and C aircraft landed in the road and the interpreter jumped out along with the CO and some Blues.

The woman confirmed what we had thought. The compound was a POW camp and had been occupied when we happened upon it the day before. During the night the NVA loaded up all of the POWs on to a deuce and a half and took them to the airfield on the other side of the village where they had been flown out to the north. We didn't even know there was an airfield there!

We were really bummed. I can't imagine how the POWs must have felt hearing us overhead before the sounds of our retreating rotor blades. They probably thought that we were abandoning them. I still wonder how many of those guys actually made it home or might have had we been successful.

Following this disappointment we headed back to O Rang with One-six as our little bird. He first went to check out the anti-aircraft pit to make sure there was nothing in it. Hovering over the lip, Chuck mentioned that there was a large tunnel leading from the pit in the direction of the comm center. Satisfied that it was empty he then flew across to the buildings by the trees.

We had found an NVA motor pool with seventeen jeeps and 2 two-and-a-half-ton trucks inside. Outside the building were five bunkers and a supply of fifty-five-gallon drums of gas or oil or a combination of both.

One-six hovered outside the doors while the maintenance crews continued to work on the vehicles inside seemingly oblivious to his presence. One-six, being One-six, couldn't leave well enough alone and his crew started stirring up trouble. The mechanics finally made the mistake of reaching for some AK-47s. It was the last move they ever made.

It was getting late and we were low on fuel, so we broke off and headed back across the border for the day.

The next morning the weather was awful. Many mornings we would find the jungle covered with low cloud, which made it unworkable. The little bird could get between the cloud and the trees, but then the Cobra would be far too vulnerable at low level to be effective.

Three teams lifted off from Phuoc Vinh and headed north to Song Be because we couldn't get in to Bu Dop. The low cloud persisted after we had refueled, so we all shut down and went for breakfast.

We emerged from the mess tent suitably replenished but much chagrined to see the cloud still lingering. One of the Cobras lifted off to do a weather check. This was routine in these weather conditions. The longer we were on the ground the farther the enemy could move and the more time it offered them to disappear into the jungle.

The cloud base was still far too low for us to do effective visual reconnaissance. When the Cobra settled back into its revetment and shut down, we decided our course of action. Someone suggested that we should go and pay O Rang a visit that morning. With brigade's blessing, two LOHs would lead us up, low-level, between the treetops and the cloud base. The Cobras would pop up on-line and expend all of our rockets on the comm center and the motor pool.

After a quick brief we mounted up and cranked the aircraft. We flew up in a gaggle of five until we neared O Rang. The LOHs headed in on-line to give the hamlet a quick look over and to make sure the NVA hadn't fortified the place during the night. Confirming that everything looked much the same as it had when we left it the day before, the three Snakes got in a line three abreast as the scouts vectored us in to the target area.

At the scout's command we all popped up from treetop level and salvoed our rockets. We expended all 149 of our rockets and O Rang disappeared in a cloud of smoke and dust.

We had a hail and farewell that night. This one not quite so eventful as my first, but this one brought on new emotions. Several of the guys whom I had gotten to know would be going home soon. It was thrilling that they had made it and to see the excitement on their faces. The presentations were always tinged with humor. The bad times were best left in Vietnam.

Chapter 11

Snake Pilot

On the first of June 1970 I was off duty and in the morning I went down to collect the platoon's mail. The content of my mail had shifted in sentiment from everyone telling me they knew what I was going through to telling me they hoped I would come home soon. They didn't understand the implication of what they were saying. The only way I would come home before March 15, 1971, would be in either a box or a black bag.

The thought of home was still difficult to deal with. In my next tape home I told my folks that *"When I get home I'll try to make up for the year that I've missed out on. I haven't been out of a uniform now in three months, day or night . . . there's nothing else to wear and nowhere to wear it to. There is nobody to impress and, as young as I am, it's pretty difficult. I guess war is difficult for everybody. I just hope it's over soon and we can all come home. No, I'm not down in the dumps and I'm not crying on anybody's shoulder. I just want to come home."*

I was still trying very hard to assimilate all of the information I had learned in the past nine weeks of flying in combat. Before I could even be considered as an aircraft commander I would have to demonstrate competency in map reading, radio procedures, getting AO and artillery clearances, working the scout, and putting in artillery, air strikes, combat assaults, and inserting and extracting the Blues. The other, more obvious, requirement was the ability to shoot rockets with precision and consistency, but we didn't get much practice in the front seat.

The next day I was back in the air. Things in the Cambodian AO had really slowed down for us. There were still small skirmishes with the NVA but the major caches had been found, and the main concentrations of NVA had either been killed or had retreated farther inland. So, the flight was nine hours of boring holes in the sky.

I had also started to think about R&R by now and where I wanted to go. Lots of the guys went to Thailand or Taipei to sow some wild oats. There was something about those slender oriental women with their long, silky, sparkling black hair flowing down their backs. I was thinking more of Hawaii and getting some friends to meet me there. Female preferably! I just wanted to be back on U.S. soil, although the girls did have their appeal.

R&R was difficult to plan, though. We could only specify if we wanted to go the first half of a month or the second half, and where we went depended on the allocations for our period.

I wanted to go to Hawaii during the later half of September to celebrate the halfway point in my tour. September 15 would be six months. Having mentioned to my folks that I was planning to go to Honolulu, they began to make plans to meet me there.

I had the list of hotels that offered R&R discounts. Rooms were being offered on Waikiki for between $21 and $25 per night. (I was earning $22.30 a day at the time.)

The R&R books mentioned all of the places to see on Oahu. Some of them were pretty inaccessible by public transportation and to solve that problem the rental car agencies also offered special deals to R&R personnel. The conditions of rental note stipulating that one had to be twenty-one years of age to be eligible made me laugh. I could go and fight their silly fucking war, but I couldn't rent a car in my own country.

That night my flight school pal, Bob James, popped in on me after getting weathered in at Phuoc Vinh. He was covered with mud up to his knees and was really pissed off. "What the hell happened to you?" I asked when I saw him. I could only laugh as he told me that walking over to the hooch he sunk in a mud puddle up to his knees and lost all his maps. He then proceeded to accuse me of booby-trapping the squadron area.

Bob was amazed at the difference between his outfit and Charlie Troop. They had to be up every morning at 7:30 A.M. to stand formation. And if the officers were caught calling each other by their first names, they were subject to an Article 15. The only time we stood formation was during an awards ceremony, a change of command, or a memorial service. As for names, we usually called one another by call sign, nickname, or first name. That was SOP. The only one whom we ever called by anything else was the CO.

Bob and I stayed up until about 2:00 A.M. talking, much the same as when I spent the night with him in Quan Loi. It never seemed to matter what time you went to bed, 4:45 always came early for the first-light pitch pull.

The weather still wasn't cooperating when we awoke. The same system that caught Bobby was still lingering in the AO. At about ten o'clock Jake asked me to go out and do a weather check. "Take Mr. Wyatt with you and show him the area," he said.

John "Mel" Wyatt had just arrived in the troop. A lanky kid from western Kentucky, Mel had yet to fly his first mission. I stopped by his room and told him, "I'm going to do a weather check, Wyatt. Red wants you to go with me."

"Yes, sir," he answered apprehensively.

"I'll meet you down at the aircraft."

I went down to the flight line to pre-flight the aircraft. Mel showed up just as I had finished. "Uhm, excuse me, sir," he said, "but aren't you going to wear your chicken plate [armored vest]?"

"Damn it, Wyatt. Quit calling me sir! I'm a warrant officer just like you are," I told him. "And no, I am not wearing a chicken plate."

"How come?" he questioned me.

"First of all, there just isn't enough room in the aircraft. Second, the damn things are uncomfortable and hot." I continued, "And finally, look at the aircraft, Wyatt. You're in the front seat and you're wearing both the chest and back plate, right?"

"Um, yes, sir," he answered.

"Damn it Wyatt, quit calling me sir," I yelled. "Now, if we get hit, a bullet will have to pass through your chest plate, go through you and your back plate, through an armor plated seat and the instrument panel to get to me. Right?"

"Yes, sir," Mel answered somewhat confused.

"So as long as you're wearing yours, I don't need one, do I?"

He looked back at the aircraft and when he turned around to me his eyes were as big as saucers.

"I guess not, sir," he gulped.

"Wyatt, quit calling me sir!"

In the morning of the sixth a formation was called on the parade ground between our hooch and the squadron TOC for an awards ceremony. I hated them. I felt so exposed just standing out in the middle of a large open area. It had been drummed into us not to loiter in open areas and now we were being ordered to do just that. After a few announcements, the awards presentation began.

"Mr. Zahn, front and center," the first sergeant barked.

I looked around a bit startled before making my way up to where he and Major Rosher were standing. It was all I could do to remember the close order drill steps to arrive where I had been summonsed.

The first sergeant bellowed,

By direction of the Secretary of the Army, under the provisions of Army Regulation 672-5-1. Attention to orders. General order number 9634, June 6, 1970. Warrant Officer One Randy Zahn is awarded the Army Commendation Medal with "V" Device for heroism in connection with military operations against a hostile force in the Republic of Vietnam. Warrant Officer Zahn distinguished himself by valorous action on 7 May 1970.

Disregarding his own safety, he courageously exposed himself to the dangers inherent in the combat environment as he directed his efforts towards neutralizing the enemy threat. His heroic and valiant actions were characterized by a great concern for the welfare of his comrades and contributed materially to the successful accomplishment of the United States mission in the Republic of Vietnam. His loyalty, diligence and devotion to duty are in keeping with the highest traditions of the military service, and reflect great credit upon himself, his unit, and the United States Army. Signed EC Meyer, Colonel, Chief of Staff.

Major Rosher then pinned on my ArCom and offered his congratulations.

The action I got the medal for took place the day after Tommy and Gary had been killed. Everybody was pissed off and smarting from losing our friends, and in situations like that people tend to go out and do stupid things. Others see it, not knowing what is going on in that person's mind, and in the next moment, there's a hero!

The truth of the matter is I was out there doing my job. I was doing what I had been trained to do, what I got paid to do, and what I was expected to do. Besides that, I had no choice in the matter. I was just a co-pilot!

Sometimes when I got back from a mission, and once the adrenaline had stopped flowing and I had time to think about the day's activities, I sat down and thought, "What a stupid shit!" or "I can't believe I did that." I don't think any-body ever went out on any given day with the intent of becoming a hero.

General Order 9634 was, in fact, a form with a few blank areas to be filled in. The action really took place in Cambodia, but since we weren't at war with Cambodia, the orders said the Republic of Vietnam.

The next night at our platoon meeting we were surprised to hear that the Navy was joining the war and would be working with us beginning on the eighth. A specially equipped Kaman HH-2 Seasprite was coming to Phuoc Vinh for a trial of new equipment. Officially it was called the Naval Airborne Munitions Detector. The crew, and subsequently we, called it the MAD bird. They called it MAD for the magnetic anomaly detector they would be carrying and we called them MAD for flying around at the height and speed that they were proposing.

The MAD was an electronic pod, originally designed for anti-submarine warfare that they lowered on a winch to a given height above the trees. As they flew around at a constant height and speed over a pre-planned search grid, the MAD would measure high concentrations of magnetic material. An operator sat at a panel in the back of the aircraft and whenever a reading went beyond a cer-tain level they would drop a smoke grenade and we would be there, not only as escorts, but also to provide immediate visual reconnaissance of the more signifi-cant readings.

It often gave erroneous readings, but on the other hand it also led us to some pretty significant cache findings. For the most part, we didn't like the mission. It generally resulted in a boring day.

Walker Jones, Cavalier One-eight, was the little bird pilot on the day of one of the MAD missions. Walker hailed from Mississippi and he talked with an amusing southern drawl and had a great sense of humor.

Walker and his crew got shot down on one of the missions and thankfully they all survived the crash with nothing more than a few cuts and bruises. The MAD bird became their rescue aircraft as they winched the crew to safety, and by the end of that day, all of us were very glad to be riding shotgun for the Navy, especially WO1 Walker Jones and his crew.

On the night of the eighth we had a floor show. Floor shows were always enter-taining in more ways than one. The bands could be Australian, Filipino, Vietnamese, Thai, or American. The American groups tended to stay in the larger more secure base camps such as Biến Hoa, Cam Ranh Bay, or Da Nang. We usually ended up with the oriental groups. It was always funny to listen to them singing in pigeon English, not understanding a word of what they were singing. And because of the oriental tongue, "rolling down the river" became "lolling down la livah."

The show was in full swing that night. The group was Vietnamese and the lead singer was a beautiful twenty-year-old girl. Just as we were really getting into the show, the electricity went kaput. After about five minutes, the air in the club became stifling and everybody went outside to await the return of the electricity.

The singer was standing off by herself so I went to talk with her. She actually spoke English very well, having graduated from high school where she studied it for two years. We spoke briefly about the failed electricity before she asked me where I was from. I told her I was from California and she said she had always dreamed of California.

Next, it was my turn and I asked her what she wanted to do with her future. Most of us would launch off into careers and aspirations. She said ruefully that she just wanted to live long enough to be somebody's wife and mother. She felt lucky that God had given her such a beautiful voice and her desire was to go somewhere for voice lessons to further her singing ability and career.

I asked her if she would like to go to the United States one day and she began to cry. She told me that ever since the war started all she had dreamed about was going to America. She said, "It must be really nice living somewhere where you don't have to worry about someone running over your back fence with a rifle or hand grenade trying to kill you. I always dream of going to the United States but it costs so much for a Vietnamese girl." She hated the war and wanted to go away . . . to any place. The VC had murdered both her mother and her father.

She asked whether I would let her write to me so she could practice her English. She couldn't afford to buy stamps and the only address I had was an APO address. Something as silly as a postage stamp prevented it from happening and after that night I never heard from nor saw her again.

Days off were getting to be quite commonplace, but I hated them. I had far too much time to sit and think and I usually thought about home. My parents would send me the *Record Ledger,* and reading it put me through lots of different and opposing feelings. I would read about friends announcing their engagements or getting married and while I seemed so close to it all, I also felt a world away. Jeanne Ball, the very first girl I ever went steady with, was getting married, and here I was nine thousand miles from home and wouldn't be there to see her walk down the aisle. To make matters even worse I received a letter telling me that my high school sweetheart, Donna Moss, was getting married. I was devastated and didn't want to believe it but I was in the wrong place to try to change her mind or do anything about it.

I started to become very depressed with the whole Vietnam thing. When I was off duty, most of my close friends were flying so there was nobody to hang around with. The PX had been an oasis, but most of the items most sought after would be gone if you weren't physically present when they opened the cartons. I wanted very much to be flying, if for no other reason than to keep my mind actively thinking about something other than home.

Kevin came in after flying and he was in a particularly good mood. Kev had a great sense of humor, but, like all of us at different times, he had a dark side. Like me with my picture of Cyndy, Kevin had a picture too. His was of his girl-friend, Carla, and sometimes he just sat there and stared at Carla's picture and I could only imagine how very much he missed her and wanted to be with her.

I would do the same with Cyndy's picture and not even realize I was doing it. Cyndy wasn't even my girlfriend! I had hoped to change that situation when I got home, but for now I could accept the big-brother relationship I had with her.

The electricity had been off for most of the day so I was pretty miserable. When the electricity goes off the fan stops and the perspiration begins. The refrigerator motor stops and the contents either get warm or spoil altogether. The hot plates were useless so I couldn't cook anything, the music stopped and all in all it made for a pretty miserable existence.

I wondered whether people ever stopped to think about all the things that we take for granted. As I grew up I could flip a switch and lights would go on. I never gave it a second thought; it was just a matter of fact. I could push a slender silver handle and the toilet would flush or turn on a tap and water would flow. Things in the refrigerator were always cold, the TV always produced a picture, the stereo played music, and there was almost always a voice on the other end of the telephone line.

And now there was none of that. I hated Vietnam.

The toilets were known as "shitters." They were housed in a corrugated tin shed with a creaking door that swung outward. There was a reason for this. When the mortars started falling, it was a lot easier to kick the door and run than pull it toward you and have to avoid it on the way out. It was nothing more than an out-house with three holes cut into wooden planks that sat above fifty-five-gallon drums that had been cut in half. The place was stifling hot, full of flies and mos-quitoes, and stunk beyond belief. Most of us had small rubber swimming pool floats to sit on to keep from getting splinters in our ass. And it was almost inevitable that whenever I went to the shitter we took incoming.

It was not an uncommon sight to see guys stumbling out the shitter door with their flight suits around their knees heading for a bunker with their naked asses exposed to all.

Since there was nothing to do at Phuoc Vinh, I went up to the transient pad by the tower and hitched a ride down to Saigon. This was only my second time in the city, but it impressed me. The streets were congested with three-wheel cyclo taxis, and beautiful girls in their colorful *ao dais* weaved their way in between, two or three on a bicycle or Vespa.

It was most bizarre to be in a combat zone with gun jeeps and armored per-sonnel carriers patrolling the streets, men in various uniforms, sand-bagged buildings, razor wire, and bunkers, and among it all were these girls. Vietnamese girls in their colorful national dress and magnificent flowing silky black hair falling to their waists. I couldn't help but stare and often caught a glimpse out of the corner of their eyes and just a hint of a smile.

I rode around the city thinking how different it might be if I was just a tourist exploring the wonders of this once magnificent city. I told the driver to take me to the PX in the Chinese district of Cholon.

I walked each and every aisle of one of the largest PXs in Vietnam and bought a few things to take back to Phuoc Vinh. They had a vastly better selection of pre-recorded cassette tapes than we had at the PX at Phuoc Vinh, so I bought a few and headed back to Tan Son Nhut to hitch a ride home.

The electricity came back on shortly before Kevin came in. I sat down to make a tape to Mom and Dad. I always tried to be as upbeat as I could when I spoke to them but I couldn't even force myself to do so today. I was just plain miserable, lonely, homesick, and depressed.

Kevin was just exuberant when he came in and asked, "Who are you talking to?"

"Mom and Dad," I said and he grabbed the mic saying, "Let me talk to them!"

"Hello! Hello, This is Randy's roommate reporting in again, and ah, hello! How are you Mr. and Mrs. Zahn this evening?

Let's see, what is it? It's Tuesday night the ninth of June nineteen hundred and seventy and I've been here exactly three months and one week today and I'm counting the minutes now, believe me. I don't like this place and ah, we just got some incoming out here and they tried to kill me again but they missed again this time.

And, um, you don't have to worry about your son because as fast as I am, he beat me into the bunker, so just call him Twinkletoes!

Uh, let's see, there's nothing much going on around here at the moment. We went flying today. Yes, well, I mean while I'm working for a living and protecting all of you people back home, your son was down in Saigon and ah, you know, having fun!

So again, you don't have to worry about him, he's keeping himself safe.

Let's see what else did we do today? Actually it's been pretty boring. We got rained on a lot and I'm very dirty and I'm hungry right now so, ah, I'll give you back to your son who's about to open me a coke and I think that's very nice of him.

So anyway good-bye and be nice and we appreciate your tapes, believe me I like them and ah, you know, well keep it up and we'll see ya around someday. Bye!"

And with his monologue over Kev handed me back the mic, grabbed his coke, and was off to God knows where. Kevin and I had become closer and closer as the days went on. Here were the two of us, who didn't know each other from Adam three months ago, from opposite sides of the country, he a Catholic and me a Jew, and I knew that we were going to be the best of friends for the rest of our lives. We seldom if ever argued about anything and just thoroughly enjoyed each other's company.

Kevin took Tommy's death very hard, and at one point was going to submit a DA Form 1049 to apply for a transfer to a different unit. There were three things that kept him in Charlie Troop. Our room, because he "couldn't stand me having the best room in Vietnam"; me, because who would take better care of him than me; and me again, because he had to take care of me!

Jake left the unit on the twelfth. Whenever somebody went home I found it a time of mixed emotion. On the one hand I was glad that they had made it through their tour and on the other it was a bit frightening. It was the ACs who went home and these were the guys who took me by the hand and showed me the things that would keep me alive for the remainder of my tour, hopefully. It was a comfort factor that I never stopped to consider. While we were out in the AO and the shit was hitting the fan, it was the AC in the backseat who kept everything in perspective, kept cool and calm (in most cases), and mentored me.

There was so much to learn and all of the ACs had their own idiosyncratic way of doing things. Most of them encouraged me to take from them what I thought would work for me. Not once did anybody ever say to me, "If you don't do it like this, you won't live" or "This is the only way to do this." It was more like, "This is what works for me, but others may have a better way of doing this!"

I had learned a lot from Jake, and Grover Wright before him, and I would miss him.

That evening Greg Allcut took over the platoon. Greg was a seasoned aviator who had done a stint in lift and also one on the ground with the Blues. He was liked and, more important, respected by all of us.

Capt. Allcut presided over his first Red platoon meeting that night. He had inherited a platoon heavy with x-rays and he would be joining us as a front seater. The scales were tipped with eight x-rays on one side and six aircraft commanders on the other.

The meeting went well and when it was over Greg wanted to see the ACs only. That could only mean one thing. They were having the ritual pow-wow where the ACs got together and decided which of the x-rays were most ready to be designated an aircraft commander.

I was to be on standby the following day with Kevin. We were essentially off, but one of us had to be available to do ground runs, maintenance operational checks (MOC), or to take an aircraft up to Song Be should there be a requirement.

We spent most of the day just lying around and reading. Shortly after lunch a runner came up from the orderly room and asked me to report to Captain T. I went down to see what was up. Captain T was so short I didn't expect to see him anywhere but in the club winding down.

"Mr. Zahn reporting as ordered, sir," I saluted.

"Nobody ordered you down here, you clown. I just wanted to have a chat. Now stand at ease. It seems the Army is a bit short of commissioned officers and is offering battlefield-direct commissions. I asked you to come down to see if you would be interested in taking a direct to second lieutenant."

I was skeptical to say the least. "What exactly would that mean, sir?" I asked.

Captain T explained, "It means you would be commissioned as a lieutenant, you'd make more money, and beyond that not a lot would change. Whatever branch you selected could elect to change your assignment but that is highly unlikely. The Army really needs pilots right now."

"So theoretically I could be flying today, take a direct and leading an infantry platoon tomorrow?" I asked.

"Highly unlikely," Captain T responded. "Highly unlikely . . . but yes, that is a possibility."

"Thanks for the offer, sir, but if it's all the same to you I think I'll just stay where I am. I can cope with somebody telling me I'll be flying another type of aircraft tomorrow, but I'm not too keen on getting told I'll be running around the jungle for the next nine months," I said in my own defense.

Captain T just laughed. "I don't really give a rat's ass what you decide, son. In two more days I am out of here, and next week at this time I'm going to be drinking beer at home. It has been a pleasure knowing you Randy Zahn . . . Snake pilot," and he stood and offered me his hand.

I returned to the hooch and Kevin asked what had happened. I told him about the dialogue I had just had with the XO and he just started laughing.

"What's so damn funny?" I asked him.

"Oh nothing. I was wondering when they'd get around to you. I've already been there and done that conversation," Kevin chuckled. "Man, the Army must think we are really stupid!"

The flying continued to be relatively boring. We weren't turning up anything new in Cambodia and mostly flew around looking for anything we may have missed.

Steve Beene was our newest AC, Cavalier Two-four, and we flew a lot together. After one long and boring day, we were flying back from Song Be. We spotted an ARVN compound several kilometers to the south. The French had built this one in their day. It was triangular in shape with lots of trenches and concertina wire.

Just as we were about to pass it the scout called and said, "Hey Two-four, I think we just took fire out of the ARVN compound!"

Steve was pretty incredulous. "What did you say?" he asked.

"We took fire from the ARVN compound down there."

Steve asked me what I thought was going on.

"Hell, I don't know," I told him. "Maybe they're getting overrun or something."

We climbed a bit to make sure we were out of small arms range and took up an orbit over the compound. Sure enough, tracers were coming out of the compound and they were certainly heading in our direction.

After a few attempts we were able to get a frequency and call sign for the unit in the compound. We were both a bit surprised when an American voice came over the radio.

Steve called, "Rocky Top One-three, this is Cavalier Two-four. I have a hunter-killer team overhead and we took some fire out of your compound. Do you require any assistance?"

"Um, Two-four, One-three, no, we don't need any help down here. I'm an advisor and it's my counterpart's birthday and we're just having a little celebration. Must be the guys having some fun and taking pot shots," a now obviously inebriated voice responded.

"Fun!" Steve yelled back. "I would appreciate it if you could tell your guys to have fun doing something other than shooting at me and my little bird."

The voice came back and said, "Don't worry about it. It's not your helicopter."

Steve was having a gross sense of humor failure. "Listen, we take any more fire out of your compound and I'm rolling in and returning fire," he yelled.

This didn't improve the situation any. "You can't talk to me like that and you don't threaten me, do you understand? I am a major in the United States Marine Corps!"

Talk about a breach of radio security.

Steve shot back, "That wasn't a threat, sir. That was a promise."

The major came back and demanded to speak to Six. "You get your commanding officer on the push right now. Do you understand? I will not be talked to like this by no damn helicopter pilot."

Steve asked me to get Major Rosher up on family fox and brief him on the situation. Ever cool and calm, he came up on the frequency. "Rocky Top One-three, this is Cavalier Six. I understand you want to talk to me?"

"I certainly do," responded the Marine. "Your Two-four element has threatened to roll in and shoot up my compound. I happen to be a major in the United States Marine Corps and a damn pilot will not speak to me like that. Now you sort this out and you sort it out now," he demanded.

Six matter of factly went over the details. "Right. I understand my team was flying over at altitude and took fire from your compound."

"Yeah, well my Vietnamese counterpart is having a birthday today and we're having a party and celebrating. His troops have had a bit too much to drink and they're just having a bit of fun."

Major Rosher went over the details again before coming back to us. "Two-four, this is Six."

"Go," was Steve's trademark response.

"Two-four, this is Six. You are not, I repeat, NOT, to expend one single round of ordnance on that compound. Do you understand that?"

"Yes, sir," Steve replied, somewhat disappointed.

"Now, if you take any more fire out of the compound you call tac air and blow that fucking compound off the face of this earth," he ordered, followed by "You got that major in the United States Marine Corps?"

There was no response and there were no more tracers! Galen Rosher had just grown another foot or two in my eyes.

The sixteenth marked the first quarter of my tour gone. It had gone fast but I had had a lot to take in and Cambodia kept us very busy. I was in the air for almost fifteen hours in the past two days and tonight I had officer of the day duty.

I didn't like anything that gave me idle time. I got in real down moods when I had time to think. It wasn't actually being in Vietnam that was so bad, it was when I stopped and thought about all of the things I was deprived of that really got to me. Just hearing a song was enough to trigger an outburst of melancholy. I still related songs to girls and how I missed them.

I was down at the TOC when the alert went off. The NVA had launched a ground probe somewhere along the green line to the north and shots were ringing out. I grabbed my flak jacket and steel pot and headed to the flight line.

The exchange went on for about twenty minutes. Nobody got through the perimeter, but that didn't stop them trying.

I was back in the TOC by the time the first light crews started showing up. I waited only until the ops officer arrived and then headed to my bed.

I woke up shortly before lunch and grabbed the tape recorder. I knew the folks would detect my mood but I still felt obliged to make the effort. I'm sure it was very difficult for my parents to understand and cope with the many mood swings I went through in my various tapes and the short letters that always accompanied them.

My mood could easily change from one hour to the next. I would have been a great case study for some psychology student: melancholy, joy, depression, sadness, anger, and an emotion that had been foreign to me before arrival in Vietnam, that of hatred. The mood swings and the fact that I sometimes lashed out at the folks on my tapes just seemed to be beyond my control.

I went to the PX and wandered the aisles looking at the same stuff I had seen since arriving in-country. At the camera counter I lingered a bit longer than usual. I brought a Kodak Instamatic with me that I bought at Kmart in Savannah, but I wanted a 35 mm camera to improve the quality of the photos I had been taking. I looked and looked and put one down after the other. I wanted one but could I justify it? Now talk about a strange feeling; here I am in the Army fighting on foreign soil and I'm worried about justifying to my parents why I wanted to spend over one hundred dollars on a camera! I received only seventy-five dollars a month in country and everything else went straight to my bank account in LA. I didn't even have a checking account so I had to ask my mom to get a check and mail it to me. They never spent one hundred dollars on a camera in their lives and I knew they would think I was being extravagant and give me shit.

Kevin came back from flying and we headed to the club for pizza and the movie. It was *Romeo and Juliet.* Just what we wanted to see, a love story.

Shortly after we went to bed we took one round of incoming. It wasn't close but it always got my attention. We had hurt them in Cambodia, but they were letting us know they were still out there.

Saturday seemed a long day. I was on last light and after dodging rain showers all day we ended up getting weathered in at Song Be. It was always disheartening to get about two thirds of the way back to Phuoc Vinh and have to turn around because we couldn't get through the weather. By the time we shut down and secured the aircraft the mess hall was out of food! It was back to ops to get a box of cold C's. It had been one of those days!

Sunday morning turned out bright and clear with wisps of ground fog making their way out of the trees. The Song Be River was completely obscured by the fog that tended to linger over the colder water for longer periods of time. It gave it a supernatural look, but less welcome, provided great cover for the bad guys to use the river for transportation. They could have floated a battleship down the river and we wouldn't have seen it.

I called ops as Steve cranked the aircraft and was told we were to proceed to Quan Loi to fly in support of Bravo Troop for the day. "Good, huh?" I asked Steve. "We get weathered in at Song Be, end up eating cold C's for dinner and sleeping on the ammo bay doors. No showers, and now, just to show their appreciation for our sacrifices we get to go and fly for Bravo Troop all day," I stated with no attempt to hide my exasperation.

"This fucking place sucks!" was Steve's response and I couldn't agree more.

We got to Quan Loi and went into the Bravo Troop TOC. After the general display of military courtesy and greetings we were given a map and Bravo Troop's shackle for the day, a nonsensical code where numbers can be converted to letters to avoid passing frequencies and grid references in the open over the radio. Then we were shown the door and told to get airborne.

Steve cranked the aircraft while I acted as fireguard before climbing in the front seat. In short order we were given takeoff clearance and with the little bird tucked up under our wing, we headed out into Bravo Troop's AO, an AO that we were totally unfamiliar with.

I opened up the map and noticed that it hadn't been posted. There were no AO boundaries, no friendly positions plotted, no nothing, just a blank map sheet.

The little bird descended out of altitude just south of what appeared to be an abandoned village. Cautiously, he made his way up to it and confirmed that it was, indeed, abandoned. But all wasn't lost. There was a road running through the village that showed signs of recent vehicular activity.

He started running the road northwesterly and I was starting to get disoriented on the map. There was nothing to navigate by and everything looked the same. Steve was talking to the little bird and I was trying to find us and write down spot reports when we noticed arty impacting a short distance away. Steve wanted to get on to arty quick to find out where it was being fired from and what the target was when he realized that he hadn't been issued with an SOI. He tried calling back to Bravo Troop Ops to get a frequency and call sign for the artillery battery. The RTO gave us a shackled frequency and call sign, but when I applied it to the shackle that we had been given it made no sense at all.

I repeatedly tried to make sense of it and nothing seemed to be going right. I now had us lost and we didn't have an SOI. I consulted the map to see where the closest firebase was that could be shooting and finally in frustration yelled at

Steve, "How the fuck am I supposed to know where it's coming from? They didn't even plot the fucking fire support bases on the map!"

Steve ordered the little bird up to altitude and gave him a direction to fly that we hoped would keep us both clear of the artillery gun–target line.

As we cleared the area we noticed a large city a bit further to our northwest. Steve asked me what it was. I said, "There are all kinds of neat reference points to navigate by up here, but none of them are on this goddamn map! We aren't even on this map sheet."

Steve thought I was bullshitting him and asked me to fly the aircraft after handing him the map over my right shoulder. "Okay," he said. "Head over to that little village to our right so we can orientate ourselves."

I flew over the village and Steve handed me back the map with a grease pencil mark surrounding the village. "That's where we are," he told me.

Looking at the map and the village he had circled I asked him, "Are you sure?"

"Hell, yes, I'm sure," he shot back.

"Steve, I don't think that's it. The road through the village below us runs southeast to northwest. The road through the village you circled runs almost due north. And the village below us has a blue close by and the one on the map doesn't," I countered.

"Dig it," Steve said. "So where the fuck are we?"

"Lost," was all I could think to say. "What's our fuel state?"

"Getting down to about four hundred pounds," he replied. "Let's go back to Quan Loi."

"Okay! Which way is it?" I asked.

"Fuck if I know. You're navigating."

All I can say at this point is that it's a damn good thing the little bird didn't know what was going on in that Cobra!

I took a guess and we headed back to the southeast since the one thing I did know was that we had been tracking generally northwesterly.

After almost two hours in the air we finally found our way back to Quan Loi. We refueled and then hovered over to the revetments and shut down. Entering the TOC I made a beeline to the map. I compared the map that they had given us with the one on the wall. "Fuck me!" I exclaimed.

Steve came over and asked me whether or not I had found out where we were.

"Yeah, I know where the fuck we were," I told him. "The map they gave us covers up to the zero zero grid line . . . like ten or twelve clicks north of here. That city we found is here," I pointed. "Fucking Kampong Cham. No wonder I couldn't find us. We were so far off the fucking map it isn't even funny!"

About that time the ops officer came over and curtly stated the obvious. "Guess you couldn't find anything out there, huh gents?"

I just gritted my teeth and headed toward the door. "No, sir," I responded before Steve could answer. "Couldn't even find ourselves!" I left their map sitting on the chair and departed but not before repeating what Steve had said earlier in the day, "This fucking place sucks!"

When we got back to Phuoc Vinh I walked into our room and, having suffered serious sense of humor failure as a result of the past twenty-four hours, I was looking forward to a quiet uncomplicated evening. Some mail would be nice.

Kevin was sitting on his bed and cheerfully commented, "The warrior returns. Want a coke?"

"That would be great, roomy. You would not fucking believe what happened to us today," I said as I told Kev the story.

When I finished telling him, he just sat there and laughed hysterically.

The mail that day included the *Record Ledger*. I skimmed the articles until I stopped at one talking about, and condemning, teenagers. That just about capped the day.

I had started a tape to the folks the day before yesterday and I felt now was as good a time as any to finish it.

"Why is everybody condemning teenagers?" I asked. *"They're throwing us all in the same big pot and they're saying we're all a bunch of stupid idiots who don't know what we're doing and causing trouble. If that's how close minded adults are . . . I don't know! Just explain to me why. You know the teenagers didn't start this war. We're just fighting it because our elder, more knowledgeable leaders started it.*

It's true, there are a lot of teenagers who are really screwed up on marijuana and LSD, some of them are in big bad clubs who go around and get a thrill out of beating up on old people and stealing their money. You'll always have the fourteen- or fifteen-year-old girl who comes home and tells her mother she's pregnant.

Have times really changed so much since you were teenagers? Really?

Take Steve and I, nineteen years old . . . teenagers. You better believe it! But think about it. Are we like all the other teenagers? Here the government trusts us with a half a million dollar aircraft. We're flying around with enough firepower to literally wipe out a whole village. We're just sitting up there more or less acting like a God. If we see someone on the ground and we want him or her to die, all we have to do is pull the trigger and they're dead.

There are a lot of other teenagers over here whose lives depend on us. If we make one wrong decision, we could cost an awful lot of people their lives.

That's not responsibility?

But did we have a choice as to whether or not we wanted to come over here? No. Did we have any choice as to who we wanted to send us over here? No. We get over here and we can't even legally buy a bottle of beer. When I go on R&R to Hawaii, I can't legally rent a car! Thank God for small things; that you'll be there and you can rent it for us.

But that doesn't matter. Here's Steve and I out here running an entire combat mission, in complete control of a combat operation. Goof up . . . somebody is going to die.

And yet, all they send us over here for is to . . . go fight kid . . . kill or be killed. What do they care?

But I guess that doesn't matter 'cause we're just teenagers like all the rest of them back at home smoking pot and all.

No. I'm not sorry I'm nineteen years old or a teenager, but I don't like to be placed in the same category as everybody else. I don't feel like everybody else. I worked to get where I am. Flight school was no picnic, the Army's no picnic, and Vietnam is damn sure no picnic. You know people are dying over here all the time, and they're not doing it for the money, 'cause it's not worth it. They're not doing it for the glory, because there isn't very much of that over here either. They're doing it because our older leaders sent us over here to do it. You know it's funny, but old soldiers never die, it's the young ones that do. I just can't understand why everyone wants to throw us all in a big pot and boil us.

We're responsible for lots and lots of lives, Mom and Dad . . . we kill people. As a matter of fact, we've killed a lot of people. This is our decision. Either they're going to die, or some of our people are going to die . . . oh, what the heck?

I'm only a teenager."

I turned off the tape recorder and went to bed.

Wednesday, June 24 was a day that none of us were looking forward to. In the Army's infinite wisdom, Vietnam was a war like no others. Commanders did a six-month tour of duty in command of a combat unit to tick a box in their two oh one personnel file. Today was the end of Major Rosher's tour as our CO and he was moving to a staff job as squadron executive officer.

During World War I, World War II, and even Korea, war meant war. In Vietnam we had a one-year tour and COs served in that capacity for six months. What that meant was that just about the time they got to really know their mission, their people and the capabilities of the unit, they were gone! Just about the time it took to become an effective leader, they were replaced with a new CO who had to go through the entire process all over again. It was a constant process that made no sense.

As soldiers we looked to our COs for leadership and guidance. In Vietnam we ended up training our commanders! It was truly a case of "I must hasten to catch my men . . . for I am their leader."

Our new CO wouldn't get to the unit until the third of July so we had a temporary CO. A captain from squadron took command of Charlie Troop for nine days and he too ticked a box.

Squadron's gain was certainly Charlie Troop's loss.

On the twenty-seventh, an announcement was made that all U.S. ground troops would have to be out of Cambodia by 6:00 P.M. on the twenty-ninth. We, on the other hand, didn't have to be out until noon on the thirtieth. There was a lot of speculation that when U.S. and allied troops moved south back into Vietnam, the NVA would be following them down to replenish their supplies and reestablish their sanctuaries in Cambodia.

We were to circle around to get well to the north and then make a final sweep through the border areas. The entire AO would be a free fire zone so we could literally shoot anything that moved.

The First of the Ninth were the first ones in, and it looked like we would be the last ones out. Our final day in Cambodia netted Alpha Troop one NVA KBH. Bravo Troop spotted three NVA, engaged them and got two kills and we spotted two individuals, engaged, and eliminated them. It seemed like the NVA weren't too anxious to mess with us again anytime soon.

And then, it was over. And what did we accomplish? From Annex K of the After Action Report from the Cambodian operation:

The 1st Squadron, 9th Cavalry distinguished itself while engaged in military operations from 1 May 1970 to 30 June 1970 in Cambodia. The men of this unit conducted ground and aerial reconnaissance in support of the 1st Cavalry Division (Airmobile) and 1st ARVN Airborne Division by leading the advance of both divisions and providing accurate and timely intelligence information to its commanders. Heedless of the intense hostile fire, adverse weather conditions, and hazardous landing zones during the sixty day operation, the 1st Squadron, 9th Cavalry struck North Vietnamese Army units with devastating effectiveness in a series of classic Air Cavalry operations. The squadron's assets were shifted as necessary, capitalizing on mobility, reconnaissance, and firepower in order to determine enemy locations and routes of march. Epitomizing determination and demonstrating a fighting willingness above and beyond the call of duty, the 1st Squadron, 9th Cavalry inflicted catastrophic personnel and equipment losses upon the enemy, thereby rendering him combat ineffective. The aggressiveness, devotion to duty, indomitable courage and extraordinary heroism demonstrated by the members of the 1st Squadron, 9th Cavalry, 1st Cavalry Division (Airmobile) are in keeping with the highest traditions of the military service and reflect credit upon themselves and the Armed Forces of the United States.

Enjoying the flexibility, mobility, and firepower provided by the helicopter, the 1/9th Cav employed the techniques of the modern cavalry doctrine. With the use of the "pink team," one AH-1G gunship helicopter and one OH-6A observation helicopter, the troops were able to cover large areas effectively. When the situation warranted, the Aero-Rifle Platoon (ARP) would be inserted to fix the enemy until a larger force could be committed to the area. The ARP would also search out bunker complexes, possible cache sites, and conduct ground reconnaissance. The squadron succeeded in bringing death to 985 enemy soldiers during this period. In addition to capturing or destroying 464 individual and crew-served weapons, over 579,000 lbs. of rice were found and destroyed or hauled back by friendly units. Other equipment such as bicycles, rafts, clothing, trucks, and various types of ammunition were also destroyed. Since many of the engagements by the 1/9th Cav were in the recon zone beyond the fixed limit of ground troops, many of the losses inflicted upon the enemy must forever go unclaimed. The instances of tremendous secondary explosions following engagements were many, and there is little doubt that hundreds of tons of munitions and arms were lost by the NVA in the recon zones.

C Troop, although coming into the Cambodian conflict after its sister units, was not to be outdone. They accounted for 284 enemy killed by helicopter, two individual weapons captured, one hundred boxes of fuses destroyed, 37 22″ diameter wheels destroyed, and 4,400 lbs. of rice captured or destroyed. C Troop was also responsible for leading ground forces into the cache site later named "Rock Island East." A scout helicopter from the troop discovered the cache while on a visual reconnaissance mission.

The valor of any unit can only be achieved through the heroic actions of every man who is a member of that unit. Below is a summary of individual valor awards earned during the period 1 May 70 to 30 June 70, which serves only as an indication of the gallant actions of the men of the First Squadron (Airmobile) Ninth Cavalry.

Distinguished Service Cross	1
Silver Star	5
Soldier's Medal	5
Distinguished Flying Cross	58
Bronze Star Medal with "V"	22
Army Commendation Medal with "V"	74
Air Medal with "V"	36

Just to top things off another formation was called at the end of the operation. A high-ranking South Vietnamese officer was on hand. It appeared that some of us were going to receive Vietnamese military decorations.

Steve and I were called up and presented with the Vietnamese Cross of Gallantry with a Silver Star device. The officer's adjutant began to read the citation:

Randy R. Zahn—Warrant Officer—US Army

Hoa tieu truc thang Chi-Doan 1/9 Su-Doan 1 Khong-Ky Hoa-Ky.

Xuat sac vao ngay 21/5/70, khi duoc lenh tham sat tren lanh tho Kampuchea, Chuan-Uy Zahn da to ra can dam truoc hoa luc phong khong cua dich, kheo leo dieu khien phi co va.

I looked at Steve out of the corner of my eye. He was trying not to laugh. He caught my eyes and gave me one of those "What the hell is he talking about?" looks.

I rolled my eyes and tried not to be too obvious as I shrugged my shoulders.

xu dung hoa tien ban chinh xac vao cac vi tri an nup cua dich gay cho chung tham bai nang vne, voi ket qua 4 Cong-quan chet tai cho nhieu kho tang va tram giao lien cua chung bi pha huy.

After the speech, the officer pinned the ribbon on me and I saluted. Months later I got the orders that had been translated:

Pilot, Squadron 1/9, 1st Air Cav Div.

Distinguished himself on 21 May 1970 when ordered to conduct an air reconnaissance in Cambodia, WO Zahn proved to be brave in the face of enemy anti-aircraft fires and cleverly maneuvered the aircraft and used rockets to strike accurately at the enemy positions. Results: 4 VC were killed in action, and several storage structures and commo-liaison stations destroyed.

Steve knocked on the door a few minutes after I read the transcript.

"Do you remember this?" he asked holding up his copy of the orders. "Nah," I said. "Just another day in the AO."

Chapter 12

Kevin Opens Up

Not having to wake up and head northeast to Cambodia was odd . . . and depressing. The Cambodian incursion had been the best flying I had done since I arrived in-country. It was the first time I felt as if we had a real purpose and we fulfilled that purpose. We hurt the enemy and we hurt them bad.

Our mission had reverted to general support of the Second Brigade in the largest portion of Phuoc Long Province. We were happy because for the first time since I arrived in-country, we would be working the AO around our own base camp. The priority was placed on supporting the ground elements with visual reconnaissance but at the same time division wanted us to try to piece together the Jolley and Adams trail systems through Phuoc Long over to Long Khanh Province. Contact was expected with the Fifth VC Division, Seventh NVA Division, and the Eighty-Sixth and Fiftieth Regional Support Groups (RSG).

There was an announcement that on the fourth, fifth, and sixth we were supposed to stand down. It would be a time for maintenance to catch up with inspections and for the pilots and aircrews to get some much needed rest. We planned to go down to Vung Tau and lie on the beach. It also would give the new CO a chance to get his feet on the ground, his briefings and hand-over done, and get himself familiar with the troop and our mission.

Kevin was having one of his days. He was pretty subdued all day and it was obvious he had something on his mind. We all went through these periods of depression and reflection but Kevin was in another world altogether.

When I got back from lunch I grabbed a book and lay down on my bed. Kevin didn't eat. He just sat on the side of his bed staring at Carla's picture, which was nothing new.

"Kev," I called as I sat up. "Can I ask you a question?"

"Sure," he replied.

"Listen, roomy! If this is none of my business just tell me, but I am really curious about something. Since we moved in here together you have had Carla's picture up there on your shelf. You look at her, you talk about her, but you never write to her and you never get any letters from her. She doesn't send you any tapes and you don't send her any. Whenever I go down to Saigon to the USO to use the phones, you never want to come along. What gives?" I asked.

Kevin slowly turned to face me. "You want to know the truth?" he asked.

"Kev, I am your roommate, but more than that, I am your friend. If you got a 'Dear John' letter . . . "

"I wish I would have," Kevin interrupted.

"You can't mean that!" I blurted back.

"Yes, I do," he said as tears formed in his eyes, "at least she'd still be alive." Then, looking at me Kevin said matter of factly, "Randy, Carla's dead . . . and that's why I don't give a shit what happens to me over here."

I sat there looking at him in dumbfounded silence. I knew from his actions and the tone of his voice that he wasn't just trying to screw with my mind.

Finally, after about two minutes I asked him, "Do you want to tell me about it?"

"Why not?" he said. He looked at Carla's photo and back at me, then he just stared at the floor. After a minute or so Kev went and picked up the picture and just held it in his hands. He began, "I was in basic training at Polk when I was told to report to the orderly room. It was January of last year, the nineteenth to be exact. I grabbed my hat and field jacket and double-timed down to the orderly room. The first sergeant was there and told me I had a telephone call and I could use the phone in the CO's office. I went in and he closed the door behind me. I didn't know what the hell was going on. I picked up the phone and it was Carla's dad. You see Carla was big in equestrian sports," he smiled. "Her dad told me that she had been thrown from her horse and had hit her head. She was in a coma. The doctors took x-rays and said there didn't appear to be any kind of permanent damage and that she should come out of the coma in a day or two. When she did, he would call me back so I could talk to her. The call came on the twenty-first, but instead of being able to talk to her he told me that she had died without regaining consciousness."

Kevin just closed his eyes ever tighter as the tears rolled down his cheeks, obviously reliving the moment.

"Kevin, I don't know what to say," I told him.

"You don't have to say anything. I've had a year and a half to get used to the idea that she won't be there when I go home so I don't really give a damn if I go home or not."

"Bullshit," I interjected. "Don't even talk like that. Is that what Carla would want? Come on, Kev, I can't imagine what you've gone through but damn it, we've seen our friends die and we've agreed that life has to go on. I know that the circumstances are different, but I'm sure that Carla would want you to be happy."

"You can't understand, Randy," Kevin responded. "Life isn't worth living without her. I want to be with Carla."

Carla Claire Hembree was born on November 16, 1950, and she died on January 21, 1969. She is buried in Gainesville, Florida. Too young.

I had experienced many new things since I came to Vietnam and felt lots of things I had never felt before. I came to cope with the loss of friends. I could cope with the rockets and getting shot at. I could handle the mortars that rained down on us, but I didn't know how to respond to my best friend who was obviously nursing a broken heart.

Plans were being made for Independence Day. Armed Forces Radio announced that they would be playing oldies all day. We were going to have our Hail and Farewell on July 4, obviously intended more for the new CO than the holiday.

I wanted more than anything to fly on the fourth. The last thing I wanted was to sit around all day listening to old music, getting melancholy and thinking about home; yet that's just exactly what happened.

Kevin was flying and as the day progressed I got more and more depressed. I felt a million miles from home. Kev and I avoided any further discussion about our talk that night but we both knew it would come up again.

The First of the Ninth was one of the last units on active duty still authorized to wear the Cavalry stetson. I ordered mine that day after lunch. I couldn't bear the thought of going back and turning on the radio again so I just walked around the base camp.

The PX was down the street from us. I popped in there and, finding nothing I couldn't live without, I went to the library. It was closed for the holiday so I headed down past DIVARTY headquarters and was amazed at what I found. A swimming pool! A real swimming pool, only a fifteen-minute walk from the hooch!

I read the sign that had been put up and found the pool wasn't open yet. It was scheduled to be open on the sixth. It was a sixty-by-thirty above-ground pool that the guys from the Twenty-seventh Maintenance Battalion, Eighth Engineers had erected.

I looked around and was a bit dismayed to find it was placed right along the green line. A sniper could have a field day! It was fortuitous that bunker twenty-two was just in front of it and next to it was a guard tower.

By the time I got back to the unit some of the teams were back for lunch. Everybody seemed to be down in the dumps. Amazing what a holiday could do to our spirits.

The new CO had arrived and compared with Major Rosher, well, there was no comparison. For Galen Rosher we would have crawled over broken glass. This new guy would have to earn our respect and that wouldn't be easy. Rosher would be a very hard act to follow.

Maj. Turner L. Nelson assumed command of Charlie Troop on July 3, 1970. He was a very distinguished looking, handsome black gentleman.

The Hail and Farewell wasn't too well received. Our spirits were down and nobody wanted to be there. We came out of the O Club after the formalities and immediately headed for our bunkers. There were guys out shooting M-16s, CAR-15s, M-60s, 38s, 45s, and anything else they could get their hands on. The place was dangerous!

"Damn, a guy could get killed around here," Rags quipped.

They were all shooting straight up in the air, but what goes up must come down! Arty was shooting flares, the guys on the green line were shooting flares, and it was an awesome sight. Tracers everywhere illuminated the night sky.

Hell, we didn't even have any fireworks . . . but that didn't stop us. After donning our flak jackets and steel pots we soon joined in the revelry and everybody felt a bit better. I hate to think what that Fourth of July cost the U.S. taxpayers.

After the fireworks, Vietnam fashion, Kevin and I went back to the room. "Sorry to have dumped on you the other night," he apologized.

"Kevin Frye, you can really be an asshole! I hate to use an old cliché, but that's what friends are for," I replied.

Kevin just sat in thought for a few moments and then said, "You know what, roomy? It's really nice to have someone who cares a little bit more than anybody else." He turned off the lights and we went to sleep.

Chapter 13

Looking for the General

The stand-down never materialized. Division wanted us out in the AO VRing. Intelligence had reported a lot of activity in the area and we didn't want to get caught with our pants down. In the morning the weather was really bad. We made several weather checks and found a herd of deer.

On the morning of the sixth, Ed McDerby, our platoon instructor pilot, told me I would be flying backseat once the weather broke. I was apprehensive at first but then I realized that perhaps I was being looked at to see if I was ready to be made an AC.

The ops officer briefed us that we would be working an area to the northeast. Highway LTL 1A ran through Phuoc Vinh and joined QL14 at Dong Xoai. We were given an area east of there to recon. We launched shortly after noon and found a bunch of cultivated fields in the area. They were quite literally in the middle of nowhere and there were no villages anywhere close by. We shot them up a bit and I guess we pissed somebody off. The little bird started taking fire. I rolled in on the area and amazed myself as I was right on target with the rockets. The scout went back in and the ground to air was no more. He spotted three dead NVA on the ground.

We flew back to Phuoc Vinh and I was a bit more confident and in a better mood than I had been. Not that I enjoyed killing, but shoot at the "little bird" and pay the price. All in all, it was a good show for my first day in the backseat.

That night we were ordered to evacuate all of the aircraft down to Bién Hoa. Once again intelligence had ascertained that Phuoc Vinh was going to get hit and didn't want to take any chances. Most of us pooh poohed it, but evacuate we did and Phuoc Vinh was hit hard that night.

All of us knew that the bad guys were holed up in Quan Phu Giao, about a mile northeast of Phuoc Vinh. They came out of the village at night to shoot at us, and by day they looked like your typical innocent civilian farmers. Masters of disguise they were.

There were large hospitals around Saigon and Long Binh, surgical hospitals and evacuation hospitals where many of our wounded from Cambodia had been hospitalized. There were also hospitals at the Air Force base at Cam Ranh Bay and it was to these hospitals that our division commander, Maj. Gen. George Casey, had set off on the morning of July 7. The hospitals at Cam Ranh treated the guys who were dying or who were about to be evacuated to Camp Zama in Japan or Tripler Army Hospital in Honolulu.

General Casey was a West Point graduate in the class of 1945. He served as a paratrooper officer with the Eleventh Airborne Division until 1948 and was decorated in combat during Korea. General Casey had taken command of the First Cavalry Division on May 12, 1970, and directed the operation in Cambodia.

Casey was a soldier's leader and cared deeply about his troops. He made a point of visiting each and every troop who had been wounded. He personally wanted to thank them for their sacrifices and dedication to duty.

Heavy monsoon rains blanketed the area, so all but essential air operations had been canceled. The only way for General Casey to get to Cam Ranh was in his staff helicopter. A rated pilot, he usually flew as co-pilot with somebody who flew more often than he was able to and was more current.

This morning General Casey would be flying an UH-1H, 69-15138 with 1st Lt. William F. Michel of the Eleventh General Support Company. Together with another UH-1, 68-16502, they set off from Phuoc Vinh at nine o'clock with an estimated arrival time of 9:45 A.M. at Bao Loc and eleven o'clock in Cam Ranh. To get to Cam Ranh they would navigate using the ground controlled approach (GCA) radar at Phuoc Vinh and Song Be, but because of their limited coverage, they were also depending on the DECCA low-level navigation system that was installed in their aircraft. DECCA was not used by any of the other services because it was notoriously unreliable. They would have to navigate through the mountains in the worst case, but hopefully they would be able to get high enough to fly in visual conditions over the tops of the clouds. GCA could provide them with radar vectors but only out to the limits of their radar coverage and the farther out you got from the radar head, the more unreliable it became.The problem with GCA was that it showed areas of shower activity, but not terrain. The mountains of the Central Highlands were covered in cloud and being pelted by the monsoon rains.

They departed from Phuoc Vinh early that morning in the hope of getting to the coast before the heaviest clouds had time to develop. They stayed with Phuoc Vinh GCA until radar contact was lost, and then contacted Song Be. They remained with Song Be GCA until they terminated radar service approximately eighteen miles to the southeast of Song Be. GCA radar was designed to allow a radar controller to assist a pilot to get his aircraft safely back on the ground by issuing radar vectors that would align the aircraft with the runway at their respective location. It was never designed for flight following.

Before reaching Bao Loc, both aircraft inadvertently flew into some clouds. Regaining visual contact with the ground they began a descent into a river valley with steep rising terrain on both sides. General Casey's aircraft was in the lead. Five-oh-two lost visual contact with them only to regain it a short time later. When the general's aircraft entered cloud again Lieutenant Michel made a radio call that they were executing a 180-degree turn to get out of the clouds and suggested five-oh-two do likewise. Five-oh-two began to climb and broke out of the clouds on top at an altitude of seven thousand feet. They heard nothing further from one-three-eight. They had flown into a large cumulonimbus cloud and disappeared. Five-oh-two landed at Da Lat a short time later and raised the alarm after one-three-eight failed to arrive and search operations were begun.

We were tasked with the search because of the expertise we had in the visual reconnaissance area. An officer from division briefed us and plans were made for four Pink teams to pull pitch at 7:00 A.M. the following morning and head up to Da Lat where we would laager from and conduct the operation. The weather was too bad to attempt any effort today.

Greg crewed us up, assigned us aircraft and collectively we got the maps that we would need for the search operation. The weather was still crap but we would wait and see what the morning would bring.

Wednesday morning came a bit earlier than normal. As usual when I knew I wasn't flying I had no trouble sleeping. If I was on a first light duty, I couldn't sleep worth a shit; just tossed and turned all night.

We all met in the mess hall for breakfast and then headed to the TOC. As the sun rose we were confronted with the rain, low clouds, and weather that came with the monsoon season.

The cloud layer was always quite thin and it was easy to get over the tops. The problem then was being certain that the clouds didn't build in size and intensity so that we couldn't get back down at the other end. Neither the Cobra nor the LOH were equipped for instrument flying conditions. Both had basic instruments in them and not a lot more.

One of the Snakes went out for a weather check and decided it was flyable. The low-level clouds were breaking up and the ground was becoming more visible. The decision was made to go, so we made our way to the aircraft where we were met by our respective crew chiefs.

While we waited for the break in the weather the pre-flight inspections were completed. This was usually a job for the front seaters. The pre-flight included starting the aircraft to check all the systems and the radios. The only thing we really couldn't check completely in the revetments was the weapon systems.

The sound of nine helicopters starting up at the same time was pretty awesome and with low clouds the sound was magnified as it bounced back from the cloud base. Two-six was leading the flight. As the platoon instructor pilot, we figured he had the most experience and were happy to have him in front.

We requested takeoff clearance and in a loose trail formation we lifted into the sky and headed east. Everybody checked in on the radio so that Two-six being flight lead knew he had all his aircraft with him. The tail-end Charlie was a UH-1 with a few crew chiefs and other necessary people on board. In retrospect maybe he should have been flying lead as the only instrument-capable aircraft in the formation.

Once we broke through the cloud layer at about eight hundred feet, the flying conditions were magnificent. A bright sun shone above and intensified the whiteness of the cloud tops now twenty-two hundred feet below us. The sky was a bright blue above, but ahead was fading to gray. More clouds.

The clouds thickened below us and we were getting more and more apprehensive. One thing a pilot did not want to do was get caught on top of building clouds not knowing exactly where he was and having no route of escape. The cloud tops were still sufficiently low this morning so that we could see the high ground sticking up through it.

We passed over a mountain whose crest was just protruding through the cloud top. I estimated its height at about twelve hundred feet. This is useful information for navigation. A few miles farther we approached another mountain only a few hundred feet below us. I could now pinpoint our position on the map. We had just passed over Xuan Loc.

"Hey Two-six," I called. "There should be a redball just below us, maybe a bit to the right. If we follow it east it'll take us right to the coast at Phan Thiet."

"Good copy," McDerby replied.

Almost as if it had been planned, we flew over a good size hole in the clouds and immediately saw the road below us. We descended down in turn in a tight spiral and reformed along the road with the Cobras now spaced out in the formation to offer protection. Tactically this was stupid. Nine aircraft flying at ground level down a road in a combat zone could prove fatal.

Luckily, we encountered no enemy activity. We did pass an ARVN convoy and a few other vehicles along the way, but we reached the coast, and thankfully, far better flying conditions.

We landed at the Army base at Phan Thiet for a quick refueling. Flying low and slow in a helicopter consumes a lot more fuel than in cruise flight because of aerodynamics and power requirements.

After consultation, we decided the best way to proceed would be to continue up the coast to the Air Force base at Phan Rang, and then follow the road to Da Lat. Navigation along that route would be a piece of cake: the ocean on the right to Phan Rang and a railroad track paralleled the road to Da Lat. A highway led to Phan Rang as well but it ran along a valley between high ground and we could be sitting ducks if the bad guys had anti-aircraft emplacements in the mountains. No, the coast was definitely a better alternative.

Phan Rang was about sixty nautical miles to the east-northeast of Phan Thiet. We followed the coast around the promontories and peninsulas out over the sea. Sharks, dolphins, and stingrays played below us as we zipped over the top of them about ten feet above the water. There was lots of chatter on the radios and the spot reports . . . "Sharks, two o'clock low," "School of dolphin dead ahead," and then Rags yelled, "Hey look everyone, look out the right wing. There's the Golden Gate Bridge!"

The remainder of the flight to Phan Rang was very quiet.

We were hungry as the blades slowed to a stop at Phan Rang. An airman was walking by the revetments and I ran over to ask him where we might get some chow. "Excuse me!" I called.

He turned and saluted. Returning the salute I said, "We're just here to refuel on our way to Da Lat. Is there anyplace close by that we could get some chow?"

"Sure," he responded. "There's the base snack bar, the O Club, the mess hall, or you can grab a snack at the bowling alley or the Fosters Freeze, sir," he told me with a smile.

"The bowling alley? Fosters Freeze?" I asked incredulously. "And how do we find these places?"

"Oh, that's easy, sir. Just go up to the corner there," he said pointing at a four-way intersection about a hundred feet away from where we were standing. "The shuttle bus comes by every fifteen minutes. Just jump on it. It goes right by the O Club and the mess hall. If you want the other places they are easy to find too. The bowling alley is just across from the movie theater and the Fosters Freeze is next to the Bank of America. The snack bar is in the building next to the pool."

I was so taken aback I couldn't speak. Talk about a different way of life! Finally I thanked the airman and asked as he began to continue along his way, "We are still in Vietnam . . . aren't we?"

We decided to fly on to Da Lat and grab some food there. The division was anxious for us to get there and start the search so we headed northwest up the valley back toward the Highlands.

The topography was incredibly different from that in our own AO around Phuoc Vinh. We were used to jungle, but here was a grass-covered valley meandering through mountains with lush vegetation and incredible scenery. There were no bomb craters and no firebases; it was almost as if they didn't even know there was a war going on.

We followed the road as it rose in front of us to more than four thousand feet above sea level. The railroad stopped at a station at the base of the mountain and there was a double-car funicular railway going up the mountainside.

We climbed with the terrain, turning almost due west and passed a large reservoir where people were skiing behind powerboats. It was as if we were in another world.

Due to the circuitous route we were forced to take because of the weather, we arrived at Da Lat long after our planned time of arrival. Da Lat was a Vietnamese mountain resort situated at an altitude of 4,931 feet above sea level. The dirt was a rust color and, surrounded by the mountains, the sleepy hamlets, and every shade of green vegetation imaginable, it made for a beautiful scene. The air was crisp and fresh and the temperature was at least 20 to 30 degrees less than what we were used to.

We shut down and were met by a lieutenant colonel from division who had arrived earlier in the day in a UH-1. As he began his brief we found that after passing up a steak at the O Club or a burger from Fosters, we were being treated to C rations. The general's aircraft was believed to have been lost farther to the west, closer to Bao Loc. The search area had been narrowed down to a box about twenty kilometers square. Da Lat did not have adequate accommodation for us all so the plan was modified to use only two teams on the search. The other two would return to our AO. The teams used on the search would return to Phuoc Vinh every evening and fly back up every morning until the aircraft was found.

It took two days of searching before the wreckage of General Casey's Huey was found. One of the lift birds actually spotted what they thought to be wreckage and called it in as a spot report. Ed McDerby, Two-six, and Ron Beyer, White, were the first Pink team on site. White went down to confirm the tail number on the wreckage. It was still visible on the vertical stabilizer, the only part of the aircraft that had not burned. It was pretty obvious what had happened, considering the weather on the day. The cloudbank that they had flown into was obscuring a mountain ridge; they flew straight into it, impacting only forty-five feet from the crest, killing everyone on board instantly. There were seven fatalities. General Casey was identified when they found his hand with his West Point graduation ring from 1945.

The burned aircraft was in itself the only consolation. A command aircraft carries a lot of secure radios and other equipment. For this to fall into enemy hands would have been catastrophic.

It was a very sad day for the First Cav. General Casey had been a respected leader and his death was a tragic accident. Five others died along with the pilots that day, including the command sergeant major. Ironically, they were on their way to visit the maimed and dying. At least they didn't suffer.

I sent a tape home telling the folks what had happened. I was tired, upset, and frustrated by the events of the past few days and my tone of voice couldn't hide that fact.

We were treated to a floor show that night. I'm not sure whether it was division's way of saying thanks for a job well done or whether it was coincidental, but because it was the day of the troop's return from the Highlands, it was suspect. And for the first time I got drunk!

On the tenth I got a tape from the folks, but because I had duty office (DO) that night I put off listening to it. I signed in at the TOC and made my first rounds of the flight line before finding a comfortable sandbag to sit on. I hit the play button and my dad started to chew my ass about something I had obviously said on a previous tape. He related that my attitude had changed; when I arrived I was so gung ho, and now I sounded so miserable.

"You said I was miserable and it didn't sound like me," I started in my reply. *"It didn't sound like me because this is only the first war I've ever been in. It's the first time I've ever been in one. So, um, yeah, I'm miserable. At times I have been more miserable than you have ever known me to be at home. That's okay. I guess I just got shot at too much that day and it kind of gives you the ass when you get shot at. You said just shoot back and make it count? Well, even when you shoot back and make them count, you're miserable. It's kind of neat, but I don't really dig killing people. I've killed forty-nine people since I've been here and it doesn't turn me on. You know I don't get excited and put nicks on my pistol or hash marks on the side of the helicopter or anything like that. Killing makes me miserable, too, believe me."*

And then our area went black. The generator had failed again. I picked up the recorder and went into the TOC. We had a small emergency generator but to do my rounds I had to carry a flashlight, which was not conducive to longevity with snipers around.

The heat and humidity were terrible as I walked around. The mosquitoes were buzzing all around my head and to make matters worse it began to rain.

Returning to the TOC was a relief. At least the fan was on and I sat myself down directly in front of it as I listened to the other side of the folks' tape. I had told them I was going to buy a car through the PX. We had Ford, GM, and American Motors dealers right on the base.

The second side of the tape was all about the merits of used cars over new cars, the cost, and so on. I listened patiently as I tried to empathize with their points of view. It wasn't until they tried to talk me into buying a Rambler Gremlin that I turned the recorder off and caught a few winks.

After breakfast I went back to the hooch. Without electricity the air inside was stifling hot, which made trying to sleep very difficult. Kevin was off that day and he was sitting there fanning himself with a large envelope.

"Come over here and fan me for a while so I can get some sleep," I suggested.

"Roomy," Kevin replied. "You know I'm you're biggest fan, but friendship only goes so far!"

"What's this friendship shit?" I asked him. "I don't even like you!"

He laughed and told me to go to sleep. I did.

I only slept a few hours before the dampness in my bed awakened me. I was soaked with perspiration. The electricity was still off when I awoke, so I went straight to the shower to try to cool off a bit. The drums hadn't been filled yet so there was no water. Recalling Steve's adage of the past, I said in disgust, "This fucking place really sucks!"

As luck would have it, the skies opened up and it started to piss down rain. I grabbed my soap and took a shower in the rain.

Kev and I went to the O Club where the emergency generator continued to power the box air conditioner. We grabbed a coke and sat down at a table. "Have you ever thought about who you want to take you home?" Kevin asked.

"Take me home?" I questioned not really understanding the question.

"Yeah. You know. Escort your body back to the States if you get greased!" he said.

"No. I haven't thought about it to be honest. First of all I have no intention of getting greased and . . . no. I haven't really thought about it."

"Well, will you take me home if I don't make it?" Kevin asked.

"Damn it, Mr. Frye, will you quit talking about getting killed. You are not going to die! Do you understand me?" I berated him.

Kevin just smiled and said, "Well, if I do, I want you to escort my body home."

"Okay. And you can get a free vacation from the war if I get it too," I responded. I had never really thought about getting killed and it was frightening.

"We have to fill out a form down at the orderly room one of these days" Kevin said.

I just replied to the affirmative, thinking that if we don't do it, we wouldn't need to. "So where are you planning to go on R&R?" I asked trying to change the subject.

"I'm not sure," Kevin said. "What about you?"

"I'm thinking about going to Hawaii and having the folks and hopefully somebody else come over and meet me," I told him.

Kevin told, rather than asked, me, "Have you heard about that stupid new directive that came out the other day? We can't wear our uniforms on R&R because, get this, we might provoke anti-war protestors. I'm sure it all has to do with that Kent State thing back in May."

"Good, ain't it?" I asked. "We're the ones fighting this fucking war and we have to be careful not to provoke the protestors? What about those fuckers provoking us? I'd love to have one of them give me shit on R&R. I'll give them anti-war."

We went to bed after spending the whole day in the O Club and woke in the morning still without electricity. It had been off for twenty-seven hours now and everything we had in our refrigerator that wasn't in an unopened can had to be thrown away.

By the fourteenth we were all getting a bit pissed off about the lack of electricity. Amazingly at about 3:30 in the afternoon, after fifty-four hours with no electricity, it came back on. I will always wonder if it had anything to do with the fact that three hours earlier division had been notified that if we didn't get any electricity they didn't get any Pink teams?

After a relatively short five-plus-hour flying day and getting three kills it was a pleasure to go into the room and be handed a cold coke again. Kevin also handed me an enormous pile of mail. "What the hell is all this?" I asked him as I took it from his hands.

"Birthday cards, I guess. It is your birthday next week, isn't it roomy?" he asked.

"Kev, to be honest with you I haven't got a fucking clue what day or date it is and quite frankly, I don't give a shit," I told him.

A lot of the guys had short timer calendars. These calendars were usually Xeroxed copies of a hand-drawn naked girl or some other such thing that was divided into 365 sections. The sections were numbered and started at 365 working down to zero. For every day we were in Vietnam, we would color in a section and although it didn't give the day or the actual date, it made reference to the only thing that really mattered.

"Well, just to keep you informed, today is Tuesday, July 14, and next Monday, the twentieth, is your birthday. In case you didn't know it, you're not going to be a teenager anymore so you won't have to get upset when people make disparaging remarks about them. You're going to be twenty years old! You old fart," Kevin laughed.

On the morning of the seventeenth the weather was appalling. Low clouds and rain covered our AO. Greg asked me to go and do a weather check. Division was anxious to get some teams in the air. I took off and headed east toward Dinh Quan, a hamlet surrounded by rock outcrops and hills of solid granite, hence its nickname of Rock City.

Getting to Dinh Quan was no problem. The AO was still unworkable so I turned around to head back to Phuoc Vinh. All the little holes in the weather I had just come through had closed in and there was now a solid wall of dark gray cloud and intense rain.

I tried to make it back, but ended up lost. The rain was fast approaching Dinh Quan so I had to go southeast to escape. Nothing looked familiar. I had been in the air for more than an hour and a half and fuel was running low. Continuing south I finally came to a river, but which one? I didn't know it at the time, but it was the Song La Nga. I knew I had gone well to the east and needed to head west. I followed the river flying relatively low keeping it immediately to the left of the aircraft. After a few minutes the river turned sharply to the north and the jungle around it got thicker and thicker.

I continued to the west and considering my fuel state I was getting worried. I flew over a rubber plantation and thought I recognized it so I maintained my heading. At last, I came upon the Dong Nai. The Dong Nai was a much larger river than the La Nga and was much easier to follow. I increased my speed, which only served to consume more of my remaining fuel. There had to be some psychology in this decision! It just seemed like the faster I went, the quicker I would get to Bién Hoa. In fact, seventy knots would have been a more prudent speed to fly to conserve fuel.

I contacted Bién Hoa approach and declared a fuel emergency. They gave me priority clearance to land but I dared not leave the river until I got to Tân Uyen, due north of Bién Hoa. At Tân Uyen I turned south and a few minutes later I crossed the green line. Landing at the POL point I let out a big sigh of relief as I looked at the fuel gauge. I had about three minutes of fuel.

The weather finally broke shortly after noon and I headed back to Phuoc Vinh, a most welcome sight. Later that day a long-awaited package from the folks arrived with three cassette tapes . . . or at least there were supposed to be. The package had been opened and the tapes were gone.

My mother's seven-page letter was still there and I was sure it would cheer me up and salvage what had begun as a pretty shitty day. In her letter she asked me if I knew what it did to her when I said I wanted to come home. She wrote, *"Can you believe that I want you to come home more than you want to?"*

I really didn't need this today and in retrospect my response was pretty inappropriate. *"No, I can't believe it because you don't know what I'm going through over here. You don't know what it's like to get mortared. You don't know what it's like to get shot at, and you certainly don't know what it's like to see your friends die . . . and I do! And that's why I can honestly say that I want to come home much more than you want me to."*

Greg had mentioned that he would arrange for me to have the day off on my birthday and at first it sounded like a great idea. Over the six days remaining before the twentieth, I flew every day except one and when we had our meeting the night of the nineteenth, I specifically asked to fly the following day. Greg said I could have the day off but I insisted.

The last thing I wanted to do on my birthday was sit around and think about home and what I might be doing if I were there. No, I wanted to fly.

We were doing a VR along Highway 322 northwest of the abandoned special forces camp at Rang Rang when we spotted a yellow logging truck hidden in the trees. The color was significant because commercial non-combatant vehicles were required to be painted yellow for easy identification. The other significant thing was that the box we were working was a free-fire zone, which meant that if anything inside the box moved, we could shoot it.

The vehicle was stationary and appeared abandoned for the time being. One of the tricks the VC and the NVA used was to confiscate these vehicles, having killed the owner or driver. They would hollow out the logs and use what appeared to be an innocent-looking commercial vehicle to transport troops (in the hollowed-out logs), arms, or munitions of war. This vehicle was definitely not here by coincidence. I was flying with McDerby and I was in the front seat. Ed said to me, "There you are Randy, your birthday present, courtesy of Uncle Ho. You have the aircraft."

I took control of the aircraft, went to pilot override on the armament control panel, and rolled in on the truck. The only way to hit it was straight on from the front because that was the only part exposed to us. Having no rocket sight in the front seat, I grabbed my grease pencil and put an "X" on the front canopy. I punched off a single pair of rockets and redrew an X where they impacted on the canopy.

I adjusted several times before the rockets were actually impacting with my makeshift sight superimposed over the explosion. On the fourth run a pair of seventeen-pound rockets crossed right in the windshield of the cab and the vehicle immediately caught fire.

We continued to circle overhead to see whether there was a secondary explosion. A small secondary erupted when the gas tanks exploded and then the logs caught fire. After a few more minutes it looked as if the whole jungle around the truck blew up. The explosion produced a fireball that rose to a height of about two hundred feet. This was definitely not a typical civilian logging operation.

I gave control of the aircraft back to Ed and in my little rearview window I saw his grin and he gave me a thumbs up. "Happy Birthday, Two-six x-ray," he said.

Unlike birthdays in the States where I would have expected to get a few presents and some free drinks, *I* ended up having to buy the bar. Then I got a reprieve. During the first round of drinks, the alert siren went off and we headed to our hooches to grab our flak jackets and steel pots. We were on Red Alert.

A short time later we were ordered to evacuate the aircraft to Biên Hoa again. Intelligence had expected an increase in activity, based on Hoi Chanh (defector) interrogations and documents that had been captured. They all seemed to point to an increase in intensified rocket, mortar, and sapper attacks on U.S. bases in the III Corp area. July 20 was not only my birthday, but it was also known in both North and South Vietnam as the "National Day of Shame." It was on this date in 1954 that the Geneva Accords were signed, splitting Vietnam.

Heavy activity was anticipated, especially at Phuoc Vinh, it being the head-quarters of the First Cavalry Division and the First of the Ninth, the NVA's most feared and hated enemy.

We parked all the aircraft at the Transient Pad at Bién Hoa. As I was tying down the main rotor blades of the aircraft, Kev came over and waited for me. "What a nice gesture," I thought. "Thanks for waiting for me," I said.

"Thanks shit. I've come to escort you to the O Club," he said. Evacuating the aircraft didn't get me off the hook after all.

When we got back to Phuoc Vinh, we found it had been a false alarm. Not a single round of incoming had impacted in the base camp the previous night. I spent most of the day answering letters and listening to the soundtrack of *Paint Your Wagon.*

When I went down for the mail I stopped in the orderly room to see if the R&R allocations had come through for September. Nothing had arrived yet.

The increase in artillery activity picked up after the twentieth. We were get-ting hit almost every night, depriving us of much needed sleep, and exhaustion was setting in. Tempers were getting short.

Chapter 14

Kevin Goes Home

On the twenty-seventh I had to fly with Double-deuce, my least favorite AC to fly with. I just never felt comfortable flying with him and we engaged in some heated words that day.

I got back to the room and Kevin could tell I was pissed off.

"Whoa! What the hell happened out there today?" he asked.

"Nothing really," I said. "I am just tired, and I fucking hate having to fly with that guy."

"I know what you mean," Kevin said.

At the meeting that night the crew assignments were given out for the next day's flying. I was to fly with Double-deuce again. I was so pissed off I just got up and walked out without saying a word.

Kevin came back to the room after the meeting had ended. I sat fuming. "Don't worry Roomy, I sorted it out. You're flying with Hubert tomorrow," he told me.

Without giving it any thought at all I just smiled at him and said, "Thanks Kev. You're a star."

On the morning of July 28, I pre-flighted the aircraft and waited for Two-eight, Hubert Kuykendall. Hubert was one of the old guys and had a reputation. He used to produce these manifesto-type documents and stick them up on the walls in the hall of the hooch. We all thought that he was some kind of communist.

Hubert was a bit older than the rest of us. With strawberry blond hair and a thick curly mustache it could be said that Hubert had an attitude. I still think he had a special recipe dinner that he ate every night to produce the world's nastiest, raunchiest, foul-smelling farts in the entire world. The closed canopy of a Snake is not exactly conducive to foul body odors, and Hubert would take great pride every time he turned the air in the cockpit green. While I, in the front seat, would gag, Hubert just sat back and laughed until tears rolled down his cheeks.

The monsoons were particularly heavy toward the end of July, so the weather remained unworkable over our AO. I went out and did a weather check and Hubert went back to bed.

We didn't get airborne until late morning. We headed out toward the eastern boundary of our AO along the Dong Nai. Kevin, along with Double-deuce and their little bird, One-six, were working closer in toward Rang Rang. I hadn't realized the previous night that Kevin had actually traded ACs with me so I wouldn't have to fly with Zeke.

Our mission was to make contact with Ranger Team Seventy-two. A LRRP had spotted some NVA on a trail that they were observing and wanted us to check it out. Our little bird ran the trail. It showed heavy recent use, and then he came upon what appeared to be some camouflaged crates. The jungle canopy was too thick to get a good visual ID on what exactly we had so Hubert called ops and requested the Blues.

The lift birds arrived on station at 1:30, and at 1:35 P.M., after they had been briefed, one-by-one they spiraled down and dropped off the Blues. They would link up with the ranger team and together they would exploit the find.

At 3:05 P.M. I heard Kevin call in with a spot report. "Grid Yankee Tango two four five five seven zero. We spotted one individual and engaged him with organics. One KBH."

The Blues moved into the area and started to uncover several crates that were hidden in hooches along the trail. It proved to be a significant find. A small weapons cache. The Blues posted a security force while the remainder of them started to open crates. The cache contained three 12.7 mm heavy machine guns in their cradles along with three spare barrels, three SKS Chicom-type 56 rifles, 127 SKS M-1944 (Chinese Type 53) carbines, nine Soviet Moisin-Nagent 1891/30 7.62 mm rifles, twelve cases of .30-caliber magazines, three tripods for 12.7 mm machine guns, twenty-four AK-47s, eight sub-machine guns of assorted make, thirteen Ross sub-machine guns PPS-43, four 60 mm mortars, four 107 mm rocket launchers, and two duffel bags of web gear.

During the exploitation no contact was made with the enemy.

"DOWN BIRD! DOWN BIRD!" It was One-six.

"Why the hell is the little bird yelling down bird?" I asked Hubert. "Who's down?"

Hubert had evidently turned down the volume on the FM radio.

"Who went down?" I demanded.

"Shut the fuck up and keep your eyes on our little bird," he snapped.

"Who went down Hubert?" I pleaded.

And Hubert just replied, "Don't worry about it."

Then came a call on our UHF frequency. "Two-eight, Double-deuce is down." It was Kevin and Zeke. "Let's get over there," I yelled at him.

He replied matter-of-factly, "We can't leave the Blues ya dumb ass!"

"Hubert, its Kevin! We have to help. Let's go!" I said frantically.

Hubert, ever the compassionate professional, said, "Shut up before I slap the shit out of you!" The lift ships were busy with the other Blues and we couldn't get our guys extracted. "There's nothing we can do!" Hubert told me, but I wasn't convinced.

As hard as it was, I continued to do my job. Not a lot more was said about the downed aircraft as we continued our mission, extracted the Blues and the ranger team, and finally headed back to Phuoc Vinh.

I jumped out of the aircraft before we were flat pitched and sprinted to the TOC. Capt. Steve Leischner was the ops officer and he had his back to me as I raced in. "Steve, where's Kevin?" I asked.

No response.

"Steve, goddamn it, where's Kevin?"

I will never forget the look on his face as he turned around to face me. "Randy, Kevin's not coming back" was all he said.

I felt the life drain from me and just stood there. I didn't speak. I didn't cry. I couldn't do anything. I was in shock.

I was still standing there when Hubert walked in the backdoor of the TOC. The rugged old warrior walked straight over to me and gave me a hug, and through the massive lump in his own throat, he just whispered, "There was nothing we could have done." And then he was gone.

The walk back to my room that afternoon was the longest of my life. I don't remember a thing about it. All I remember was standing in front of our door for what seemed like hours, but in reality was probably only a minute or two. I walked in as I could feel the swelling in my eyes. Closing the door behind me I put my helmet down, and turning around I saw Carla's picture. She seemed to be smiling more than I remembered. I sank to my knees as I covered my face with my hands. The only words that would come were, "Oh my God." And then I cried.

I cried as I had never cried before. "WHY? Goddamn you. Why did you let this happen?" And I cried some more.

Greg knocked at my door and came in. I just looked at him and cried again. I don't remember the whole dialogue of the conversation but I do remember him telling me that I would not be flying the next day. I needed time to grieve.

I told him before he left, "Greg, Kevin and I had a conversation the other week. He wanted me to escort his body home."

"I'll see what I can do," he replied before the door closed behind him.

The official report of the crash says,

66-15305 was on a visual reconnaissance mission on 28 July 1970, when it experienced an engine failure at YT262568. The Aircraft Commander reported his initial difficulty by twice calling "Going down" to an accompanying LOH that was flying recon at treetop level in the same area. The LOH immediately climbed to altitude to relay the message to Charlie Troop Operations and to follow the AH-1G down. The AH-1G, estimated to be at two thousand feet and approximately two kilometers north-northwest of a large open field appeared to be in a normal autorotative glide at approximately five hundred feet indicated at which time the LOH's altitude surpassed that of the descending AH-1G. The LOH pilot monitored emergency procedures as was called off by the AH-1G after their initial transmission. The gunner asked the Aircraft Commander if he wanted the fuel and electrical systems turned off to which the Aircraft Commander replied "Yes" though there is no means of shutting off the fuel from the forward compartment of the AH-1G aircraft. While still over the trees the aircraft was observed to assume a radical decelerating attitude with a subsequent loss of airspeed and rotor RPM. The aircraft's momentum carried it just clear of the trees where it settled vertically with zero airspeed and rotor RPM.

Chuck landed his LOH next to the Cobra. It was on its side and beginning to burn. Chuck and his crew managed to get Kevin out and then Mark. They both died on impact. The aircraft had quite literally fallen out of the sky.

I couldn't bring myself to make a tape and tell my folks yet, but I sat down the following day to write them a letter. *"I didn't quite get this done the other night and God only knows why I didn't finish it yesterday. It was a bright sunlit beautifully clear day the twenty-eighth and then clouds, thunder, lightning, and rain struck. Mom and Dad, yesterday at 4:15 Kevin was killed in a crash. I don't have to tell you how it affected me, as I'm sure you can imagine.*

The room is dark and lonely now. It'll never be the same without Kevin's voice. I'll never forget him. He was like a brother to me. God, how I miss him. I still find it so very hard to believe.

You learn something about life every day I guess and growing up. I just wish you'd have told me that growing up is so damn hard to do. Can't there be an easier way than to be forced to watch your friends die? Why does every lesson have to be so matter-of-fact? Why did Kevin have to die? WHY?"

Anger started to show itself later as I sat down to record a tape of the event. *"Yesterday was a rather hard day in my life . . . not rather. It was. Yesterday we were flying out over our Blues, who I've told you once before is our ground recon unit. We were over them, and once they're on the ground, you cannot leave them. They have to have cover. So there we were. Then we got the . . . call that I've heard numerous times before . . . Down Bird. However this time it appeared it was a new kind of down bird for me. It was new to me because one of our Cobras had crashed. It didn't get shot down. It had an engine failure, which is the easiest thing to recover from in a helicopter, if you just do what you're taught, do what you're trained to do. Everybody here knows exactly how to put them in the trees. We know how to put them in rivers. We know how to ditch them at sea, and we know how to put them down where we have an area . . . a smooth area.*

Well yesterday at 4:15, to put it bluntly, somebody fucked up. And because of it . . . my roommate is dead. Yes, Kevin was killed in a crash yesterday, just because somebody screwed up. He panicked. I'm not going to condemn him because I don't know how I would have reacted and God only knows I hope I never have a chance to find out.

All I know is that I lost a damn good friend yesterday. It hit me real real hard. Like a brick wall. I still find it pretty hard to believe that he's gone. I'd much rather look at it that Kevin DEROSed. He went home.

Man, this place is so senseless, so worthless. I'm getting so sick of watching my friends die for no damn reason at all. We're not doing any good over here. They're not trying to win this . . . war.

The other day we went and found some dinks and they wouldn't give us a clearance to fire so we said, "Okay, then we're not going to work." That's no way to win a war.

Yeah, I got some dinks down here so you know where they're at the next time you want to go and look for them.

It hit me and Rags especially, more than anybody else, hard. But like Beeny once said, and Steve doesn't know it yet because he's on R&R, but like he said and you've heard it too . . . life, it just goes on.

I've learned from it something that you've tried to teach me for so many years. You've got to live life day by day. Don't worry about what's going to happen tomorrow when you still have today to live.

There's really not much more I can say except I'm going to miss him and I'm sure his parents will too. He was really a great guy."

There are no words that can describe what I felt that day. Twenty-one years later, my wife Kim and I sat down to listen to all the tapes that my folks had saved for me. Kevin's voice was there with his infectious zest for life and sense of humor. And while Kim sat and laughed listening to his monologue, I cried. She didn't understand why and she asked me.

"Kevin is going to die in two weeks and I can't stop it." I said through my tears. "God, I want him back, sweetheart."

Kim, knowingly, kissed me on the forehead and left me alone with my grief. It was as if Kevin was still alive and I knew what was going to happen and when. I wanted to change the course of history and prevent it. I knew I couldn't. It was the most helpless feeling I have ever experienced.

Kevin knew he was going to die. Perhaps in some small way he wanted to die. His mother, Irene, sent me a copy of a letter that Kevin had written to her and her now-deceased husband, Warren, before he left to go to Vietnam.

"Mom and Dad,

I address this specifically to you, my parents, but it is an open letter to all who have been close to me.

By now you have been contacted by telegram and appropriate personnel extending the regrets of the Department of the Army.

I guess you must feel pretty miserable right now, I can see that. But what is done, is done. I am gone for a little while, but look at it this way, we will be together again, it will not be in the too distant future. Life is short, eternity is so awesome in its "length."

My thought is that what people refer to death and the life hereafter is but an extension of our life now.

However, that part of our lives is carried on in a spiritual form. We cannot see or touch this spirit. Not being able to understand in our human minds an inanimate form, not being able to touch or feel it, this spiritual form suddenly acquires the quality of displacement, that is, we place it in a faraway land called heaven, purgatory, or hell.

Did it ever occur to anyone that these lands conjured up by our simple imaginations are not as far away as we might believe? If we were to believe this, then the souls of those who have departed prior to us must not be so very far away.

Death interests me. All fear of it dwindled away a long time ago. The saying goes, "that anyone who does not fear death is either a liar or insane." I disagree; this loss of fear comes in the form of a simple realization, not with the fanfare or boasts of a hero, for I am no hero.

Understand my death. No, do not just accept it, understand that I am close to you now, and that one day we will be together again.

I used to think of heaven as a place where you knelt around all day in white robes with wings on your back and praying.

I now see it as a long trail through a forest. The road stretches forever, no restrictions, no boundaries. People are free to stop, look over the countryside, and write, paint, do anything they please.

It is good to remember past times, but plan for the future. Use memories as a foundation on which you may build the future. The past, present, future—good, bad, beautiful, and ugly—are all one and the same. It is but our narrow minds that distinguish one from another.

I could never claim a patriotic motive for wanting to go to Vietnam. My driving force was more out of loyalty to those of my age who have gone before me and failed to return. It is a stupid war. But who can tell me what war has never been stupid.

My dream of flying has been fulfilled. I was an officer in the United States Army. What more could one ask for? I am proud of my accomplishments."

I am proud to have had Kevin Mark Frye as my roommate and friend.

On Thursday morning, we had the memorial service for Kevin and Zeke. Major Nelson asked me to give Kevin's eulogy. It was something I wasn't looking forward to but I knew that I had to do it. I also mentioned to the major about the conversation that Kevin and I had had just weeks before about escorting each other's body home. I was told, "We will talk about that later! And by the way Mr. Zahn, will you please pack up Mr. Frye's personal belongings?"

Giving Kevin's eulogy was one of the most difficult things I have ever done in my life. I wish I could remember what I said, but I can't. I was numb throughout. Packing his belongings and the picture of Carla came a close second. It was a gut-wrenching task. It made it seem so final.

The first time I ever spoke to Kevin's mother was in 1998. I had lost track of her address and only after much effort and a lot of help from friends was I able to locate her in Jacksonville, Florida. Once I had her telephone number, it sat next to the telephone for weeks. If the truth were known, I was scared to call her. I was afraid that all those emotions would resurface and I didn't know whether she would be able to handle that. I also didn't know whether I could.

When I finally made contact with Mrs. Frye, we had a very nice, and long overdue, conversation. We spoke about Kevin and our individual feelings and memories. During the conversation Mrs. Frye learned about the conversation Kevin and I had that night, so many years ago, before his death. I told her what Kevin had said about Carla and her not being there when he came home.

Mrs. Frye told me she felt that Kevin had had a plan and somehow he fulfilled it. And then she told me that Kevin is buried in Gainesville, Florida . . . in the same plot with his beloved Carla. He is where he wanted to be all along.

And again, I wept.

Chapter 15

The Red Towel Boogie

The landline rang in the TOC. It was the 227th Assault Helicopter Company operations officer asking if we would assist them in searching for one of their aircraft. He got a report that one of their aircraft had gone down and decided to organize a search since they hadn't heard from the crew for twenty hours.

Twenty hours! We were dumbfounded. When we had a bird go down we launched every aircraft we had that was flyable . . . and some that weren't. It didn't matter where we were, what we were doing, or what we were wearing. We dropped everything and hauled ass to the flight line.

One day we got a "down bird" call for one of our scouts. Felix Poindexter was in the shower when the siren sounded. He grabbed his helmet and, wrapped in nothing more than a large red towel, he ran through a formation of enlisted troops, jumped in an aircraft, and took off.

Ed McDerby was already on station over the downed aircraft when Felix arrived. Asking whether everything was okay, McDerby replied that it was, but he needed to go back to Phuoc Vinh. Felix asked him what was wrong and Ed told him, "My X-ray just puked all over the front seat and the stench is making me sick!"

Felix told Ed that he would relieve him and almost simultaneously noticed that the fuel gauge in his aircraft read zero.

Grabbing the aircraft logbook, Felix opened it up to the DA Form 2408-13, the Aircraft Inspection and Maintenance Record, and noticed that the aircraft was carrying a circled red X condition for the removal of the fuel sensor probe. A red X inside a circle indicates a fault and the aircraft may be flown only under defined limits. The conditions for flying the aircraft after the removal of the fuel sensor probe were ensuring it was full of fuel prior to takeoff and then being back on the ground in no more than an hour and a half of flying time.

So there was Felix . . . barefooted, wearing a red towel, in an aircraft that he had no idea how much fuel it held. The standard fuel load that we refueled to after a mission was twelve hundred pounds. This would give us about an hour and a half of flight time and in the event of a scramble meant we didn't have to waste time refueling before we took off.

McDerby had left the area on the way back to Phuoc Vinh. Felix let him go, knowing that if he really didn't have any fuel he never would have made it back anyway. About thirty minutes later another aircraft came out and Felix headed back to Phuoc Vinh. He was one hell of a sight, standing out at the POL point refueling his aircraft in his red towel.

That's what Charlie Troop was all about, when one of our own went down, nothing stopped us.

The weather broke on the second of August and we got airborne about mid-morning. The return to my normal routine so soon after Kevin's death made it easier to accept. When I was in the air I was totally focused on the mission. There was no time to think about anything else.

The rains began again and we got weathered in at Bién Hoa. With the change in our AO the previous month, our liaison officer had moved to Bién Hoa to be co-located with the Second Brigade HQ.

We grabbed his jeep and headed over to the Air Force side of the base to grab some chow. After lunch I went over to the Admin building to see what I could find out about R&R allocations. Time was marching on and I still had no news to send home. My parents' co-workers were being very good about changing their vacation plans to allow them to come to visit with me in Hawaii. I didn't want to inconvenience them any more or longer than absolutely necessary.

There were still no allocations.

We flew back to Phuoc Vinh, and after the normal post-flight paperwork and activities, I headed back to the hooch. I hated going back there. I had accepted Kevin's death, but I didn't have to like it. I opened the door and stepped in to find a very tall black man sitting on what had been Kevin's bed.

As I walked in he immediately jumped up and introduced himself. "Hi! I'm Bobby McNeal. Las Vegas, Nevada. I've just come over from Bravo troop. I guess I'm going to be your new roommate."

"Hi Bobby, I'm Randy Zahn."

"Yeah, I know," he responded. "I went to flight school with Danny Rager. He said you could use some company."

"He's right about that," I told him. "Make yourself at home!"

Bobby Mc was a big man, about six-foot-three and as solid as a rock.

After I cleaned up and grabbed a coke we began to get to know each other. It would be a lie to say I wasn't a bit apprehensive about rooming with a black man. I was. It had nothing to do with prejudice, and everything to do with lack of familiarity.

We spoke about our backgrounds and how we came to end up in the Army and at Charlie Troop. At one point Bobby just sat down on the edge of the bed and started laughing.

"What's so damn funny?" I asked him.

Bobby looked at me and said, "Man, oh, man. Talk about a minority area. We have a nigger and a Jew living together!" I joined him in laughter.

On the fourth we were working well to the east in Binh Tuy Province when the scout spotted four individuals. They took cover and we rolled in hot with seventeen-pounders. When the scout went back in to the area he found two NVA and three VC soldiers whom we had killed.

The area showed lots of use and we decided to put in an airstrike. Binh Hoa launched a flight of F-100 Super Sabers to work with us. After they had expended their ordnance we covered the area with artillery. Adjusting the marking rounds we issued the "Fire for Effect" order and cleared the area to go re-arm and re-fuel. When we returned to the area at 1:10 the scout found casualties. The artillery had killed one VC while the Air Force was credited with three VC kills.

My hours had been piling up again so I was given the next day off. I decided to go down to see Major Nelson that afternoon.

"Excuse me, sir," I said. "You said we would discuss my escorting Mr. Frye's body home later and since I had today off I thought—"

"There is nothing to discuss, Mr. Zahn," he interrupted. "Mr. Lamont will be DEROSing in a few days. I've arranged to have him escort Mr. Frye's body."

"But you don't understand, sir," I pleaded. "Kevin and I were very close and I promised him I would escort his body home if anything happened to him. I owe him that."

"Will that be all, Mr. Zahn?" the major asked.

"Sir. I lost my best friend last week and now you're telling me I can't keep the promise I made to him?" I asked angrily.

The major just sat there, and without even looking at me repeated, "Will that be all?"

"That will be all, sir!" I stated and turned and walked out without saluting.

I was livid when I went and collected the mail. There was a tape from home and on it my brother asked, "What are you guys doing over there besides having a ball?"

I completely lost my cool as I responded *I'll tell you what we're doing. Let's put it this way. If you think it's so much fun over here, get your ass on a plane and come on over and try it for a while. I've got an extra bed in my room now too and if I tell you how it became extra, I'll guarangoddamntee ya you'll change your mind!*

For the moment, I had forgotten all about Bobby. Emotionally, I wouldn't allow myself to get close to anybody again. Bobby and I got along great and I enjoyed his company, but deep down I just could not let myself get too close to him or anybody else.

Beeny fell for the direct commission deal. He was given a direct as a second lieutenant in the infantry and within days he was removed from flying status and given a platoon in Delta Troop. He would be flying jeeps for the rest of his tour.

The next day we were back working the same area and I logged another ten plus hours. Greg was getting ready to go on R&R and suggested we have a platoon party before he left. There were about thirty of us in the Gun platoon—pilots, crew chiefs, and armament specialists. Some of the guys took a UH-1 down to the commissary in Saigon and bought a hundred steaks and several cases of cokes, 7 UP, and beer . . . all for the thirty of us.

Saturday night, August 8, Phuoc Vinh got hit hard again with 81 mm mortars. The 81 mm that the VC used were manufactured in North Vietnam. They were exact copies of the U.S. 81 mm M-1 mortar. It was a particularly popular weapon with the VC and the NVA because it could be broken down to three, one-man loads—making it easily transportable.

The incoming and harassment was picking up to the point where we were getting hit almost every night. This night we were lucky. Most all of the rounds impacted at the other end of the base camp. Eight soldiers were wounded, one seriously.

Though the incoming could be devastating, generally it took its real toll in sleep deprivation. Artillery is an indiscriminate weapon. It doesn't care who it kills or wounds and, fortunately, it isn't all that accurate. Having said that, after it impacts, it takes a while for the adrenaline to ebb so one can get back to sleep. Fortunately, I didn't have to get up in the morning. My hours had accumulated and once again I was grounded for three days due to fatigue. I had flown thirty-eight hours in the past few days.

We were awaiting the arrival of some new pilots any day now. We were really short, which served to put more hours on those of us who were there. Division didn't care that we were short of crews. They just wanted four teams in the AO.

Rumors were starting to circulate that we would be moving soon. The Twenty-Fifth Infantry Division was standing down, packing up, and heading back to the States. Word was that we were going to move into their base at Cu Chi. We weren't too enamored with the thought. Phuoc Vinh wasn't exactly the height of luxury, but it was home.

Greg left for R&R and Lt. Larry Grover, being the next highest ranking officer, took over the platoon in his absence. Larry had come to us from Alpha Troop after taking a direct commission. He was of medium build with blond hair, and he played a guitar. Oftentimes I went to bed being serenaded by Larry's guitar from the other end of the hooch.

The R&R allocations finally came in on the eleventh; my dates were September 25 through October 1.

"And, oh, by the way. You're being assigned a collateral duty. You are the new Unit Fire Marshal," our new XO, Capt. Fred Joles, told me. The fire marshal job was basically a shit detail and although I can't prove it, I think it fell on my shoulders due to the unceremonious way I departed the CO's office the week before.

Fred came to the unit after Captain T left. A schoolteacher from Michigan, Fred was slightly older than the majority of the warrant officer pilots. He soon acquired the nickname of "Mother." He looked out for his people, often in conflict with the CO.

I went down to Saigon that afternoon. I wanted to call Mom and Dad and give them the details of my R&R. I knew they were as anxious as I was.

When I got back it was pissing down rain, but by now I was used to the monsoons. Hardly a day went by that we didn't shower in the rain.

Beeny came over after dinner. "What are ya doing?" he asked.

"Not much. Why?" I asked.

"I'm going to take a patrol out into the rubber plantation at about twenty-one hundred. We have an LP out and we can't make contact with them. We're going to take some supplies and new batteries for their radios. Ya want to come along?" he asked.

"How do you know they need supplies if you can't make contact with them?" I queried. "Where exactly are they?"

"Last contact we had was at about four-thirty. Their radio was weak so I think their batteries have gone dead. We're going to take them some new batteries, cokes, and some extra ammo," he told me.

"And what if it isn't their batteries?" I inquired.

"Then we'll probably find four dudes. You want to come along."

"Where are they?" I asked again.

The area just to the southeast of Phuoc Vinh had been a big rubber plantation before the war. It was one of many owned by the French firm Michelin.

"They're about four clicks inside the Michelin almost due east of us," he finally told me.

Before I even had time to think about it, I blurted out, "Sure! When do we leave?"

Steve told me to meet him on the road behind the O Club at nine o'clock sharp. "You'll ride with me in the command jeep," he said. "And don't forget your sidearm, steel pot, and flak jacket," he reminded me as he left the room. "I'll get you an M-16."

I had never been on the ground outside the base camp, except at Fire Support bases. In retrospect I probably should have asked Lieutenant Grover if it was okay, but I didn't. I was riding in the right rear seat of the jeep. Over the rear wheel well on the left side of the jeep was the radio. The second jeep had a pedestal-mounted M-60 machine gun, and the third carried a 107 mm recoilless rifle.

Leaving the main gate, Steve signaled a halt. He turned around and gave the order to "lock and load." Rounds were chambered in all of the weapons. The next command was "move out!"

I became pretty nervous. Nervous, hell! I was scared shitless! The village of Phuoc Vinh was off to our right as we made our way down the normally dusty road. With the monsoon rains the dust had turned to rust red mud.

About a quarter of a mile from the gate we turned off to the left. The jeeps were blacked out and it was so dark I couldn't see a thing at first. I don't know how the drivers could see the road in front of them. As my eyes began to adjust to the dark, shapes began to appear. We were traveling along a road lined with trees on both sides—rubber trees.

Behind us were two more jeeps although I couldn't see them. The headlights had cat-eye slits that provided just enough light to illuminate the bumper. The jeeps themselves were nothing but silhouettes. All was silent except for the sounds of the motors almost idling along at a snail's pace. I began to think about mines and all sorts of things. What the hell was I doing here?

We continued along in silence . . . my head swiveling from side to side, looking. I could just make out the horizon through the trees. The longer we were out the better my eyes adapted to the dark. There was nothing to see but silhouettes. Looking to the left I saw something move. A head. A head had popped up from the brush. My heart raced and I was raising my M-16 when a flashlight beam flashed on and off twice. The jeep came to a halt. I didn't know what the hell was going on.

One of the guys in the second jeep flashed back a signal. We had made contact with the patrol. Having delivered the supplies, the patrol installed the new batteries and a commo check was made. We turned around and headed back to Phuoc Vinh. This was the most dangerous part of the mission, having to backtrack our original route.

I was never so happy to be back inside the front gate. The headlights came back on and Steve turned around and said, "Pretty bitchin', huh?"

We got back to the company area and Steve could tell I was pretty shaken. "What's the matter?" he asked.

"Steve, do you have any idea how close I came to popping that guy tonight? If he waited another second to signal you I would have killed him," I said. "I didn't know what to expect. I didn't know when we were going to make contact. I almost killed one of your guys."

"Oh wow!" Steve said as he headed to the club.

It was good to get back in the air the following day. I flew backseat with Lieutenant Grover. It was a long day, 10.3 hours. We flew into the night and when we got back to Phuoc Vinh Lieutenant Grover told me he had spoken to the other ACs after the meeting the night before and he was going to recommend to Greg that I be made an aircraft commander, upon his return.

August 14 was a different day. I had the day off to do my fire marshal duties in preparation for a Command Inspection. I went around checking all of the fire extinguishers and making sure there were no obvious fire hazards. Obvious fire hazards? What a joke! We lived in wood-frame hooches with plywood walls. The walls in many of the rooms were stained with tar paper and jet fuel. Every room had small arms ammunition, grenades, captured 50-cal rounds, mortar shells, and more. The whole place was a firetrap.

At two o'clock division commandeered our maintenance hanger for a floor show. The USO sponsored this one . . . Miss America 1970.

Pam Eldred, Miss America, from Birmingham, Michigan, was indeed there with her six runners-up. They sang, danced, and mingled with the troops. Miss California performed and as she made her way into the throngs I approached her.

"Hi," she said smiling at me. "Where are you from?"

She was a lot taller than the average female, with beautiful long blond hair and the pearliest, whitest teeth I'd ever seen.

"Hi," I replied. "California. Where are you from?" I asked her.

"Yucaipa," she told me. "Do you know where it is?"

"Sure. I've been through there a few times," I told her.

We spoke for about a half-hour. I asked her what she thought of Vietnam. She said, "When they told me we would be coming to Vietnam I didn't know whether to welcome it as a good opportunity or to be frightened." She continued, "I could never possibly remember the names of all the guys I've met, but I will never, never forget their faces."

They had only been in-country for two days and by her own admission they were seeing the good side. Then she asked me, "What do you do over here?"

"I fly Cobras," I told her.

"What's a Cobra?" she asked.

"It's a helicopter gunship," I said. "There are some parked just over there." I pointed to the revetments.

"Oh! Those are those cute skinny things!" She said innocently.

"They may be skinny," I laughed. "But if you were on the receiving end of one you wouldn't think they were so cute."

She was looking forward to going home. Before she left to mingle with others she gave me a big smile and a kiss on the cheek, and said, "It was really nice meeting you. Come and see me the next time you're in Yucaipa! We'll talk about our experiences here."

They stayed for another hour and talked while some troopers packed up their gear. Their stage equipment was loaded into a C-7 Caribou cargo plane, but we got to fly them back to Bién Hoa. I flew left seat in a UH-1 with WO1 Mike Smith, another Californian. As she disembarked from the helicopter at Bién Hoa, Miss California gave my arm a squeeze through the window and another smile.

I saw her several times in the following years . . . on TV and in the movies. Her name is Susan Anton.

When we got back from Bién Hoa, there was a message to see Lieutenant Grover. I knocked at his door. "Come in," he said putting down his guitar.

"Hi Larry. You wanted to see me?" I asked.

"I sure did," he said and offered me a seat.

"I've been thinking about what I said when we flew the other day. We are really short of pilots and I'm not waiting till Red gets back. The other ACs and me all agree that you deserve to be the next AC, so I'm having the orders cut. Two-six has signed you off. Tomorrow you're in the backseat as aircraft commander. You have Lamont's aircraft, zero-six-eight. There are a few call signs available so pick the one you want."

I was ecstatic. Making the grade as an AC in the Red platoon of the First of the Ninth was no small thing. Some guys flew a whole tour and never made AC.

"Larry, I want to be Two-four," I told him.

Grover Wright had DEROSed only a month after I arrived at Charlie Troop. In that month I flew with him several times and I learned something on each and every flight. He was dedicated to the mission and cared about his X-rays, the scouts, and the lift birds. Whenever I asked him something I always got an answer with an explanation. "This is why we do this" or "Don't do that because . . ."

Grover was a teacher—a professional—and I respected him immensely. I just wish our tours had overlapped a bit more. Grover Wright was Cavalier Two-four and for that reason and none other, I wanted the call sign. To do it as much justice as Grover would be my destiny.

I never knew what Grover thought of me or indeed, whether he even remembered me. We reconnected in 1999, and in February of 2000 he sent me an e-mail with a poem that he had spent two months composing:

Randy Zahn,
The 9th Cavalry Sky Trooper,
. . . changing of the guard

At times I close my eyes and I can still see you,
a Sky Trooper in command of all that you do.
Flying in formidable chariots of rotor blades and steel,
with friendship bonds that were never spoken of, but there to feel.

You must admit you were among the country's best in heart and skill,
patiently hand-hewn in the gladiator craftsman's art and will.
Your senses were unspoiled with reflexes faster than light,
in a mature and strengthened body honed for a warrior's fight.
I saw you stand in defiance as you faced the ultimate fear: the loss of your
*   life,*
while you had yet to experience its simple normalcy and mere strife.
Concepts of courage, honor, and pride were earned by your just deed,
they were not just words to describe goals someone wished to seed.

I remember the first day you joined us: your smile, your presence, and wit,
and eagerly sought to soar in the clouds, fire rockets, cannons, and just plain
*   spit.*
In days you were no longer the virgin warrior, untried and unproved,
but a Sky Trooper in a black Stetson cavalry hat for whom all would move.

I feared for the day I and some would leave the troop for the States,
for who would replace us and protect the scouts, blues, and the lift-bird fates?
Your skill and professionalism quickly relaxed my concern,
as I watched you take command, protect our troop, and continue to learn.

Now, many years have past and all the tigers are gone from play,
and I close my eyes and I can still see you there, as if it were today.
These remembrances will keep you forever as you were back then,
as current memories will never change you from the youthful warrior I knew,
and still get to call my friend.

I was moved beyond belief. For in some small way I too was a hero to my hero.

On August 15, 1970, having been in-country exactly five months, I became Dashing Cavalier Two-four.

Special Orders number 252 Extract:

ZAHN, RANDY R WO1 100B0 Trp C 1st Sqdn 9th Cav WAGTCOA AVN

Apt as: Aircraft Commander in AH-1G type aircraft.

I logged 5.8 hours of flying time that day as AC. The rain pretty much curtailed any flying in the afternoon. After lunch I was told to report to the aid station and to bring my shot record with me. I went in and the medic told me I was due a plague shot.

Plague was the one shot I remembered from BCT. It felt like somebody had taken a blowtorch to my arm and I could barely move it for two days. It hurt like hell!

Doctor Joseph Eckert, our squadron flight surgeon, came into the room. "Hi, Randy. Give me your shot record. We'll get the formalities over with and then I'll get the injection."

"Sure, Doc," I said.

Taking the shot record from me, he signed it acknowledging the 2 cc of plague vaccine that represented the normal dose.

I picked up the card and began to walk out. "Thanks, Doc. I'll see you later," I told him.

"What do you mean you'll see me later? I haven't given you the injection yet," he said.

"Yeah. I know. My folks might have raised ugly children, but they didn't raise stupid ones," I told him. "You may have been dumb enough to sign my shot record before I got the shot, but I'm not dumb enough to take the shot after you've signed it. I'll take my chances with the plague thanks," and I left.

In the morning it was still raining. Nobody was flying. Outside the hooch there was a sea of mud. I spent the day sleeping, listening to music, and answering mail.

"It is five months to the day since I have seen U.S. soil. It sure doesn't seem like it's been that long but I'm glad it has. Just think, one more month and this whole thing will be half over. Once I get home I will wake up, as I know this year is only a bad dream. All these things couldn't have really happened, could they?"

1st Lt. Harvey Hopkins, our new Blue Platoon leader, was from Covina, California. I never understood why those of us from the same geographic areas became so close, but we did. Harvey and I had become good friends and spent a lot of our time together. Bobby was on R&R in Australia, so Harvey, or "Blue," as we called him, slept in his bed a few nights while he was gone.

On the night of the seventeenth, we headed over to division headquarters across the street from our area. There were two house trailers toward the back of the compound. "Where the hell are we going?" I asked him.

"You'll see," was all he would say.

We approached the first trailer and Blue stopped and knocked on the door. A Caucasian girl with long brown hair opened the door. She was wearing cutoff blue jeans and a halter top. I thought it was an apparition. "Oh, hi, Harvey. Come on in," she said as she moved aside.

"Randy, this is Joanna and this is Margie," he said pointing at another girl. "Ladies, this is my good friend, Randy Zahn. Cavalier Two-four."

The girls, Americans, were Red Cross volunteers. The Donut Dollies! Their accommodation was U.S.-made house trailers complete with kitchens, bathrooms with tubs, and a living room with proper furniture and air conditioning.

I was amazed. We stayed and chatted until half past midnight before excusing ourselves. Harvey and I went back to my room where I made some Kraft macaroni and cheese. He just sat there with a shit-eating grin on his face. "So? What do you think?" he asked.

"What do I think about what?" I asked in return.

"The girls," he said.

"They're nice," I told him. "Why do you ask?"

Harvey became known as the "King of the Donut Dollies." We spent more and more time with them at night. It was surreal coming back from flying combat missions all day, jumping in a hot bath, and then sitting down to watch TV in an air conditioned house trailer with round-eyed girls.

Floor shows took on a new meaning, too. The girls came to the shows with us so we could dance too. There were four Dollies altogether, Joanna and Margie in the one trailer and two other girls, Peggy and Judy, in the other.

I could never hope to understand what would motivate young, attractive girls to put their lives on hold to go to a combat zone with no pay. They traveled to the base camps and fire support bases to offer, in most cases, nothing more than a smile and a friendly face, not to mention passing out donuts, which is how they got their name.

The more I got to know them the more I admired what they were doing. Some of the guys thought they were husband hunting but they had a more patriotic motive than that. This was their way of doing what they could to show their support for the troops and, in some small way, knowing them enriched my life.

Days off were getting fewer and farther between. We were still short of pilots so that most of us flew every day. On the twentieth I would once again exceed 140 hours and be grounded. I could use the rest.

I hitched a ride down to Bién Hoa to go to the Air Force base exchange. After having dinner at the Officer's Club I got back on a C-123 flight to Phuoc Vinh. At the platoon meeting that evening the CO stopped in. He told us that we would be working extra long hours in the AO for the next few days but he didn't tell us why. He wasn't wrong. I flew 29.9 hours over the next three days. The mental fatigue involved with combat flying is devastating. As an AC, flying the aircraft had to become an extension of our body. There was so little time to think about physically flying the aircraft that it had to be automatic.

Back in flight school all of my capacity had been taken up just manipulating the controls. I didn't have any spare capacity to think with, and I certainly did not have the clarity of mind to make life-and-death decisions. Now, flying the aircraft had become automatic. It was like waking up in the morning, a motor skill. Something I could do without giving it any real thought. I could feel the aircraft; I knew the sounds and the smells. I could tell when it was in balance without having to look at the turn and slip indicator.

Having confidence in the machine my ass was strapped to had a lot to do with the crew chief. I was lucky. I had a good one. Marshall Maring hailed from Washington state. He was so damn skinny I used to be afraid that the rotor wash of the helicopter would blow him over as I hovered into the revetment. I called him "Bones." Bones was an exceptional crew chief. He took care of our aircraft, 68-15068, as a mother would take care of a child. Not only did he do all of the maintenance and inspections, but also he would clean the canopy, wax the rotor blades, wipe up spills, and generally keep the aircraft exceptionally clean. There was never a day I went down to the aircraft that he wasn't there.

On the morning of August 24, we all gathered in the TOC for a brief. "Gentlemen, take a map and pay close attention," the ops officer said. "We have a special assignment. Vice President Agnew will be in Saigon this week. He arrives tomorrow. We have been tasked to VR the areas surrounding Saigon," he continued. "We will be laagering out of Nha Be, which is a Navy Seawolf base on the Saigon River about ten miles southeast of the city. Re-arm and re-fuel will be there along with ground support personnel. Don't fuck with the Navy. Treat them with the same respect that you will expect from them. And gentlemen . . . if anything happens to the Vice President, if he so much as stubs his toe, they are going to hang our asses."

The area around Saigon is mostly river delta, a generally flat area covered with rice paddies. For us, there would be no place to take cover and we had to rethink our tactics. The rivers around the city had a curfew on them. After four o'clock all local traffic had to be off of the rivers and any sampans we found were subject to search by the national police.

Nha Be provided another example of the difference between the services. The Air Force had their pools, air conditioned billets, banks, and theaters. The Navy also had air conditioned billets and whole lobsters at meal times. Like us, they had to pay for their meals. We paid five cents for whatever we could manage to find, which, more often than not was C rations. The sailors paid sixty-five cents for a whole lobster, but at least they shared them with us.

We got back quite late that night after flying for 11.8 hours. I entered my room to find a blue envelope among my mail. I had seen one like it before but I couldn't remember where. It was postmarked in Jacksonville, Florida, and the return address had a smiling mouth where I would have expected to see a name.

I opened it and began to read. It was dated August 21.

"Dear Randy,

Nothing like getting a letter in a strange handwriting.

You are very familiar to our family because Kevin often wrote about you.

Mrs. Frye wanted me to write to you. First of all, to say thanks for making Kev's brief tour of duty a pleasant one. I'm sure it wasn't all that great but that's what Kev wanted us to believe.

Needless to say it will take a long time for us to learn to live with just a memory.

I must say the Army has been very generous for Kev's sacrifice. And they certainly believe in a lot of paperwork!

My sister and I often collect all sorts of goodies to send to Kev and we both feel that if you would like something please feel free to say—"I have a craving for pretzels, etc."

Unlike some sour grapes over here we support you all.

I am enclosing a write-up that was published in our paper. Unfortunately the whole letter was not published. In it, Kev wrote of guys like you and Chuck Frazier before he even got to know you.

My dear nephew wrote a fourteen-page letter trying to help us understand his death. It was rather weird to be reading his letter in the past tense.

Myron Lamont stayed with us for four days. He told us just what a fine group you are. Doesn't that make you feel great?

Well Randy, I'd like to say again if any of you would like some CARE packages feel free to send in a request—we are all deeply appreciative of what you boys are doing.

> *Sincerely,*
>
> *Kevin's old school teacher aunt—*
> *Bobbi*

P.S. In the clipping it said 'the result of enemy action' which we do not know. Consensus of opinion from The Telegram *by editorial staff."*

After carefully folding it up and placing it back in its envelope I switched off the light and went to bed. Once again, missing Kevin.

On the twenty-fifth, my scout and I took off from Nha Be and were heading out to the area we had been assigned to recon when we flew over a small hamlet and saw about thirty or forty people wearing black pajamas with coolie hats. They were all carrying weapons of some sort.

Some of them appeared very anxious as we circled overhead. I made contact with the brigade ops officer to report our find. After a few minutes he assured me that they were Ruff Puffs, South Vietnamese Regional Popular Forces. These were South Vietnamese troops under the command of the province chief. How he could be so certain they were friendlies I didn't understand, but as we left the area they scattered in all directions.

The operation made for very long days, anywhere from seven to twelve hours of flying. The next day I scared myself so bad I called it quits early in the afternoon. Some ground troops had located an unexploded five-hundred-pound bomb along a trail close to a dock on the river. It had been booby-trapped and they wanted me to blow it up. I moved the scout well clear of the area before I rolled in. Hitting a five-hundred-pound bomb half submerged in the muck isn't easy at the best of times, but I succumbed to what could have been a fatal lapse in judgment: I got a dose of target fixation.

I made two runs without hitting it with rockets and decided to use my 20 mm Vulcan cannon. I could walk the rounds onto the bomb and, simply by kicking the pedals, I would be able to cover a good deal of the ground around the bomb, and hopefully hit it.

I rolled in again and became so focused on hitting that damn bomb that I lost track of my altitude. My x-ray yelled, "Pull up" and I reacted immediately.

I pulled out of the dive and began to climb out. There were trees alongside the river and they were above me when I pulled out of the gun run. Had I hit the bomb, the explosion would have blown us out of the sky!

We got back to Nha Be to refuel and my legs were shaking. Only two teams were needed for the post four o'clock river patrol so I volunteered to go home.

I hovered into the revetment and there, as always, was Bones waiting for me. As the blades slowed to a stop, he grabbed the tip, placed the tie-down hook in its hole, and tied the blades down.

"How'd it go today?" he asked.

"Okay," I said. "Except I almost lost us our aircraft."

"Yeah, I know," he said smiling at me.

"What do you mean you know?" I asked him. I took off my helmet and unbuckled my shoulder harness before bleeding the hydraulic accumulator.

As I climbed out of the aircraft Bones grabbed my arm and with a smile said, "Come here."

I followed him to the rear of the aircraft where there is a stinger that comes out of the rear of the tail boom. Its purpose is to prevent hitting the tail rotor on the ground. Wedged between the stinger and the tail boom itself was vegetation . . . green brush that the tail had gone through as I pulled out . . . green brush that grew to a height of about three feet.

I looked at Bones sheepishly and all I could manage to say was "Fuck me."

South of Nha Be the following evening I had river patrol. It was about four forty-five when we spotted a sampan heading up the river. The procedure after four o'clock was that one of our lift ships would hover close to the vessel, everybody on board the boat had to show their ID cards, and anything in the boat that was covered had to be uncovered for inspection. The lift birds also carried a national policeman.

They approached a sampan with three individuals in it, all clad in black pajamas and coolie hats. With the Huey hovering close by, the policeman hollered at them through a loud hailer. They ignored him. They carried on like there wasn't even a helicopter there. They didn't even look up.

The policeman hollered again and again and still they ignored him. The door gunner on the Huey opened up with his M-60 across the bow of the sampan but still they ignored it.

"Hey Two-four. These fuckers won't stop," the lift pilot told me.

"Have your gunner walk his 60 around the boat and see if that gets their attention," I told him.

I could see the water dancing around the boat as the bullets ripped through the surface. Still they continued.

"See if you can stop them," he called.

"Move off over the shore and I'll put a pair of rockets in front of them," I said.

The Huey moved off along with my LOH as I rolled over and dove at the boat. The rockets impacted about fifteen feet in front of the sampan creating a cauldron effect in the water. The sampan bounced and swerved through the disturbed water but still they continued without giving us a glance.

"Hey Two-four. This police dude wants you to blow these assholes out of the water."

"You got it. Move off to the north, and little bird, move south. Cover me," I instructed.

"What the fuck are you going to do?" they asked.

"Watch and see," I told them.

I descended and brought the aircraft to a hover along the riverbank. Then I turned and waited until the sampan crossed the nose of the aircraft. They were about three hundred feet out in the river when I pressed down my thumb. The rockets left the tubes with a loud WHOOSH and three sets of eyeballs turned and looked straight at me. They were as big as saucers and then they were no more. Pieces of sampan and bodies rained down as I took off. "Let's go home," I said.

The operation around Saigon ended on the twenty-eighth. The Vice President of the United States went home not having stubbed a toe and I wasn't even there to wave good-bye.

The next day I was told to report to the first aid station. Doc Eckert, still a little pissed off, called me.

"Morning Two-four," he said as I walked in. "You're grounded again."

He handed me another HQ CAV FL 89 form, a medical restriction from flying duty, two more days off for exceeding 140 hours in the previous month. It suited me fine. Zero-six-eight was having a one-hundred-hour inspection so I spent the day on the flight line waxing the aircraft while Bones completed the inspection.

On the way back to my hooch the orderly room clerk called out to me, "Hey, Mr. Zahn! I have something for you." I walked in and was handed a MACV Form 439-R, Permissive Orders for Out-of-Country Travel. My R&R orders had finally arrived.

On the thirtieth we got word that division was forming a new troop of the First of the Ninth. It would be designated as Echo Troop and be based at Lai Khe.

The bad news was they were taking personnel from the existing troops to make up the numbers, and in the shuffle Bobby Mc and Rags left Charlie Troop.

Harvey moved in with me as soon as Bobby had left. Our new room was designated California West.

In the shuffle we also got a few new people in the troop. One of them arrived in the morning. His name was Larry Edeal, another Californian. Larry and I had gone to Cobra School together and became good friends during the time we were in Savannah. The red hooch was full so Larry got a bed in the lift hooch with the UH-1 pilots. I introduced him to the guys and then we went to the club to grab a cold drink and a pizza. I had to fly that afternoon. I flew six and a half hours, which marked a milestone in my aviation career. I had logged my one-thousandth hour of flight time. So much for being grounded.

I had OD again on the thirtieth so I would be up all night. After dinner Larry came down to the TOC and we sat and talked. He had heard the same horror stories about the squadron as everybody else had and was a bit apprehensive.

"What you've heard is true to a degree," I told him. "I've heard all the BS about the life expectancy of pilots in the squadron and all that other crap. Don't believe it. Take it from one who knows Lar. In a day or two you won't want to be in any other unit in Vietnam."

We talked till the early hours of the morning when Larry left to go to bed. I had the day off after OD so I would sleep during the day.

The last day of a month always made me feel better when I got to tear off another page of the calendar. This month was especially satisfying. In twenty-five more days I would be back in paradise.

On September 1 Echo Troop, First of the Ninth Cavalry was organized using assets from both the squadron and the division. The bulk of the personnel and aircraft came from Delta Company of the 227th Assault Helicopter Battalion.

Initially they tried something new because they couldn't get enough Hueys for the Lift Platoon. They used the Hueys that were assigned to Division Artillery (DIVARTY) but this proved unsatisfactory. If an aircraft got shot down, the Blues needed to respond immediately—not when DIVARTY could break away their Hueys.

They took the one UH-1 they had assigned to their maintenance platoon and one each from the other troops, to give them a total of five.

Echo Troop spent the bulk of their time supporting Bravo Troop in Binh Tuy Province in addition to providing VR coverage for DIVARTY in AO chief.

Things in our AO were fairly quiet . . . except at night. The base camp continued to get hit almost nightly and everyone was getting pretty antsy from sleep depravation.

On September 4, I walked by the aid station on my way back to the hooch. Doc Eckert stopped me and handed me another FL89. Two days back in the air and two days back on the ground. It was Steve's birthday and since I didn't have to fly the next day I took him over to Eleventh Group HQ and bought him a steak dinner. We sat and chatted as we ate and he filled me in on Hawaii.

I had made reservations at the Waikikian, which was next door to Fort DeRussy, the R&R Center. Our rooms would cost $19.50 a night. One of my best friends from school days, Mike Rosenthal, was coming over with the folks and I was really looking forward to seeing him. I really wanted Donna to be there but I knew there was no chance of that now.

After dinner Steve and I jumped back in his jeep and went over to the outdoor movie. A screen was set up outside and Steve pulled the jeep up behind the seats.

"Hey Beeny," I said, "I know I just bought you dinner and it's your birthday and all and now we're playing drive-in, but promise me you won't try to kiss me."

"Oh wow! How are you going to act?" Steve asked as we both laughed.

We got back to the troop area about eleven o'clock and had a drink at the club before turning in.

I woke up late on the fifth. Normally I would have tried to make a tape to the folks but my machine's recording capability was broken, so all I could do was playback on it. I listened to some music and sat down to write a few letters. I made it through two before lying down and falling asleep. Harvey woke me for dinner. After we ate, Harvey suggested we play volleyball over at division. Steve and Larry joined us along with Moose, one of the Blue's pet monkeys. We walked over to division with Moose holding our hands and went to the court. It was vacant and the ball was in a box beside the court. Harv went to see whether the girls wanted to play, but they weren't in.

We played two-a-side and Moose thought it would be great fun to try to catch the ball as it went over the net. He scurried up one of the poles and while we were playing that damn monkey kept running back and forth along the top of the net, tightrope style. He would jump at the ball when it went past and more often then not lost his balance and grabbed the net to keep himself from falling.

After a while we tried to knock him off with the ball and he started squawking really loud and making a big commotion. We were all laughing so hard we damn near pissed our pants.

Larry and I were both off the next day so we went to Saigon. We got off the helicopter at Hotel Three and went across to the movie theater. One of my favorite movies, *Paint Your Wagon,* was playing. After the movie we caught a lift up to the Red Carpet pad at Long Bién. This was MACV's headquarters and their club was posh. We walked in and went up to the bar.

"Excuse me," I said to the guy next to me. Then I looked at him. "Frank?" I asked astonished.

"Randy!" he said in surprise. "What the hell are you doing here?"

Frank Gallagher and I were in a car club, the T-Timers, together back in Tujunga, California, when we were in high school. I hadn't any idea he was a pilot. I introduced him to Larry and asked him to join us for dinner. We reminisced and all in all it turned out to be a wonderful dinner, steak and lobster.

We got back to Phuoc Vinh after dark and headed for our rooms. As soon as I walked into the hooch the phone rang. "Red Hooch, Mr. Zahn speaking, sir," I answered.

It was the TOC. "Hey Two-four, grab your gear and hot-foot it down here. We have a mission for you," the ops specialist told me.

"What? Now?" I asked.

"Yes, sir," he responded.

I went to my room to grab my flight gear. Harvey wasn't in.

I stopped by Bones's room on the way to the TOC. He was out too.

"What's up?" I asked the ops officer when I walked in.

"The Blues are on the ground just northwest of Gary Owen. Echo of the Eighty-Second had a bird go in this afternoon," I was told. "I want you to go out and cover them until we can get them out of there."

I lifted off at 10:00 P.M. On the way out to the area I established contact. "Blue. This is Two-four."

"Hey, Jewish. This is Bluish, nice to hear your voice. Haven't you got anything better to do tonight?" Harvey whispered into his handset.

"Yeah, I do actually," I chided. "I'm going to RTB (return to base) and go visit the girls."

"Don't make me laugh, goddamnit," Blue admonished me. "The dinks will hear me."

"Tough shit. I need a new roommate anyway," I told him.

Basically I flew donuts in the sky above them until 1:00 A.M. when another Snake relieved me on station. We never left the Blues on the ground unprotected. I touched down at one-fifteen and as usual, Bones was waiting.

"Where the hell were you at this time of the morning?" he asked.

"Bones, I'm tired," I told him. "I'm not flying tomorrow . . . or today, whatever the hell today is. Put her to bed and you can do your daily tomorrow."

I went straight back to my room, took off my boots, and fell asleep. A short time later the mortars started falling. I could tell they were impacting a long way off. I didn't even get out of bed. I just turned over and thought, "fucking gooks."

Monday, September 7 was my dad's sixty-third birthday. I sat down and wrote him a long letter since I couldn't make a tape. Dad and I had always been close and having his youngest son in Vietnam was taking its toll on him. He was an emotional man who wore his heart on his sleeve, and the closer we got to reunite in Hawaii the more nervous he became.

On the eighth One-six was my little bird. We were working an area south of Rang Rang along Highway 322. I could read Chuck's aircraft as he worked. I knew that when he first got on the deck he would be flying relatively fast and in large orbits. As he and his crew became more comfortable with the area, he would slow down and his circles became tighter until he was just barely crawling along at a hover.

There was a lot of discipline both internally in the aircraft and among the team. The radio stayed silent unless somebody had something to say.

Chuck reported some use in the area before spotting an enemy soldier, who raised his AK-47 to shoot at the LOH. It was the last thing he ever did. A moment later, One-six screamed, "Taking fire!" The tail of the LOH kicked up and I had rockets on the way. I worked the area over pretty good and told Chuck to go back in.

"Hey One-six," I called, "If anything happens out here we're in center of mass two five four five. Rang Rang is on a heading of three five zero about ten k's."

I made it a habit of telling my scout where we were working and the heading and distance to the closest place to land. The scout crews didn't carry maps and if things really got out of hand and they needed to land, it was useful for them to know where to head and about how long it would take them to get there.

"Roger that," One-six responded.

And almost immediately thereafter, "Takin'—" and the radio went dead. I saw his tail kick and I rolled in again. As I pulled out of the rocket run I looked over my shoulder and was relieved to see the LOH still in the air. Radio contact had been lost. I saddled up on him and escorted him back to Rang Rang. The aircraft was shot up pretty badly. As he began to touch down the whole aircraft lurched to the left and kicked up a big cloud of dust.

I landed beside the aircraft and gave control to my x-ray. I jumped out and ran to the LOH. "You all alright?" I asked as I approached the aircraft.

I was relieved to hear that everyone was fine. The VC had walked a 30-cal machine gun right between Chuck and his observer, taking out all of the radios and most of his instruments. Bullets also penetrated the main gearbox, which is why he made such an abrupt landing. The transmission had frozen as soon as he touched down. Chuck looked unfazed. "Get one of the lift birds over here to take me back to Phuoc Vinh," Chuck demanded.

And then he asked, "What happened after I got hit?"

"I expended all my rockets on the area," I told him. "There's another team on station now."

"Good," Chuck said. "Let's get back so I can get another bird!"

"Haven't you had enough for one day?" I asked him.

Chuck just smiled at me. "Hell, no," he said. "We have some unfinished business down south."

An hour later we were back in the air over the same area. As I approached the area I got a brief from the other team. There was a lot of stuff down there, and they had taken fire sporadically since they'd been on station.

"Three. This is Two-four. Saddle up the Blues and get them out here," I said. "Get me a section of fighters out here and a section of max to escort the lift ships in. I'll start an arty prep now."

"Roger that Two-four," came the response.

"Big Red Three-seven, this is Cavalier Two-four. Fire mission. Over."

"Cavalier Two-four. Big Red Three-seven. Fire mission. Out."

"Roger Big Red, grid two five five four five four. We have personnel in a bunker complex. Fire one Willie Pete for marking. I will adjust. Over."

"Roger Two-four. Grid two five five four five four. Personnel in bunkers. One Willie Pete to mark. Will call shot. You adjust."

"Roger Big Red," I replied. "One-six, hold to the east. We have arty on the way from Rang Rang."

"Roger that," Chuck said as he headed east.

"Cavalier Two-four. Big Red Three-seven. Shot. Over."

"Shot. Out," I responded.

"Two-four, Three-seven. Splash. Over," Arty advised.

"Splash. Out."

The shot and splash calls are standard calls. The artillerymen compute the time of flight of the missile until impact. They call when it leaves their tubes, "shot"; and again when the round should impact, "splash."

The white phosphorus round impacted short and left. "Big Red. Two-four. Add one fifty right one hundred. Mark it," I said.

"Add one five zero right one zero zero. Wilson Pickett." And a few seconds later, "Cavalier Two-four. Big Red Three-seven. Shot over."

"Shot. Out," I responded.

"Splash. Over," he informed me.

"Splash. Out."

The round impacted right on target. "Big Red Three-seven. Cavalier Two-four. Bingo. Fire HE with delayed fuses. Fire for effect. Over," I ordered.

"Roger Two-four. Delayed HE. Fire for effect. We'll give you eight rounds. Will you give us a BDA?"

"Roger that Three-seven. I have a Pink team on station. We'll BDA," I told him.

It was pretty awesome watching 155mm artillery rounds impacting, seeing the initial explosion and then the shock waves moving out in concentric circles from the point of impact.

"Cavalier Two-four. This is Phantom Raider Four-one."

"Phantom Raider Four-one. This is Two-four. Go," I responded.

"Roger that, Two-four. I have a flight of fox-fours en route to your location. What have you got?" the Phantom pilot asked.

"Right, Four-one. We're at grid Yankee Tango two five four five. I had a scout get shot up pretty bad. Looks like we have a bunker complex. We've been taking some ground-to-air. Small arms. Arty is prepping the area now with HE. As soon as I shut them off, I'll get my little bird back in there for a BDA. I have Blues en route with a section of max. I'd like you to prep the LZ for me please," I briefed him.

"Roger that, Two-four. We should be with you in zero-two," he said.

"Sounds good, Four-one. Can you hold high and dry for a while?" I asked him.

"No sweat, GI," he chuckled.

"Cavalier Two-four. Big Red Three-seven. Fire mission complete. Over."

"Roger that, Three-seven," I told him. "Stand by for a bomb damage assessment."

"One-six. Two-four. You want to head back into the area and see what we've got? Arty is complete and they're waiting for a BDA," I told Chuck.

"Roger that. We're on the way."

"And listen . . . kind of make it quick. There's a section of F-4s on the way out and the lift birds should be checking in any minute."

"Roger."

"Two-four, Three-nine on family," WO1 Mike Smith checked in.

"Hey Three-nine. What's your ETA?" I asked.

"We should be there in about one zero. What's up?" he asked.

"Cavalier Two-four, this is Blue Max Five-one."

"Roger Three-nine, stand by. Blue Max Five-one. This is Cavalier Two-four. Go ahead."

"Two-four, Five-one. I have a section of Snakes. We were bounced off of Song Be. What can we do to help?"

"Right Five-one. I have my lift ships en route to insert the Blues. Their ETA is in one zero. I'd like you to saddle them up and escort them in on the insertion. I've prepped the area with arty and I have a section of fast movers waiting to prep the LZ. My little bird is doing a BDA now. As soon as he's done I'll get the F-4s in so you shouldn't have to hold too long. How copy?" I asked.

"Solid Two-four. We'll see ya in about one zero. We're just abeam Dong Xoai now."

"Two-four, One-six. The arty has uncovered quite a complex down here. There are several eight-by-ten bunkers partially damaged and we have lots of blood trails down here. No bodies that we can see."

"Roger One-six. Go and check out the area about a hundred meters at your four o'clock. How's that look for the Blue birds?" I asked.

Chuck turned to his right and asked if he was over the area. "Here?"

"Yeah. What does it look like?" I asked again.

"It's a good two ship LZ. They can touch down. Low grass with a few stumps. Fairly flat," he told me.

"Roger that. Okay. I want you to mark the LZ with a pete and then come on up to altitude for now. I'm sending in the Air Force."

"Okay," he said. "Just say when."

"Phantom Raider Four-one, this is Two-four. You boys ready to go to work?" I inquired.

"Roger that, Two-four."

"Great. My little bird is on the deck now. He'll mark the LZ with a pete. Looks like your best approach will be south to north with a left break. The complex will be at your two o'clock. We haven't taken any fire since before the arty. We've got a lot of blood trails, so there are folks down there and we might have pissed them off," I told him.

"Roger. We're over the area now. Have your little bird mark it and move off to the southwest. We'll be in as soon as you give us an all-clear. I'll give you five hundred pound HEs on the LZ, then we'll nape the complex."

"Roger that," I said. Switching radios to UHF I called Chuck. "Okay One-six. Mark it and move off to the southwest." I watched the white phosphorus grenade explode in a billowy white cloud. For being so deadly, it was beautiful. The LOH high-tailed it out of the area.

"Okay Four-one. You're cleared in hot. I'll hold southwest with my little bird."

The Phantoms dove in steeply, dropping their ordnance right on target. Trees toppled over, enlarging the LZ, and once again the shock waves were awesome. On their second run they adjusted about one hundred and fifty meters to the northeast. The napalm exploded in a massive ball of fire and destruction.

Major Nelson came up on my UHF frequency, the frequency that was reserved for the Pink team.

"Two-four. This is Six. Sit rep," he requested.

"Six. Two-four. I'm busy now and I'd appreciate it if you'd vacate this freq." There was no response.

"Two-four. Raider Four-one. We're expended. Will you send us a BDA?" he asked.

"Roger that, Four-one. I'll let the Blues give you a proper one. Thanks for the help."

"Any time. Good luck out here today," he said as the Phantoms climbed back into the heavens and headed back to Bién Hoa.

"Three-nine, you up?" I asked.

"Go," Smitty answered.

"Right. I have a good lima zulu for you. The little bird hasn't taken any fire in a while. There are blood trails so there are people down there. Max will saddle you up and escort you in. I want you in one ship at a time, five second breaks at my command."

"Roger. Good copy," he replied.

Smitty left the frequency to brief the other lift pilots.

"Hey Two-four, One-six," Chuck called.

"Go."

"It looks pretty quiet down here. Nothing's moving. Looks like it'll be a cold insertion," he said.

"Roger. That'll make the Blue birds happy!"

"Cavalier Two-four. Blue max Five-one."

"Hey Five-one. Where ya at?" I asked him.

"We're just coming up on four UH-1s. Looks like they're out of Papa Vic. They your boys?"

"That's them, Five-one. The fast movers are clear. They've softened the LZ up a bit and my little bird says its pretty quiet right now. The Blue birds will be going in single ship at five-second breaks. Can you handle that?"

"Sounds good to me," he responded.

"Okay Two-four, Three-nine. We have arrived."

I had watched the birds' approach in loose trail formation. The Blue Max Cobras were right behind them.

"Okay, Three-nine and Five-one. Come up channel two. I want everybody on the same frequency. I want everybody talking to everybody else."

"Hey One-six, the Blue birds and Max will be joining us on uniform for the insertion," I told Chuck.

Before he could respond the other aircraft began to check in. "Two-four, Three-nine. Channel two."

"Rog Three-nine."

"Two-four. Max Five-one is with you."

"Great stuff. Okay One-six, give the Blue birds an LZ brief and let's get to work."

"Okay Three-nine, this is One-six. The LZ is the open area just to my right. You should be able to get pretty close to the ground. The bombs blew some debris around so watch it. Doesn't seem to be anybody around. I'd approach from east to west. We're popping smoke."

"Roger that One-six. Good copy," Smitty replied.

"Okay guys, this is Two-four. Let's do it."

The insertion was poetry in motion. The lift birds broke off at five-second intervals and did a high overhead approach spiraling down over the LZ to reduce their exposure. The Cobras rode shotgun on both sides as the first Huey approached the LZ. The miniguns were blazing until the rockets left the tubes.

The first aircraft descended into the LZ and rolled from the heel of the skids onto the toes and he was off. The Blues unassed the aircraft as soon as the heels had touched; they knew there was no time to waste and they had to set up a defensive perimeter for the rest of the insertion. As soon as the first aircraft cleared the LZ the second one was descending below treetop level. The insertion went off without a hitch like a beautifully choreographed ballet, one that we had rehearsed many times before.

The Blues spent the day exploiting a very recently and heavily used bunker complex. They found a couple of dead VC and other articles of war. As previously reported, there were lots of blood trails but as they so often did, the VC had just disappeared into thin air. After several hours, the Blues were extracted without incident. When the last lift ship was out I came back on the radio. "OK, guys! Let's go home."

We got back to Phuoc Vinh a short time later. As I was shutting down, Bones came up with a cold coke for my x-ray and me.

"Thank you, bud," I told him as I climbed out of the cockpit. My back was a bit sore and I was very tired. I filled in the logbook. We had flown for twelve and a half hours.

Chapter 16

"You're Just a Kid!"

The next morning I awoke late. I was scheduled for a night-training sortie that night, so the day was free. I reviewed my paperwork for R&R. I wanted everything to be ready when the time came. I had only two more weeks until I had to report to Biên Hoa. I also spent some time bringing my logbook up-to-date. I had been grounded off and on for the past two weeks and now I could see why. My total time was now 1,066 hours and I had flown 151 hours in the past four weeks. Those four weeks included all the days I had been grounded too. It was no wonder I was so tired. R&R would certainly be a welcome break.

As a result of the twelve-and-a-half-hour day I had flown, I was grounded again. I still had to fly the night training mission. McDerby flew front seat as the IP and we went out and did some night flying and a few radar approaches.

The following morning I slept in until eleven o'clock. Sleep was something I never seemed to get enough of. After lunch I went to the mail room and picked up a letter from my parents. My cousin, Norman Carabet, our family doctor, had put both Mom and Dad on tranquilizers for their nerves. They were at their wit's end.

The morning of September 12 was hot and humid. The monsoon rains began around ten o'clock. I ran out to pull down the plastic sheets to prevent the water from blowing in through the screen. By the time I got back in I was soaked. My next door neighbor, 1st Lt. Van Joyce, was in his room, so I went over to chat. I had recently got some new cassette tapes and we listened to them as we talked. We talked about surfing and Hawaii. We talked about girls and flying. We talked about anything that came to mind. It was a nice relaxing day.

The Blues were called out to secure a CH-47 Chinook that had crashed a few miles east of Phuoc Vinh. As dusk approached it became apparent that division wasn't going to be able to get the aircraft out that day. I took off to cover them after having an early dinner.

"Hey Bluish, this is Jewish. Over."

"Hey roomy, we have to stop meeting like this," he answered. "Can you find out when we're going to be extracted?"

"Sure. Stand by," I told him.

"Three, this is Two-four," I called on family fox.

"Go ahead Two-four. This is Three."

"Any idea when the lift ships are launching to pick up the Blues?" I inquired.

"Um, yeah, Two-four . . . Six says we're leaving them in tonight. They're to secure the downed bird until they lift it out tomorrow."

"What the hell do you mean we're leaving them in?" I asked.

"Hey Two-four. Don't shoot me. I'm just the messenger," he said.

"Blue, Two-four."

"Go ahead, buddy," he answered.

"Word is that the old man says you're supposed to stay there and secure the hook until tomorrow," I relayed.

"What kind of bullshit is this?" Blue asked.

"Hey bubba, I don't like it anymore than you do but I'll be up here as long as you're on the ground," I reassured him.

A short while later the family fox beckoned. "Two-four, this is Three."

"Go ahead," I answered.

"You're supposed to RTB. We can react quickly if the Blues get into trouble. They're only a few clicks out of base," he ordered.

"That is bullshit!" I protested. "Since when do we leave the Blues on the ground unprotected? Negative RTB. I am staying on station."

"Hey Two-four. Can it and get your ass back here. I'm not asking, I'm telling. If you have any questions you can see the old man when you shut down."

"Bullshit. I have nothing to say to him," I muttered.

"Blue, Two-four. I've been ORDERED to RTB."

"What?" he asked.

"Yeah. The CO told me to get my ass back on the ground," I said rather dejectedly.

"Okay," Blue responded apprehensively.

"Listen," I told him, "If anything happens, if you hear anything or get lonely, you call ops and tell the RTO to call me and I'll be back out here ASAP. I don't give a fuck what the old man says."

"Okay, buddy. We're going to get hunkered down. I'll see you in the morning," Harvey told me.

"Yeah. If not before. You guys keep your heads down. I'll see ya at first light," I said.

Reluctantly, and against my better judgment, I called the tower and headed for home. I was still seething when I got back to the room. I grabbed a coke and sat down to try to make sense of what seemed a stupid decision. I couldn't.

About 11:30 I put on a tape and hit the rack. It was Dennis Yost and the Classics IV's Greatest Hits. Spooky was playing at 11:45 when KA WHOMPF!

"Shit! That's close," I thought as shrapnel and dirt began to rain down on the roof. I rolled off the bed onto the floor. KA WHOMPF again. This time it was closer. "That's two," I thought and headed for the bunker. Incoming always had come in volleys of two. There would be about a ten- or fifteen-second lull and then two more. I ran to the side door of the hooch. As I pushed open the screen

Randy Zahn, Cavalier 24, at Phuoc Vinh, 1970

Randy Zahn's mount, 068, in flight

Close-up of the 20mm Vulcan cannon mounted on 068

The Arch at Phuoc Vinh, 1970

The campaign blade of the First of the Ninth Cavalry in front of the headquarters building at Phuoc Vinh

The author's room at Phuoc Vinh; note photograph of Karla on the shelf to the left

Runway zero nine at Phuoc Vinh, 1970

A taping session in the author's room (from left to right): Tom Whiddon (KIA), Randy Zahn, and Steve Beene

Ground fire from this village in Cambodia (the remains of which can be seen to the left) claimed Tom Whiddon and his crew on May 6, 1970

North American OV10 Bronco Forward Air Controller (FAC) flown by George Lamperti, call sign Rash 26

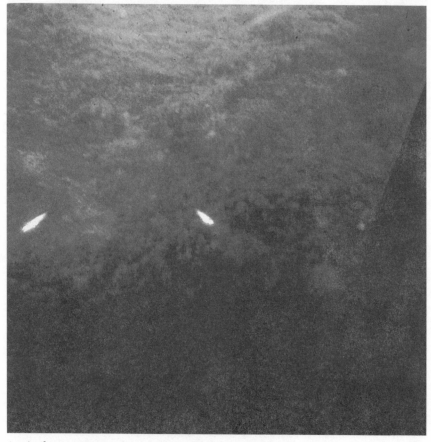

A pair of seventeen-pound rockets streak toward their target

Two "deuce and a half" trucks burning after the Trai Bai ambush

Awards ceremony following the ambush contact at Trai Bai airstrip
Decorations are being presented by Maj. Gen. George Putnam (center, in fatigues with Cav hat) who addresses Charlie Troop commander Maj. Keith Ball
Then, from left to right: CW2 Chuck Frazier, 1st Lt. Jim Williams, CW2 Larry Edeal, CW2 Randy Dyer, CW2 Randy Zahn, WO1 Al Sellers, CW2 Robert James, unknown

Fire Support Base Buttons at Song Be, with Nui Ba Ra looming in the background

1st Lt. Van Joyce (killed in action March 12, 1971) in front of 068, Tien Ngon, January 1971

Randy Zahn, left, and WO1 Cowles (Wally) Waldron

Charlie Troop now
Back row, left to right: Galen Rosher, Ronald "Dexter" Evans, "Uncle" John Craig
Center, left to right: Randy Zahn, Ronald "White" Beyer, Fred "Mother" Joles
Front row, left to right: Sam Hinch, Al "Big Al" DeMailo, Mark "Babysan" Hilton, Ross Rainwater

door to run to the bunker, something, and to this day I don't know what it was, told me to hit the deck. I dove to the ground. Every significant episode of my life flashed before me in record time. I sensed smoke and debris flying around before I heard the third KA WHOMPF. It was excruciatingly loud. My ears were ringing. I struggled to get up. As I ran toward the bunker I felt a strange sensation on the right side of my face. I couldn't make out what it was, and my leg hurt like hell, along with my back and my neck. When I got to the bunker door I stopped to see what was causing the sensation. As I brought my hand up to my face it was covered in blood.

Ron Beyer, White, grabbed me and pulled me inside. He laid me over a footlocker before pulling a two-foot splinter of wood out of my right temple. When I hit the ground the plywood wall next to me had splintered and projected this piece into my head. As I ran it flopped up and down, causing the sensation I had felt. I was shaking pretty badly. I was in shock. My ears were still ringing as more rounds impacted outside. The red hooch was ablaze and rounds of ammunition were cooking off in all directions. The incoming continued in one of the longest volleys we had ever experienced. At about 12:45 a jeep pulled up and took me, Van Joyce, and Cowles (Wally) Waldron over to Fifteenth Med. Medics ran out to bring us inside. They opened a large sliding door and we entered the triage room. It was in a huge bunker. A doctor came over and placed a cotton bandage over my right leg and did something to my back and my neck. I couldn't tell what. He cleaned the area where the splinter had been, gave me a few shots, filled out a tag, and tied it to my ankle. When he had finished, a medic came over and wheeled the cart I was on out into a waiting area.

"No fucking way," I said as we left the bunker.

"What's the matter?" the medic asked me.

"I just got my shit blown away and now you've brought me back out into this fucking hooch. We're still getting hit, goddamnit. You take me back into that bunker," I demanded. He left me there.

At approximately 1:30 A.M. a medevac Huey landed at the pad outside the door. I was placed on the aircraft along with Van, Wally, and a few others.

It was about a fifteen-minute flight down to Long Binh. The air felt wonderful as we flew. We landed at the Ninety-Third Evacuation Hospital and once again I was whisked off to triage. Somebody read my tag and unwrapped the bandage on my leg. He looked at my back and then he explored my neck. I could hardly keep my eyes open. I was tired and still in semi-shock, although not in very much pain. A medic tried to start an IV in my right arm.

"Holy shit," I winced. "That fucking hurts."

He was trying to insert a 10-gauge IV needle. It was about as big as a garden hose and hurt worse than my wounds. Once he got it in he sighed. "Darn. It's clogged. I'll have to pull it out and reposition it."

He tried again with the same result. As he was about to try for a third time I looked him square in the eyes. "You touch me with another fucking needle and I'm going to come off this table and—"

"What's going on here?" a man said from behind a surgical mask.

He took one look at my arm and dismissed the medic. "I'll do this one," he said. All I could see was his eyes. He apologized for the pain he was about to inflict. "I'm afraid I can't do this without it hurting but do it I must. We have to get some fluids in you." At four o'clock, I was wheeled into surgery.

CKAAH. CKAAH. "What the hell is that noise?" I thought. I was really groggy and not too with it.

CKAAH. CKAAH. I looked around and everything was blurry. An oxygen tank sat next to my bed with a brown tube attached to it and a smaller green tube attached to the brown tube. I grabbed the tube and followed it with my hand. The other end was inserted into my right nostril and every time I breathed, it made the noise. I pulled the brown tube off of the oxygen tank and the green tube out of my nose. Then I pulled them apart and threw one in one direction and the other one in the opposite direction.

A nurse came over. "What are you doing?" she admonished me.

I stared at her through glazed eyes.

"That tube helps you breathe," she told me. I was out again.

When I woke up the second time and was a bit more coherent, I looked around me. I was in a ward that was shaped like an X. The nurses' station was in the center of the wings so they could observe all four wings of the ward.

"Welcome back, neighbor," somebody said.

Van was in the bed beside me. He was a good-looking guy who came to Vietnam from Hawaii, where he had been living. He was well up in the rankings of top surfers on the island. Van had been in-country for almost two years and had flown damn near every type of helicopter the Army had in-theater, the Cobra being the last on his list of want-to-flys.

"Hey Van," I acknowledged. "What happened to you?" I asked.

"Ah, I just got a bit of shrapnel in my forearm. No big thing," he told me.

And from the other direction, "Hi. When are we getting married?"

"What?" I asked incredulously.

"Well. You told me you loved me and asked me to marry you and I just want to know when you have in mind?" a nurse smiled.

"Get married? What are you talking about? I don't even know you," I said. Van was laughing.

"Did he or did he not ask me to marry him?" the nurse asked Van.

"You did, Two-four. Honest. I heard it with my own ears," he said.

I just looked at him and then back at her. "I guess I don't remember," I apologized.

"That's okay," she said. "Demerol does funny things to people. I am Anne Liberatore and I'll be taking care of you while you're here. Everybody calls me Annie."

"Hi Annie. I'm Randy. Randy Zahn."

Annie was cute with short brown hair and a roundish face, glasses, and a great smile.

"Hi Randy," she responded with a firm squeeze on my arm. "Lunch will be here soon. I'll see you in a while. Do you need anything now?"

"No thanks," I said and then, "Shit! I'm supposed to go on R&R in ten days! Will I still be able to go? Oh God, they haven't notified my parents, have they?" I asked as my mind raced.

"I'm afraid that'll be up to your surgeon. R&R that is," she said. "About notification, you'll have to ask your unit." And she retreated to the nurses' station.

I looked at Van and asked him, "Did I really ask her to marry me?"

That afternoon the surgeon who had operated on me came by. He asked how I was doing and told me about my wounds. "You had a nasty wound to your outer right thigh. A piece of shrapnel . . . this piece," he said reaching to my bedside table and picking up a jagged piece of metal, "entered about mid-thigh. It went through the muscle and hit your femur. That's the big bone in your upper leg. Luckily there is no damage to the bone. I got it out as you can see, and I debrided the wound." He stopped to make sure I was still with him.

"I haven't closed the wound. The VC has a nasty habit of urinating on their shells or wiping shit on them. It's a primitive form of biological warfare, but it works. It can cause a really nasty infection," he continued. "One of the nurses will change the bandage and irrigate the wound twice a day for five days. Then I'll get you back into the OR and close it once we're sure there is no infection. You also had a small piece of shrapnel that hadn't actually penetrated your back. It broke the skin and it looks nasty, but I disinfected the area and it should be fine. There is also a small piece of metal in your neck. It is just under the skin and it'll work itself out. The body has a wonderful way of rejecting foreign bodies. No need to make another incision. Now, do you have any questions for me?" he asked.

"Yes, sir," I said. "I do. I'm supposed to be going on R&R on the twenty-fifth. I am supposed to report to Bién Hoa on the twenty-third. Will I still be able to go?" I asked tentatively.

"Where are you going?" he asked me.

"I'm meeting my parents and a good friend in Hawaii," I told him.

"Well, the stitches won't be out by then but you can go to the ER at Tripler in Honolulu and they can remove them. And you may not make the twenty-third. We'll get word to Cav Rear and if I have to I'll drive you to the plane myself," he reassured me. "But two things: one, no swimming until the stitches are out; and two, you won't be able to fly for at least a month. We'll just have to wait and see how that muscle heals."

"Thank you, sir," I smiled. "Thank you very much for everything."

"It's my pleasure. Who are you with anyway?" he asked.

"Charlie Troop. First of the Ninth, sir," I bragged. "I fly Cobras."

"Christ," he said shaking his head. "You're just a kid."

I was anxious to call my folks. I knew that if the Army had contacted them they would be extremely upset.

"Annie, is there a phone anywhere close by that I can call my parents from?" I asked.

"Sure," she told me. "There's a MARS station here at the hospital but you have to put your name on a list and they'll let us know when they want you to come over. It could be any time of the night or day," she added. "But don't be too anxious. You're not going anywhere for a day or two." I slept for most of the rest of that day.

In the morning I was awakened for breakfast. We ate at tables in the ward. Even in the hospital the Army didn't provide breakfast in bed. About mid-morning a blond nurse came over to my bedside. "Hi! I'm Cathy," she introduced herself.

"Where's Annie?" I asked.

"Your fiancée?" she joked (I hoped). "She's off duty today. I'm going to change that bandage and have a look at your wounds. Your leg is still open," she reminded me. "You want to have a look?" she asked.

"Not just now," I said without hesitation. "Maybe in a day or two. Not now, thanks."

Cathy removed the bandage painlessly. She had a squeeze bottle with a clear solution in it that she squirted into my open leg. It was a weird sensation. Not painful . . . just weird. She seemed to be at ease with what she saw and bandaged it back up. "It looks just fine," she reassured me. "You get some rest now." She had a beautiful smile.

After lunch I took a nap. Somebody woke me. I looked up and it was Major Nelson, Captain Joles, and Steve. "Forgive me for not getting up and saluting, sir," I said.

"Don't worry about that. How are you doing?" the major asked me.

"Not too bad, sir," I told him as I sat up. "I don't think I'll be flying for a while. What happened last night?" I asked.

"The red hooch took two direct hits. There's nothing left of it. It burned to the ground," they told me.

"Looks like the round that hit you impacted just about on Blue's pillow!" they continued.

"Blue? Shit! Are they still in the AO?" I asked.

"No. They came in this morning," one of them said.

"What did Blue say when he found out?" I asked nobody in particular.

Steve spoke up. "He didn't say anything. We didn't tell him. He just walked around the corner of the aid station and when he looked up and saw what was left of the hooch he stopped dead in his tracks. He asked if everybody got out okay and we told him that five of you were wounded."

"Five? Who besides Van and Wally and me?" I asked.

"Wyatt took a bit of shrapnel and so did Kent Thomas," I was told.

"So what did Blue say?" I asked.

"He asked about you and when he found out you got hit, he didn't say anything. He just cried."

"Cried?" I exclaimed. "Wait till I see him . . . the wimp!"

I sat there and tried to imagine how I would have felt if the roles had been reversed and I decided I would have cried too. It was nice to be cared about. They had to be getting back, but said they'd come to visit again. Before they left Steve grabbed my hand. "Man, I was worried about you. We lost Tommy and Kevin. I couldn't handle losing you too." And he left. I knew exactly where he was coming from.

It wasn't until the next day that I was able to get a phone call through to home. Mom answered "Hi doll, how's everything?" she asked.

"I'm fine, Mom. How's things at home?" I asked.

She started to talk about irrelevant things before I realized that my dad wasn't on the other phone. In the past when I had called, no matter who answered, the other would go to the other telephone almost instantly. After a few minutes of talking I asked, "Mom. Where is Daddy?"

"Oh, I didn't want to tell you. You have enough to worry about, but since you're on the phone . . . " she trailed off.

"Tell me what, Mom?" I asked her anxiously.

"The other day Dad got to work and he was shaking all over. He was a nervous wreck. His boss sent him home and called me at work. I went home to meet him," she told me.

"What happened?" I asked again.

"Norman put him in the hospital for observation. He's on the verge of a nervous breakdown. He's so silly. He was sure something had happened to you." And almost in the same breath she asked, "Where are you? In Saigon?"

"No, Mom. I'm in the hospital too," I told her.

"Who are you visiting in the hospital?" she asked.

"The surgeon," I replied.

There was silence on the other end of the line.

"Mom, I got wounded the night before last. I'm okay though. I just thought I had better call in case the Army decided to send you some dumb telegram or something," I explained.

She began to cry. "Are you sure?" she asked me.

"I'm sure, Mom. I'm okay. I got hit by some shrapnel but they got it all out and I'll be fine."

"Where were you hit?" she asked.

"It doesn't matter," I said.

"Don't you dare tell me it doesn't matter. Where?" she yelled and then, almost as an afterthought, "I can't tell your father. He'll have a fit." Mom was bewildered and in shock. She didn't know who to be more worried about, my dad or me.

"Mom. Don't say anything to Dad. Not a word. I'll tell him when I see him in Hawaii," I suggested.

"Will you still be able to go?" she asked.

"The doc says there is no reason why I can't. Nothing has changed . . . except I may be limping a bit when I get there."

"Oye vey," she exclaimed. "What next?"

"Mother, listen to me. I am okay and Daddy will be too. Just don't say anything. I'll be fine. I love you both and I'll see you in a few days," I tried to reassure her.

"I love you too, doll boy," she just managed to get out through her tears.

We hung up and I thought, "Oh shit."

Van went back to the unit on the fourteenth and I continued to make good progress recuperating. Annie came over to my bed that evening and said, "We're having a party tonight. Want to come?"

"I'd love to," I told her, "But what will I wear?"

"Haven't you got any clothes with you?"

"I arrived with a pair of underwear and they cut those off of me. According to my CO that was the last personal possession I had. I lost everything else in the fire."

"Don't worry," Annie told me. "I'll get you some fatigues. What size boots do you wear?" she asked.

"Nine and a half, wide," I told her.

She put a finger to her lips and smiled as she turned to walk away.

"Annie!" I called after her.

"Shhhh," she said. "I'll see you later."

Just before supper they put a small Vietnamese girl in the bed next to mine. She had been burned somehow. After supper Annie returned with some clothes for me. "Put these on and I'll be back in a little while," she told me.

I did my best to get dressed under the covers on my bed. I was afraid somebody might see me and ask questions. Putting on my pants was fun, not being able to bend my leg. And my boots? Impossible.

Just about the time I finished getting dressed, a female lieutenant colonel approached.

"Now I am in deep shit," I thought.

I pulled the covers right up under my chin and tried to appear nonchalant. She walked straight over to me and bid me a "Good evening."

"Good evening, ma'am," I replied.

"How are you tonight?" she asked.

"I'm fine, thanks," I told her.

"May I sit on your bed?" she asked. "I'd like to visit with this young lady," she told me nodding toward the little Vietnamese girl.

"No problem," I told her, holding the covers that much tighter so she would not see that I was fully dressed. Annie walked in the back door, took one look, did an about face, and disappeared out the same door she had just come in. Ten minutes later, the colonel left, but not before thanking me for the use of the bed. As soon as she turned the corner Annie came back in and we were out the back door like a flash. The party was in the bachelor officer quarters (BOQ) and mostly docs and nurses, although there were some Dustoff pilots there as well. One came up to Annie and whispered something to her. She grabbed my arm and just said, "Forget it. I have me a Cobra pilot!"

Obviously, I wasn't able to dance but I enjoyed the change and got back to my bed about midnight. The hospital gave me a nice break until one night when I heard incoming impacting some distance away. The ward I was in offered no overhead protection and having just recently been hit I freaked out a bit.

I spent some time writing letters. The sixteenth marked the halfway point of my tour and I lay there thinking, "This is a hell of a way to celebrate the countdown!" And then the realization hit me full force and I started to get a bit teary-eyed. Annie came over to change my bandage and irrigate the wound.

"What's the matter?" she asked.

"I guess it just hit me," I told her.

"What hit you?"

"I came very close to being killed the other night."

I told Annie what had happened and about the "something" that made me hit the ground when I normally would have kept running. If I had been on my feet the shrapnel would have pierced my abdomen. It would have been all over except for the funeral. Annie got up after the bandage change. She gave me a peck on the forehead and said, "It wasn't your time, big guy." And she left.

In the morning on the seventeenth I was taken back to the OR and the surgeon closed the wound and sutured my leg with stainless steel stitches. I was sick from the anesthesia when I awoke in recovery. When I got back to the ward there was a letter and tape waiting for me. It was from Mom. Dad got out of the hospital on the fourteenth. She hadn't told him anything and he asked why I hadn't written or sent any tapes and Mom made excuses for me. Mom wrote, *"It seems like all Dad does is think, talk, and live Randy."* It was getting more and more difficult for her to keep it a secret from him.

Major Nelson and the First Sergeant (TOP) came to visit on the eighteenth. They brought me some more mail and something I never wanted.

TOP began to read:

14 September 1970 General Orders Number 200

The following AWARD is announced: Randy Zahn is awarded the Purple Heart for wounds received in action in the Republic of Vietnam on 13 September 1970 by direction of the President under the provisions of AR 672-5-1. Signed Roger H. Drue, 1st Lt. Adjutant.

Major Nelson pinned the ribbon on to my pillow and offered his congratulations.

"Congratulations?" I asked, "For what? For getting wounded?"

TOP reminded me that I would have to get a new ID card, dog tags, flight gear, a new weapon, and anything else I lost.

"What exactly did I lose, TOP?" I asked.

"Son, you're lucky you got out of there with your life. The explosives, ordnance, and demolition (EOD) people checked out the impact craters. A 75mm hit you. You were lying about seven feet from the point of impact. If you hadn't been flat on the ground, we would have been picking up little pieces of Cavalier Two-four. You are one lucky son of a bitch."

"Thanks TOP," I said. And under my breath I said, "Thanks something."

The surgeon came in to see how I was getting on. He told me all had gone well and there was no reason I couldn't go on R&R, but "You can't go swimming until the stitches are out and no flying until after you get back and come to see me," he reminded me.

"Doc," I said "Any chance of getting a pass for a day. I'd like to go up to Phuoc Vinh and get some clothes and stuff to take with me as long as I'll be going straight from here."

"I'll arrange it," he said. "You have a good time and I'll see you when you get back."

"Yes, sir, and thanks again," I said as he departed.

I called the unit and asked them to send an aircraft down to pick me up. On the morning of the twenty-second, one of the lift birds came down. I still had my borrowed fatigues, thanks to Annie. First stop was at Bién Hoa to get a new ID card and dog tags. When I got back to the aircraft I asked, "Can I fly this thing back to Phuoc Vinh?"

"You up to it?" the AC asked.

"We'll find out," I told him.

We climbed in and I fastened my harness. After starting the aircraft I lifted into the hover. "So far so good," I said and we took off.

After landing at Phuoc Vinh, we shut down and headed to the TOC. "No flying, my ass," I said. The guys were glad to see me. I walked around to the hooch and there wasn't much left of it. Burned out with metal twisted from the heat, there was nothing there but rubble. I went to the club to see who was there.

"Two-four!" It was Harvey. "Goddamnit buddy, don't you ever do that to me again," he admonished me.

"Hey, it wasn't my idea to get blown away," I reminded him.

"Blown away?" he asked. "I'm not talking about that. I don't give a shit if you get yourself greased. Don't you ever leave me in the AO like that again."

He walked over to me and put his arms around me . . . hugging me. "Shit, Jewish, I was worried about you man. How are ya doing?" he asked.

"I'm okay, Blue. I'll be fine," I told him. "You're missing out pal. There are some nice nurses down at the Ninety-Third."

"You little fucker," he laughed. "You don't miss a trick, do you?"

"Hey, I learned from the best, man," I responded.

Steve walked in. "Hey Randy, how you doing?"

"Fine Steve, just fine. I have a favor to ask of you."

"What's that?"

"All those new clothes you bought when you were in Hawaii. Can I borrow them? I lost everything in the hooch," I told him.

"No sweat man. You can have all of it."

"Thanks Steve, you're a pal," I said thankfully. After a few more greetings it was time to get back. I opted to be a passenger on the way back to the hospital. The breeze felt great. That evening Annie and I went to the O Club at the Ninety-Third. We got a pizza and sat off in a corner talking. We promised that we would keep in touch after I went back to Phuoc Vinh. When some of Annie's friends came to join us, I excused myself saying I had to get up early. I guess I felt intruded upon and didn't want to show it.

After breakfast on the twenty-fourth, a Ninety-Third Evac jeep delivered me to Bién Hoa. I was on my way back to Paradise.

The bus, complete with chicken wire, took us to Camp Alpha at Tan Son Nhut the night of the twenty-fourth. Sleep was impossible, I didn't even try. We were leaving very early in the morning on flight P208. The Pan American Boeing 707 was the most beautiful sight I had ever seen. I climbed the boarding stairs and found a window seat close to the front of the aircraft. "Gentlemen: Welcome aboard flight 208 to Honolulu, Hawaii. For those of you who may have forgotten, that it is in the United States of America. We should be airborne soon and our ETA in Honolulu is 12:55 P.M. on the twenty-fifth. Sit back, relax, and get some rest."

The engines started and we began to taxi. A short time later the wheels slipped the surly bonds and a cheer erupted throughout the cabin. I tried to visualize the reunion with my parents but all I could think about was Tommy and Kevin. Their deaths seemed so senseless.

My parents and Mike arrived in Hawaii the day before me. They were instructed to go to Fort DeRussy, not the airport. Upon our arrival we had to process through public health, immigration, and customs, and then board Army buses to take us to Fort DeRussy.

The flight seemed to take forever. My leg hurt from the pressure of my pants on the stitches. I did my best to make myself comfortable before I dozed off. It was bright and beautiful as we descended into Honolulu. When we landed, nobody cheered. Most of us remained seated—lost in our own thoughts. Some of those on board that day would be seeing wives they hadn't seen in months and, in some cases, children. Others would be greeting fiancées, girlfriends, and like me, parents. It had been more than six months since I last saw my mother and father and I'm sure they had guessed, and I knew, that I had changed. I might have been twenty years old, but I felt much older.

After the formalities were completed, we boarded the buses that I was happy to see had no chicken wire covering the windows. MP jeeps escorted us with lights flashing for the twenty-minute drive to Fort DeRussy. The jeeps weren't so much for our benefit but for the crowds awaiting our arrival at the R&R center. The MP radioed our location to those waiting for us at DeRussy as we made our way through the streets of Honolulu.

As the buses pulled into the parking lot people were lined up in two rows, gauntlet-like, along a pathway. The buses stopped in turn with their doors between the rows of people. I was uncomfortable. I watched the guys seated in front of me get off the bus and the two lines disintegrated. People were everywhere and there was laughter, hugs, and tears. I carefully made my way down the steps and stopped. The last thing I needed was someone bumping into me in his or her excitement. I moved forward cautiously, a bit dazed. I looked around and all of a sudden my dad was in front of me. He just stood there with tears in his eyes and his mouth agape. I limped toward him but he just stood there looking me up and down. I'm sure he was counting arms and legs and hands and feet. Finally, he hugged me like he had never hugged me before. He was crying.

"Mommy just told me," he said choking back his tears. "Are you all right, babe?" he asked and then he kissed me.

"I'm okay, Dad," I told him. "I'll be fine."

Mom and Mike came over. They had agreed to give Dad and me a few minutes alone. We hugged and exchanged greetings. I had such mixed emotions I don't know what I was thinking.

There were more formalities to go through before we were able to leave the R&R center, but as soon as they were over we went to the hotel. The Waikikian was a small Polynesian-style hotel. The rooms had verandas that were partially obscured by lush vegetation. Quiet and quaint, the rooms had ceiling fans and no TVs. I unpacked and sat down exhausted. My body was still in another time zone.

Mom and Dad came over to our room and the questions began. Dad wanted to know what had happened to me and when. He understood why Mom hadn't told him but he didn't like it. I told them the whole story when Mike posed a question, "What time was it when you got hit?"

"11:45 at night," I said. "I was in bed."

He looked at me and then at my Dad.

"Joe, what time did you get to work that morning?"

Dad replied nonchalantly, "Quarter to eight, the same time I always do."

Mike stated rather than asked, "There is a fifteen-hour time difference between LA and Vietnam, isn't there?"

I looked up understanding the implication of what he was getting at. "Wow!" I exclaimed. "I don't believe this."

Mom and Dad hadn't twigged. Mom asked, "What are you two talking about?"

"Mom, don't you see? Daddy arrived at work feeling like something had happened to me. Right?"

"Yeah, so."

"When you consider the difference in time zones, Daddy got that feeling at almost the exact same time that I got wounded," I explained.

We didn't do much that first day. I just wanted to unwind. Mom and Dad went back to their room and Mike told me what was going on back at home. As he talked I began to realize that I wasn't nearly as interested in what was going on at home as I was concerned about what was going on at Charlie Troop. Mike didn't ask much about Nam although I could sense his curiosity. I didn't volunteer anything because I knew he would be unable to relate to what I had experienced in the past six months.

On Saturday we went to the beach at DeRussy. I sat there, unable to go in the water, taking it all in. There were lots of people around. Guys with girlfriends and wives, hugging and cuddling, kissing and holding hands. Little children were running around and frolicking in the water. I felt strangely out of place, but I realized that it wasn't because of the couples. I just didn't want to be there.

We picked up our rental car before lunch and went to the Ala Moana Shopping Center that afternoon. I bought clothes but I was more interested in the girls than I was the clothes. Some of the native Hawaiian girls were stunning.

We went to Duke Kahanamokus for dinner that night and had a wonderful meal. It was a relaxed atmosphere, but I couldn't rid myself of the inner turmoil. After dinner we went back to the hotel. Mike went to bed and I went for a walk. I wanted to be on my own. I needed to be alone.

After breakfast Monday, Mike drove the two of us over to Tripler Army Hospital to get my stitches removed. That done, we headed back to the hotel, changed, and went to the beach. I dropped my towel on the beach and dove through the breakers. It was exhilarating and refreshing, but I still wasn't happy.

At dinner that night we made plans for the rest of the week . . . the rest of the week? I only had two more full days before I had to head back.

I was compelled on Tuesday to visit Pearl Harbor. Despite the fact that I was a history buff, I needed to go. We went after breakfast. Pearl Harbor and the *Arizona* Memorial are places of beauty and solace and I felt better just being there. On the morning of December 7, 1941, these same waters were filled with burning fuel, death, and destruction. And for some reason I could relate to that. Mentally, that was where I was at—which is why I felt so strangely out of place lying on a beach watching those happy couples.

I couldn't relax. I couldn't enjoy myself. I knew that I had to go back and I wanted to. I knew that my lengthy absence because of the hospital and R&R only increased the workload on the other guys. I felt like I was letting them down. I didn't know what the next six months would bring. How many more of my friends were going to be killed or wounded? And once again I began to feel the same things I felt six and a half months ago when I passed through this place: fear, apprehension, and loneliness. I wondered why we were even allowed R&R. The concept of taking a vacation from the war seemed ludicrous, but then we weren't fighting a war according to the politicos in Washington.

My flight back to Vietnam was scheduled to depart at 9:00 A.M. on October 1. I was happy to be leaving early in the day so we didn't have to linger around too long.

I didn't sleep much that last night. I was out of bed and in the shower by six o'clock. Mom, Dad, and Mike took me to the airport. Their flight was leaving shortly after mine. Nobody spoke much until the announcement came for all military personnel traveling on the charter flight to Saigon to report to the gate. Mom and Dad didn't want this to happen. I, on the other hand, wanted to get on the plane and back to Phuoc Vinh.

I wondered whether they had given me a lobotomy when I was in the hospital.

Chapter 17

Down Bird! Down Bird!

After stopping at Guam for an hour to refuel, at 5:30 in the afternoon on October 2, I was back in Saigon. It was too late to get back to Phuoc Vinh that night, but I called the Troop and asked them to send a Huey down for me the following day.

I was confused, annoyed with myself, and a bit conscience stricken that I had been such poor company in Hawaii. I was also feeling guilty that I actually wanted to come back to Vietnam; I was feeling anxious, as this really was the beginning of the end of my tour of duty. And when I got back to Phuoc Vinh on Saturday, I was feeling depressed.

It was great to see the guys and to learn that no one had been wounded or killed during my absence, but the next week was going to be one major hassle.

During my R&R I had missed the September Hail and Farewell and the opportunity to say good-bye to Greg. Our paths must have crossed in Bién Hoa, but I didn't see him. My Officer Efficiency Report was waiting for me. It had been signed and sealed, and on my first morning back it was delivered. It had covered the period from June 22 through August 12. Ed McDerby had been my section leader for the period and as my rating officer, he had to fill out an OER when he gave up the section to Capt. John Craig, whom we affectionately nicknamed "Uncle John."

Both Ed and Greg had sections to fill out and I was pleased with my evaluation. They scored me in the ninety-sixth and ninety-fifth percentiles. Overall a good report.

Capt. Dick Skaaden was the new Red. Dick had been a warrant officer who had taken a direct commission. He was on his second tour of duty in Vietnam and arrived in the troop just in time to see me get blown up and hauled off to the hospital. About average height, Dick was slender and blond, a sign of his Scandinavian heritage. Soft spoken, he conducted the meeting with quiet confidence. I found this reassuring.

I hadn't found a place to call home yet. My room was gone and all physical memories of Kevin went with it. Harvey met me at the club after our meeting.

"Hey buddy. How ya doing?"

"I'm fine, Harv. Where do we live these days?"

"The hooch has been rebuilt on the same slab of concrete and they've saved the same area for you!"

"What do you mean for me? Where do you live?" I asked him.

"I've moved into the lift hooch," he told me.

"They're fucking crazy if they think I'm moving back in there, man. The gooks have that place zeroed in!" I exclaimed.

"Yeah. No shit! Why in the hell do you think I moved into the lift hooch?" he laughed.

I didn't have much choice where I slept that first night back. I grabbed a bed and I was out. I would have loved to wake up and go fly, but that wouldn't happen for another week. There was so much to do first. I had to check in with Doc Eckert. I had to find a new place to live. I had to go back to Bién Hoa to have new flight gear issued to me, and then back to the Ninety-third Evac to get a clearance from the surgeon. Once he cleared me I would have to take a currency ride to satisfy McDerby that I hadn't lost the touch.

I had to fill out a personal claim form for the Judge Advocate's office, who handled the administrative side of things. When I started to think of all the things I lost I became even more depressed. The pictures of Tommy and Kevin could never be replaced nor the pictures I had taken in Cambodia. My photo of Cyndy was gone and the war trophies I had managed to accumulate were no more.

I hadn't been back in-country for twenty-four hours and already I was pissed off.

There was very little I could do without gear, so I just loafed around for those first few days back. Even if I had my flight gear I still couldn't fly until I had been medically cleared. The family car was going down to Bién Hoa on Tuesday, so I made plans to go to flight gear issue and get all my new equipment.

My leg was healing well. The limp was almost completely gone and I was pain-free. Despite everything else, I did have something to be thankful for.

Larry and I talked about Hawaii. I told him about my week, and once again my emotions were playing havoc with me. I had to sort out in my own mind whether the reason I didn't have a good time in Hawaii was because I missed the guys and the camaraderie we shared in Vietnam, or was it because I had to return to Vietnam?

I went back to the hospital on Wednesday to see the doctor. He had told me to allow a month from my second surgery, but I was feeling good and my leg appeared to be healing fine. I was anxious to see Annie so I went back to my ward. Annie was off duty. I made some inquiries only to find that my surgeon was on R&R. Feeling let down, I went back to Phuoc Vinh.

At the meeting that night Dick asked me how I felt about flying and I told him I was fine. The rest of the guys had been flying their asses off and they needed a break. I was scheduled to fly with McDerby the following day.

After breakfast we flew over to the airstrip at Chon Thành to run through emergency procedures and takeoff and landing profiles. It was as if I had never been out of the cockpit and Ed complimented me on my performance. After the ride we returned to Phuoc Vinh to refuel before going out on a mission. It felt great to be back in the air.

I told Red that I was happy to fly despite not having my medical clearance from the surgeon—and fly I did. I took off on the morning of the ninth feeling exhilarated, refreshed, and anxious to repay the debt I owed the NVA for my stay in the hospital.

The next few days are a bit of a blur. I flew every day for a week. The only toll my absence had taken showed itself through fatigue. I had never realized the mental fatigue involved in flying hour after hour of combat, but after a three-and-a-half-week absence, I knew it now.

During that week I found a new home too. I moved into a large bunker that had two bedrooms. Dick and John Craig, my section leader, lived in one room and Larry and I moved into the other. The bunker was about thirty by thirty with the bedrooms adjacent to each other on opposite sides of the bunker. The area in the middle was living area. It had a bar and kitchenette, for lack of a better description. It wasn't as nice as the room I had shared with Kevin and Bobby and Blue, but it was heavily fortified and would stand up to anything but a direct hit from a 122 mm.

One thing that had changed since I was in the hospital was our mission. Intelligence had documents that had been removed from dead NVA and VC soldiers. These captured documents provided evidence that the headquarters of the NVA in South Vietnam was holed up in our AO.

Known as the Trung Uong Cuc Mien Nam—more commonly translated as Central Office for South Vietnam, or COSVN, this elusive controlling political body had hop-scotched its way around southern South Vietnam and Cambodia, always a step ahead of us.

During the war with the French, COSVN was located in the extreme southern tip of the country. In 1955 it moved to Tay Ninh. Supposedly autonomous and under control of dissident southerners, this was pure propaganda fiction. COSVN and the war, in general, had always been firmly under the control of communist Hanoi.

Virtually everyone was flying all day every day looking for the elusive COSVN or the Subregion Five (SR5) element, as we called it.

On Sunday, October 18, I had a relatively new guy in my front seat, WO1 John Fink. One-two, Bill Cahill, was our little bird that uneventful day. Bill was a good scout pilot. Hailing from Massachusetts, he was one of those guys you just couldn't help but like.

As busy as we were and as much as we were flying, we didn't need any hassle from our own ops officer, but that's exactly what we got. For the first time since I had been in the troop, we had a non-aviator as an ops officer. We had just completed our last mission for the day and as we landed to refuel the radio crackled back to life, "Two-four, I have another mission for you. I want you to go down to vicinity of grid one eight four one. Your contact is Painful Hovel Seven-seven. Go check out their NDP," Captain Mike LaChance ordered.

"Hey One-two, guess what?" I asked Bill on our uniform frequency. "We have another mission."

"You've got to be shittin' me," Bill replied. "Man, I have to take a shit."

"Okay. Let's go shut down. I can use a break too," I told him.

I acknowledged the mission order, "Roger. We're gonna shut down for one five after we refuel. We need a break."

Bill went to the shitter and I went in to the TOC. "What's up?" I asked Mike.

"Not much. Bravo Company, Second of the Seventh are hunkering down and they just want us to have a look around," he told me.

"Have they been in contact at all?" I asked.

"Don't know."

Bill came back and we waited for his crew to return. His observer that day was SP6 Doug Strait and his gunner was Sgt. Rae Bailey. When we had all reassembled I said, "Let's go and get this over with. It's Sunday. Today's supposed to be a day of rest."

"Dig it," Bill said with a big smile.

We walked out together and as Bill was climbing into his seat I asked, "Hey Bill, aren't you wearing your chicken plate?"

"Nah," he told me. "There isn't anybody out there to shoot at me anyway!"

I had never recalled seeing a scout pilot go out into the AO without his chicken plate on, but if that was Bill's decision there wasn't much I could do about it. Departing Phuoc Vinh, we headed southeast. I called, "Painful Hovel Seven-seven. Cavalier Two-four."

"Cavalier Two-four, this is Hovel Seven-seven, go."

"Seven-seven, I have a pink team en route to your house. Understand you want us to check out the neighborhood?" I asked.

"Roger that, Two-four. There's a lot of activity to our west, but we don't have enough time to check it out before the lights go out," he told me.

"What kind of activity? Have you been in contact?"

"Negative contact, but there are definitely non-friendlies in the area."

"Roger that."

"One-two, Two-four."

"Go!"

"Listen good buddy, these guys are in their NDP and want us to check out the area to their west. He says there are bad guys west of their house. Once we identify them, keep your speed up and tell your crew to keep their eyes and ears open."

"Okay," Bill responded.

"Hovel Seven-seven, this is Two-four."

"Go ahead Two-four."

"We are approaching your area and I need to get a good ID on you guys before it gets much darker. Can you pop a smoke?" I asked.

"I'd rather not, Two-four."

"Understood. Can you hear me approaching?"

"Roger that. We hear you," he confirmed.

"OK, give me a vector to your house and a bingo when I fly over you. Can you do that?"

"Roger," Seven-seven said. "We are on some high ground with a clear view. I see you now. Turn to your ten o'clock. Okay, Two-four, you're going to cross a small blue with a little clearing on the east side."

"Got it," I acknowledged.

"Good. There's a little hill just across the clearing. We're king of that mountain," he said.

"Good copy."

"Okay One-two, you see the little clearing just under me now?"

"Roger. Got it," Bill responded. "I think this is the area that White was in the other day. He said there is all kinds of shit out here."

"OK, the friendlies are on the hill just east of the clearing. Make a low pass and see if you can spot them. We don't want to give their position away if there are bad guys in the area."

"Roger that."

"John, put a grid of this area up on the canopy for me," I told my x-ray.

I watched Bill as he descended over the area. He made a low fast pass and then turned the aircraft over on its right side.

"Two-four, One-two. Have you got me in sight?"

"Silly boy," I said. "Of course I have you in sight."

"I know. Dumb question. Watch the birdie nooowwww . . . Bingo the friendlies!"

"Got it," I said. I immediately looked for landmarks to help me remember their location. The last thing I wanted to do when working for friendlies was to get disoriented and end up shooting them. Bill began to check out the area in front of the NDP. Fast at first, he started to reduce his speed.

"Hey Two-four, the shadows are pretty bad down here. It's hard to see anything."

"Roger. If it gets too dark and you get uncomfortable, come on up and we'll head for the barn," I told Bill.

A moment later, "Hey Two-four! You know the area I was just at?"

"Roger."

"Well, there were a bunch of dudes down there shooting at me," Bill told me.

"So, why didn't you mark it?" I admonished more than asked. This was a new twist for me. Not once in my eight months in-country could I remember a scout taking fire and *not* yelling "taking fire," marking it with a smoke, and hightailing it out of the area.

"John, where the hell is that grid I asked you for? Get me a grid of the area. NOW!" I told my front-seater. I didn't like the way things were going.

"Okay, Two-four." It was Bill. "I'm going to make another run and mark it this time."

"Just be careful, goddamnit," I said.

"Seven-seven, this is Two-four. My little bird just took fire to your west. Did you hear or see anything?" I asked.

"Negative."

Bill started his second pass.

"John, get me a fucking grid of this area." This was my third request.

Bill never completed his pass. As he approached the area, he came under intense ground-to-air fire and was literally blown out of the sky. His aircraft exploded before it hit the trees.

"DOWN BIRD, DOWN BIRD!" I yelled over family fox.

"Wow! What was that?" John exclaimed from the front seat.

"Hovel Seven-seven, Hovel Seven-seven. This is Two-four. My little bird just went in about a click to your west. He's on fire."

"Roger that Two-four," and with his mic still keyed I heard him yell "Saddle up, we're moving out."

"That was the little bird, you asshole. If you were doing your job and watching him you would know that. Now get me a grid," I yelled into the intercom.

"Damn. And I didn't bring my camera," John exclaimed.

I couldn't believe my ears. "You motherfucker," I spat.

"One-two is down in the vicinity of Painful Hovel," I told ops trying to give them an idea of our location. "He exploded before he hit the trees. The aircraft is on fire. Friendlies are a click away moving toward the aircraft!"

"Roger that, Two-four, we're launching the Blues."

Blue himself was actually airborne already. He was in the back of Don Armstrong's (Cavalier 46) Huey along with a Canadian film crew.

"Hey Two-four, this is Two-three." It was Larry.

"Hey bud, get your ass out here. I need some help."

"Roger that. I'm on the way with White. What happened?"

I related the story to Larry. "I've been up Guard since they went in. Negative beepers. I don't think they made it out. The little bird blew before they even hit the trees."

"Hang in there. We'll be there shortly."

"Okay listen, it's getting dark. I'm going to go down low level and make a few passes. I don't know where the hell he even took fire from. He never marked it the first time. I'm going to make a few low passes to see if I can see anything."

"Two-four, Two-five." Uncle John checked in.

"Hey Two-five, beat feet on out here roomy. This might be a long night."

I dove out of altitude toward the burning LOH and leveled off about a hundred feet above the trees at one hundred and fifty knots. Rolling right and then left, looking, looking for anything. Bill, his crew, bad guys, anything. I made three passes and on the third one I saw some muzzle flashes to my right.

Pulling back on the cyclic, we rocketed back up into the air in a cyclic climb. As the airspeed dropped off I kicked the left pedal and we fell to the left in a hammerhead turn. Diving almost vertically back toward the area I let loose with about six pair of rockets. More muzzle flashes. Cognizant of the diminishing light I pulled out before I normally would have, but with reduced light my depth perception was pretty poor.

"I'm going to put on my landing light. You may be able to find me faster," I said as we climbed back up to altitude.

"I've got you," said Larry.

"Ditto," John called.

Before I knew it, there was another LOH down on the trees.

"Who's the little bird?" I asked.

"White," replied Ron Beyer.

"Hey White. I don't think they made it out of there. I couldn't see anything and there has been negative contact on guard."

"Roger. I'll go and have a look," he said.

"Just be careful. It's getting dark and there are lots of bad guys down there," I warned.

"Two-four, this is Seven-seven."

"Go ahead, pal," I said, almost having forgotten about him.

"Roger, we're just getting ready to cross this blue. We could use some help finding our way to your little bird."

"Okay, I have another little bird on the deck right now. As soon as he checks out the down bird, I'll get him over to you," I told him.

"Hey White, Two-four."

"Go ahead."

"Listen, Painful Hovel Seven-seven is up, I shackle, delta mike lima november. Can you vector him to the little bird?" I requested.

"Roger that. Where they at?" Ron asked.

"They're back at your six on the blue."

"Why the hell are they moving at night?" Ron asked.

"Good question. I told him that One-two was down and he told his troops to saddle up and they're on the move."

By the time White found the grunts there were five Cobras in a daisy chain flying a circle around the downed little bird. We must have looked like hungry vultures. White was still helping the grunts when One-six swooped in. He wasn't on the deck for thirty seconds when he yelled "Taking fire!" I looked at the LOH and then I looked around me. I hesitated. Everyone hesitated and then, as if it were choreographed, we all rolled in at the same time. The jungle just blew apart as the rockets from five Snakes exploded in unison.

"Shit!" I yelled. "Everybody break right. I say again, everybody break right!" As we continued our rocket runs we were coming ever closer together, like the spokes of a wheel coming toward their hub. There was never a greater potential for a mid-air collision.

Low on fuel, I turned the mission over to one of the other Snakes and headed back to Phuoc Vinh to re-arm and re-fuel. Before the night was over we put down artillery and an airstrike. We had ARA work the area over as flare ships and a Nighthawk bird, a UH-1 with a two-million-candlepower Zeon light, illuminated the area. Painful Hovel Seven-seven hunkered down again until first light. One of his troops had drowned trying to cross the river. We flew until almost midnight before returning to Phuoc Vinh. There was nothing more we could do and all of us were exhausted. I had flown eleven and a half hours, five of them at night. I was angry. Bill and the others were almost certainly dead and John, my x-ray, had failed to do his job properly. Anger overcame my exhaustion.

"John," I said to my x-ray. "When we get on the ground, you had better get the fuck out and run as fast as you can or I'm going to shoot you."

And I would have.

Nobody slept very well that night. We were not in the habit of coming home when one of our crews was still on the ground.

At first light, four hunter-killer teams and the Blue birds lifted off en masse. They were going to insert the Blues to link up with the Painful Hovel crowd. I wasn't scheduled to takeoff until later in the morning, as I hadn't gone to bed until after two o'clock.

They arrived on-station at about 6:00 A.M. and the bad guys were waiting for them. White and One-six went down to start the recon and almost immediately came under intense ground-to-air fire. One-six took several hits and headed to FSB Pershing, not far away, escorted by White and two Snakes. They landed uneventfully and shut down to inspect their aircraft. There was the normal banter going on about Chuck being a magnet ass, when one of the crew chiefs found two bullet holes in the belly of White's aircraft. He hadn't even known he was hit.

The Blues were inserted in a LZ while the Snakes flew a cloverleaf pattern that guaranteed continuous protection to the lift aircraft. Sometime late that morning the Charlie Troop Blues linked up with the soldiers from B Company, Second of the Seventh, and together they began to push toward the downed LOH. The going was slow. There were booby traps everywhere. At one point a large explosion was observed in the trees. A call was made to the ground troops. Hovel Seven-seven responded. One of his troops had tripped a booby-trapped ammo can full of detonator fuses that wounded seven soldiers. They called for a dustoff aircraft and a short time later got a call from a UH-1 from the 227th. He had just come off of Pershing and heard the call.

Larry was on station, "Cavalier Two-three, this is Fat Albert."

"Fat Albert, Two-three. Go ahead."

"Roger that, sir. I just lifted from Pershing and am only a few minutes away. Can I be of any assistance?"

"Do you have a JP on board?" Larry asked.

"Negative."

"We have a bunch of WIAs and there are no touch downs in the area. Best I can offer is a hover hole, but I don't know how you'd get the wounded on board the aircraft."

"We can link the seat belts together," he offered.

"Okay!" Larry briefed him on the tactical situation and ensured him that the scouts would be down there to help keep the bad guys' heads down. The UH-1 hovered down into the hole, chopping off branches of trees as he descended. He made two runs with wounded back to base before he would be relieved on station by a hoist-equipped medevac aircraft. Fat Albert was recommended for a Distinguished Flying Cross for his efforts.

Once the wounded were all evacuated, the ground troops began to move again.

Ron "Barney" Vestal (Cavalier 13) and I lifted off of Phuoc Vinh after an early lunch. Mel Wyatt was in my front seat. The other team was getting short on fuel.

"Two-three, Two-four," I called.

"Go ahead."

"Rog, One-three and I are en route. Should be with you in about ten minutes. What have you got?" I asked.

Larry briefed me and I then told Barney to call White for his brief. When we arrived on station, Mel tested the turret before I let Barney descend. The two LOHs fell into a trail formation as White pointed out what he had found so far.

"You be careful down here, One-three," White cautioned. "I think the bad guys are hiding in these bunkers."

"Roger that," Barney told him. Larry and White headed back to Phuoc Vinh as I took over the mission.

"Blue, Two-four," I called.

"Go ahead, Jewish."

"Hey, it's me up here now. One-three is my little bird. Two-three and White di-died back to Papa Vic for some fuel and chow. Everything okay down there?"

"Rog. There's shit all over the place down here. I don't know exactly what we've got yet, but it's the best camouflage job I've ever seen," Blue told me.

"Okay, be careful down there."

"You bet!"

Barney continued his VR. His observer that day was Corp. David Bryant. Bryant had only two days left in-country but insisted on flying because he was best friends with Rae Bailey. He wanted to find him, or at least get some revenge. Larry and White had been gone for only twenty minutes when One-three yelled, "Taking Fire!" There was smoke trailing from his aircraft as I rolled in.

Barney was pretty frazzled. "Two-four, One-three. My observer's hit. I can't tell where. There's blood all over everything. I need to get on the ground. I can't see anything."

Mel had the map and vectored Barney as I called operations. "Roger that," Mel responded, "Just keep going straight. There's a grassy area next to a river about a click away."

"Shit. I think my observer's dead."

"Fuck!" I screamed at nobody in particular.

I called ops, "My little bird's hit. He's putting the aircraft down. His Oscar has been hit. Crank me up some arty and get me a flight of fighters out here. Launch the Blue birds!"

Mel kept his cool and continued to give Barney vectors. It was so nice to have a competent and experienced x-ray in the front seat.

"Two-four. This is Six. Sitrep." It was the CO.

"Not now," I responded.

Mel asked, "Why does he always ask for a sitrep? Doesn't he listen to what the hell is going on?"

Barney had just cleared the trees when his engine quit. I made a low pass over him to make sure all was well and then noticed some movement in the trees just east of his position. Two people emerged from the downed LOH, both from the right side, and took up defensive positions.

"Mel, I've got movement in the treeline. People running. Shit!" I exclaimed.

"Where the hell are the lift ships?" I asked. "We've got movement in the trees about fifty meters from the little bird. We need to get these guys out now!"

I made a dummy rocket run to keep the NVA at bay while preserving my rockets to escort in the lift ship, and only then did we realize that the folks we saw running were Americans! Barney had landed in the middle of an American infantry company.

"Two-four, this is One-three on guard." It was Barney.

"Hey One-three. Nice to hear your voice, how you doing?"

"My observer's dead," he told me. "They shot him in the head."

"Okay. The lift ships are on the way. Just keep your heads down. There are some GIs in the trees to your west. I say again . . . GIs in the trees . . . don't get antsy and shoot them."

Other teams had begun to arrive on station and I briefed them on the situation and location from where Barney took fire. I wasn't about to leave Barney and his crew. Between the radio calls and putting in an artillery barrage, keeping track of who was where and watching over the downed crew, Mel and I were kept very busy.

"Hey One-three, Two-four," I called. No response. "One-three, Two-four on guard!" Still nothing.

"Son of a bitch! We're going down to take a look, Wyatt," I told Mel. "Keep your eyes open."

I dove out of altitude and broke out just over the trees. We came in from west to east. Breaking out over the clearing, we passed only about a hundred feet over the downed LOH. Neither Mel nor I could see Barney or his gunner.

"Shit. Not again!" I said in dread.

"Can we get a goddamned lift bird out here?" I yelled at ops. "Today? One-three-Two-four," I tried again.

"Hey Two-four, this is Four-two." It was WO1 Dave Farrell.

"Go ahead, Four-two. Where you at?" I asked.

"While you were doing whatever it is you do up there, I swooped in and picked up your downed crew. We're half way back to Phuoc Vinh," Dave told me.

"Did you see a Huey, Mel?" I asked.

"Nope," he responded.

"What do you mean you swooped in, Four-two?"

"We landed next to the LOH. We have One-three and his gunner on board. They're fine . . . we have his Oscar too. He's dead. I'm QSY to Phuoc Vinh."

I was amazed. Farrell had landed next to the downed aircraft and was on the ground for a matter of seconds before he had the entire crew of the LOH on board and, flying at treetop level, was half way back to base. Neither Mel nor I ever saw him. It wasn't until later that afternoon that the ground element finally got through to the LOH that had been shot down the previous day. The aircraft was burned out. About one hundred meters west of the crash site, the search and recovery element located SP4 Rae Bailey's body. Bill Cahill's body was found east of the crash site. He had been decapitated. There was no sign of Doug Strait. Three flight helmets were found in the area around the crashed LOH. One had been destroyed by fire, and one by the explosion. The third was found in good condition.

Wreckage of the aircraft was strewn about fifty meters from the point of impact in all directions. The ground troops made an extensive search throughout the entire area. No sign of Doug Strait was found.

A week after Cahill's LOH was shot down, a U.S. element was moving through an area about a half mile north of the crash site. They found the large prints of an aviator's boot intermingled with the prints of an enemy force. It was never determined whether the print belonged to Doug Strait or perhaps to an enemy soldier wearing an aviator's boots. Because one helmet found at the crash site was in good condition, and because no sign of Doug Strait was ever found and because of the footprints, the very real possibility that Strait had survived the crash and was taken as a prisoner of war had to be considered.

Among the bodies of the enemy that had been killed near the site of Bill's LOH was that of a male Caucasian. Inside his shirt, and stained with his blood, was a Soviet flag. We had killed a Russian advisor and the flag hung in our Officers' Club from that day on. Advisors, who the Russians had always denied providing, would never have been found in anything other than a higher headquarters. There had to be other high-ranking officers there too.

Unbeknown to Bill, and to us at the time, he had discovered COSVN.

Doug Strait was never found. His body was never recovered and on November 17, 1975, he was officially declared dead.

In the end, the complex that Bill Cahill and his crew had discovered before their deaths turned out to be a massive complex covering almost a square mile. There was a hospital complex, administrative centers, and classrooms. The biggest prize was all of the documents that were discovered. The NVA didn't have time to take them during the firefight. It led us in the following weeks to cache sites, complexes of various types, and troop concentrations.

When it was all over, though, I would have rather had Bill, Rae, and Doug back.

Chapter 18

Steak Out

Echo Troop moved over to support the brigade since we were tied up with the COSVN thing. On the morning of the twentieth, one of their hunter-killer teams was reconning a river northeast of Phuoc Vinh when they spotted nineteen individuals in an open area—all had packs and weapons. The Cobra rolled in and killed ten of them.

At 2:10 that afternoon they inserted their Blues and immediately captured an NVA officer. It was almost as if he were waiting at the LZ. About 4:00 P.M. the Blues made contact with two more NVA. After a short firefight, they killed the enemy soldiers and discovered that one had been a forward observer. They had made contact with an NVA artillery unit.

The Echo Blues continued their ground recon and made further discoveries: weapons and packs, flour, documents, firing tables, and a map of Phuoc Vinh. The officer the Blues had captured was an NVA warrant officer. More than that, he was the commander of the artillery company that had blown up our hooch. Upon his return to division headquarters at Phuoc Vinh, he began to talk. He was tired of running around the jungle eating rice soup and bugs. He was tired of getting shot at and running from us. He decided to *chieu hoi* and change sides.

On the twenty-first, he went out with the Echo Troop Blues and led them to a 75mm recoilless rifle. Not just any 75mm, but the gun that had hit our hooch!

That same morning we lifted off to head back to the COSVN area. There was still a lot of ground to cover out there. About mid-morning I got a call to return to base.

"What's up?" I asked.

"Just RTB and shut down when you get here," I was told.

After we shut down we went into the TOC and were told to report to squadron headquarters. Maj. Gen. George W. Putnam, Jr., the new commanding general of the First Cav, was coming over for an Impact Ceremony. A civilian film crew from CBS was there too.

We formed up on the parade ground and awaited the general's arrival. He didn't keep us waiting long. Major Nelson greeted him with a salute. He faced us and put us at "Parade rest." Taking up the more relaxed stance, General Putnam began to tell us what the ground troops were finding out in the AO as a result of our find and what a significant find it had been. A short time later the command sergeant major (CSM) bellowed, "Attention to orders!" and we snapped to attention.

Several awards were given out before I was called. "Mr. Zahn. Front and center!"

I positioned myself in front of the general and saluted.

The CSM began to read:

General Orders number 18674. Award of the Distinguished Flying Cross.
TC 439. The following award is announced.
Zahn, Randy R. Warrant Officer WO1, United States Army. Troop C, first
Squadron (Airmobile) ninth Cavalry.
Awarded: Distinguished Flying Cross.
Date of Action: 18 October 1970.
Theater: Republic of Vietnam.
Authority: By direction of the President, under the provisions of the Act of
Congress, approved 2 July 1926.
Reason: For heroism while participating in aerial flight evidenced by volun-
tary actions above and beyond the call of duty in the Republic of Vietnam. Warrant
Officer Zahn distinguished himself by exceptionally valorous actions on 18 Octo-
ber 1970, while serving as pilot in the Republic of Vietnam. Warrant Officer Zahn
made repeated rocket attacks on enemy positions after one of the helicopters had
been downed by the hostiles. Again and again he attacked until his ammunition
was expired and he was replaced by another gunship. His outstanding flying abili-
ty and devotion to duty is in keeping with the highest traditions of the military
service and reflects great credit upon himself, his unit, and the United States Army.
Signed G.E. Newman, Colonel, Chief of Staff.

I was incredibly proud as General Putnam pinned the DFC on me. He shook my hand and congratulated me.

"Thank you very much, sir." I saluted. "I was only doing my job."

He smiled and said, "Then keep up the good work!"

"Yes, sir."

Fifteen minutes later we all cranked up and were heading back to the AO.

Besides the discovery of COSVN, activity in the AO was picking up. The enemy was moving back in in force after rebuilding some of their sanctuaries in Cambodia.

I was feeling depressed after losing four members of the scout crews in the past few days. I had had only one day off since I came back from R&R and started flying again, and I was very tired, having flown ninety-five hours in just under two weeks.

After we finished our missions that afternoon I took a much-needed shower and sat down to write the folks a short note before dinner. It would be my first chance to write in the past week.

"Dear Mom and Dad,

You'll have to forgive me for not writing but we've been real busy and in the air all hours of the day.

We ran into some big NVA complex of some kind the other day and have been at it every day. It means quite a bit to us as we lost a good friend out there two days ago. He was my little bird so you can see I was in no mood to write.

Your questions will have to go unanswered until I get more time to write and rest. I'll try to finish up the tape soon also.

Must get some sleep. Write soon.

All my love, Randy."

After finishing the letter I went to the club for dinner. I went in and walked up to the bar to order. Sitting at the bar next to me was a lieutenant from squadron and the NVA warrant officer.

"What the hell do you call this?" I asked the lieutenant.

"He's decided to work with us," he told me. Smiling he said, "I don't know when the last time was that he had a steak!"

I couldn't believe it. This guy was responsible for blowing up our hooch, almost killing five of us and here was a lieutenant from our own squadron buying him a steak in our club.

"I don't either," I said. "But he had better eat it fast."

"Why?" The lieutenant asked.

"Why? Because I am going back to my bunker to get my 38 and if this asshole is still here when I get back, I'm going to shoot him. That's why!" I yelled as I got up to leave. I was livid. I did go back to my bunker. I did get my 38 and I did go back to the club. But I didn't shoot him. They were both long gone.

"What a fucked up war!" I said to no one in particular. I didn't eat that evening: I had lost my appetite. Still angry, I went back to the bunker and went to bed.

I finally got a day off—two in fact—beginning on the twenty-fifth. I went to the auto sales office next to the PX. Gary, one of the salesmen, related the ins and outs of purchasing a car through the exchange. The factory had to receive full payment at least ten weeks prior to delivery, insurance had to be pre-arranged, and so forth. I decided I would put two thousand dollars down and finance the rest.

"You do realize you'll need a co-signer for the loan, don't you?" he asked.

"Co-signer? What the hell for?" I asked him.

"Because the bank won't give you the money without one."

"Why not?" I asked incredulously.

"Because you're a minor!" he said rolling his eyes. I could only laugh.

The next day we were told that the Third Squadron of the Seventeenth Cav were being placed under the operational control of the First Cavalry Division and were assigned to our squadron.

With this enhanced capability we were now task-organized to provide visual reconnaissance support for the entire division. Alpha Troop of the Third of the Seventeenth was released to the First of the Ninth and their HQ assumed operational control of Bravo Troop and us. I never could figure out what the Army was trying to accomplish with all the mixing and matching but there were greater military minds than mine that made these decisions. We were two separate troops doing the same mission, although the Third of the Seventeenth scouts flew the bigger, slower, and under-powered Bell OH-58A Kiowa.

The OH-58 had failed to win the military light observation helicopter competition in 1964, losing out to the more agile OH-6. After an extensive redesign and subsequent success on the civilian market as the Bell JetRanger, the Army went back on its decision, despite the fact that the engine installation in the JetRanger was causing problems at high speeds.

I always wondered if Lyndon Johnson had anything to do with that decision. Textron had recently purchased Bell Helicopters, and before he became president Mr. Johnson had been on the board of Textron. I don't think it is any secret that President and Mrs. Johnson made millions of dollars out of the Vietnam War.

Despite the fact that we were doing the same job, the first order of business was an extensive period of training. Our Blues had to train their Blues in rappelling, the use of Maguire rigs, and the rigging of aircraft for extraction.

The aircrews were interchanged on a daily basis to facilitate area orientation training, use of signal operating instructions, understanding of the First Cavalry Division rules of engagement, and to teach them the techniques that we had so successfully employed in our AO. The training was hard going. We started by pairing one of our scouts with one of their Cobras while their scouts flew as our little birds. It became obvious early on that we had completely different methods of operating. Our scout pilots were very uncomfortable flying with them because their Cobras flew so much higher than we did, and I hated flying with their scouts. They flew so damn fast we could hardly maintain visual contact with them and I don't know how they ever spotted anything on the ground. They never went slow enough! Suffice it to say that each and every unit that flew in Vietnam had their own ways of doing things. They adopted procedures that worked for them as we did for us. I preferred our way.

We flew every day since our AO had almost tripled in size. It now consisted of both the First and Third Brigade's areas of responsibility and most of our contacts were still with the SR-5 element of COSVN and the Seventy-fourth Artillery.

It rained a lot the last week of October. We had lots of weather holds and several of the flying days were cut short due to the heavy rains and low cloud bases, but the flying hours continued to mount. When I returned to base after flying seven hours on the thirty-first I was, thankfully, grounded for three days once again due to the 140-hour rule.

A bunch of us were off the following day so we jumped in a Huey and went to Saigon. I wanted to call home. We landed at Hotel Three, the main heliport within the Tan Son Nhut airfield complex. Van and I walked to the main gate and grabbed a cyclo down to the USO on Tu Do Street. There was always a queue of people waiting to use the telephones.

I woke Mom and Dad up at some ungodly hour, which they never seemed to mind.

On the way back to Tan Son Nhut, Van and I were stopped at an MP inspection point. The MP was checking identification cards and dog tags. Some soldiers would go to Saigon and lose themselves in the underworld of drugs and prostitution, while civilians dressed in uniforms to gain access to the military installations. The MP saluted smartly and requested, "May I see your ID cards and dogs tags, please?"

"Sure," Van replied.

We removed our dog tags and handed them to the MP as we removed our ID cards from our respective wallets. Van and I continued to talk when I noticed the nametag on the MP's shirt. I looked at him more closely before I winked at Van and said, "Ya know Van, you'd think these damn MPs could find something better to do then fuck with combat troops who are doing nothing but minding their own business."

Van played along. "Yeah, assholes. All of them."

I continued, "These fucking REMFs who live in their damned air conditioned billets and all. They wouldn't know a war if it slapped them in the face!"

The MP was getting angry.

"You'd at least think these fuckers would give a break to guys they've known all their lives," I said.

At that, the MP took a double-take at my ID card. He looked up at me, back at the card, and then said, "Holy Shit! What in the hell are you doing here?"

Van cleared his throat and said jokingly, "Don't you mean what in the hell are you doing here, SIR!"

The MP started to apologize as I got off the cyclo and went to him. We shook hands. Ron Moen and I had known each other since we were five years old and attended Pinewood Elementary School in Tujunga, California, together. We spent about twenty minutes talking about old times and whom we were corresponding with, what was happening at home, and so forth. Before Van and I headed back to Hotel Three, Ron and I made a plan to get together again in a few weeks.

On my second day off I didn't get much relaxation. There were lots of rumors going around about us moving. In the course of one week we heard we were moving to Di An, Cu Chi, Phan Thiet, Phu Bai, Bear Cat, and to the infamous A Shau Valley. There were also some that said the entire First Cavalry Division would be standing down and would be home before Christmas. But one thing was fact, we were having an Inspector General's inspection on Monday, November 9, and everybody was jumping through their asses. Many of us had unauthorized weapons and we had to either hide them or get rid of them. Most hid them for the day.

I had to do my fire marshal thing and make inspections, ensure there were adequate fire extinguishers throughout our area and that they were in date, the correct type and size, and so forth. According to regulations I was also supposed to hold a fire drill. I faked the paperwork on this one. Fire drills in Vietnam? Give me a break.

The major was coming down on everybody and everything. We were in a combat zone and he tried to prepare for the inspection as if we were Stateside. As each day passed Major Nelson tried to implement more and more Stateside Army standards.

On November 3, I went down to the flight line. I had to get out of the area and away from the CO. Bones was doing some maintenance on the aircraft and I decided to wax it. It was a lot of work but it kept me busy. I liked spending time with Bones and our aircraft. He and I got to be closer and I was able to draw from his knowledge and learn more about the systems and workings of the aircraft.

Larry and I had recently adopted a scrawny black cat. We named him "Mauser." Mauser had come to us lost, frightened, and hungry; his ribs protruded from beneath his skin. We took him to the vet for shots and started feeding him. We also made sure that our hooch maid understood the consequences if Mauser went missing too. He would have made a good meal for a Vietnamese family! Mauser soon began to put on weight and his dull thin coat began to fill in with thick and shiny jet-black hair. In return for our care he kept us company and Mauser kept our rats and mice at bay and feasted on the cockroaches that tried to move into the bunker.

Larry was off the following day and we decided to go to Saigon. Larry wanted to call his wife Trish and I wanted to call Cyndy. As we were signing out the orderly room clerk asked, "Haven't you heard? Saigon is off limits to the Cav now."

"What do you mean . . . off limits?" Larry asked.

"Some general has put it off limits to combat troops. We aren't allowed down there anymore," he said.

"So we can't go use the only damn phones in the country to call home anymore?" I asked.

"I guess not, sir," he said as he shrugged his shoulders.

"Well, how do you like that shit?" Larry asked as we walked out.

Platoon meetings were held in the living area of our bunker nightly and I was ready for the meeting tonight. Our roommate, Dick Skaaden, was our platoon leader. I didn't want to lay into him but I was really pissed off about this new restriction.

"Hey Dick! What's this shit about us not being able to go to Saigon anymore?" I questioned.

Clearly taken aback, he asked, "What are you talking about?"

Larry and I related to him the conversation we had in the orderly room that afternoon and it was obvious that this was news to Dick. Our meetings were always held after all of the platoon leaders had met with the CO and the operations officer and he had more news for us. "Flight time is going to be cut back starting on the fifteenth," he began. "Spares are in short supply, and with no spares we can't keep the aircraft in the air. Next," he hesitated, "the 'old man' wants us to stand inspection once a week."

"WHAT?" everybody asked incredulously.

"Yeah, he wants us in formation and he plans to inspect us once a week," Dick continued.

"Well, fuck him!" somebody said.

"That isn't all," Dick continued. "He wants us to start wearing our chicken plates when we fly."

There was silence in the bunker.

"Hey Dick," I stuck my neck out, "With all due respect, why don't you invite him to spend a day, one whole fucking day, in one of our front seats with his chicken plate on? Does he have any idea what the hell he's even talking about?" I asked as I got madder.

"The scouts and lift pilots wear theirs and he wants us to wear ours," Dick said in his defense.

All of us, without exception, refused to wear our chicken plates. The matter was closed as far as we were concerned. After the meeting Larry, Dick, and I stayed put. John went to the club. Dick wasn't too keen on his position as platoon leader. He had all of our respect but he would rather have just been a pilot. Larry and I gave Dick and John grief all the time. Both had been warrant officers on their first tours of duty and both took direct commissions. They claimed it was for the money. Both were married, both had infant daughters, and both were great guys.

On the morning of the fifth, I would be flying with Dick for the first time. We took off at 6:00 A.M. and by nine o'clock we were back on the ground. The fog had rolled in. We were working an area about sixty miles east of Phuoc Vinh in the foothills of the Central Highlands. When the fog had cleared, we took off again and headed back to the east. The sky was crystal clear and the visibility was unrestricted. I decided to take Dick on a tour. I kept the little bird at altitude and we went up into the mountains. We flew over Bao Loc and on up to DaLat. It was a beautiful day and we played.

That night, after our "hard day" in the AO, we were treated to a floor show. Dick, John, Harv, Larry, and I went over early and got a table right up front. Before the show began we got three rounds of drinks so we wouldn't have to get up during the show. The group was from the Philippines and the female lead singer was beautiful. Usually the lead singers were good-looking girls and some-times they did more than sing. The show was well received and half way through it we were feeling no pain. During one of the songs in the second set, the singer started to strip. We cheered her on as she removed her micro-skirt and blouse. Next went her bra as she continued to dance and sing in the only piece of clothing that she still wore . . . her frilly underwear. As the next song began, the underwear came off as she gave up the mic and began to dance across our tables in the nude and taunting us with her actions and her breasts.

She stepped onto our table and danced above us as we gawked at her. Her breasts were gyrating and she squatted only inches from where my head rested on my hands. I could smell her perspiration as she taunted me. Her crotch hovered inches above me as she grabbed the back of my head. I raised my head off of my hands and she turned around immediately. Where her crotch had been only a second ago was now her nicely rounded butt and I couldn't help myself. Wrapping my arms around her legs I pulled her backward and bit her on the ass! She screamed and jumped off the table, yelling at me, as I fell backward off my chair laughing so hard tears were rolling down my cheeks. The guys were cheering, hooping, and hollering as I left the club. I had to go pee before I wet myself. After relieving myself I went back to the bunker and my tape recorder and switched it on.

"Hey, Dad? Dad? You really would have been proud of me tonight Dad. I bit a girl on the ass!"

I was blitzed! I spoke for a few more seconds and hit the rewind button. After the tape had rewound I hit play and was greeted with total silence. Confused, I tried again.

Record. *"Dad, Dad, can you hear me? I bit this girl on the ass. The singer. You would have loved it, Dad!"* Rewind. Play. Still nothing. Again I tried. The battery light was on, the mic plugged in, and by now I had the volume up about three-quarters.

"DAD? DAD? Can you hear me, Dad? I bit a girl on the ass, Dad. Are you there?" I yelled. *"Can you hear me? DAD?"*

Rewinding the tape again, I turned the volume up full and hit play. From what seemed like miles away, I heard a very faint voice . . . "Dad, Dad. . . ." Looking around to find where the voice was coming from, in my stupor, I noticed that the earplug was plugged in and lying on the floor under my table. As I pulled it closer and closer my voice got louder and louder. I unplugged the earphone from its jack and hit play once again. The sound of me screaming was enough to knock me off my chair for the second time that evening.

Picking myself up, I looked in the mirror and said, "You stupid shit!"

Record. *"Dad. I'm going to sleep. I'll talk to you tomorrow."*

Chapter 19

Major Disagreements

On Friday, November 6, we began a new mission. We were tasked by division to conduct Eagle Flights. The province chief had put all of the roads off limits to the locals after 6:00 P.M. The incentive he used to gain compliance was us. At six o'clock a Cobra, a LOH, and an H-model full of ARVNs took off to patrol the roads surrounding Phuoc Vinh. It was kind of like playing highway patrol. The idea was that if we spotted any vehicles on the roads we would stop them so the ARVNs could be landed to inspect them. If the vehicle didn't stop, it was left up to the discretion of the Cobra AC how to bring them to a halt. People walking along the road were usually shot by the ARVNs. They took no prisoners. We hadn't been finding much in the AO since our encounter with COSVN, so this new mission was welcome because it was different and relatively easy— at least it should have been.

The lead up to the IG inspection was tedious on everyone. Major Nelson took on a new persona and decided he was going to change virtually everything. He and the operations officer decided they were going to start running the missions and that's when the trouble began.

During the afternoon of the seventh, I was out on a mission when I got a call from operations. They had bounced the Blues and ARA and told me to insert them at a grid coordinate.

"What's the target?" I asked, "And who did the recon?"

"Negative known target. Just insert them," Captain LaChance told me.

"Understand we have no known target, nobody has VRed the area, we haven't checked out or prepped an LZ and you want me to insert them cold turkey?" I asked.

"Roger that," he replied.

"Who is my contact for the Blues?" I asked.

"It's Three-five."

"Roger . . . break. Three-five, Two-four on family. Come up channel two."

"Two-four, this is Mom. Go ahead."

"What in the fuck is going on?" I asked. "Since when does ops bounce you guys to insert the Blues without a target?"

"He told us you bounced us!" Fred replied.

"Negative. Ops called and told me you and ARA were en route, gave me a grid, and TOLD me to insert the Blues."

"You're calling the shots. What do you want to do?" Fred asked.

"We're down to bingo fuel so turn around and I'll see you back at base. I need to get on to ARA and send them home too," I told him.

After re-fuelling, we went back and shut down. I walked into the TOC and no sooner had I walked through the door than Mike jumped on me.

"What in the hell do you think you're doing?" he asked.

"I'm not doing anything," I shot back.

"I gave you a mission and you wasted the assets. You don't run this troop, Mister. You do as you're told!" he yelled.

"No, sir," I yelled back. "YOU wasted the assets. I do NOT put the Blues on the ground without a target. I do NOT put the Blues on the ground without a recon of the area. I do NOT ask for the Blues to be bounced until the prep has been done. I do NOT tell anybody to do anything without a proper brief. I do NOT bounce the Blues when I have no fucking fuel in my aircraft and I do NOT do what you say just because you say it." I was so mad I just walked out.

That night at the meeting Dick told me the CO had chewed his ass out because I was sarcastic on the radio. As the meeting continued, Major Nelson walked in.

"Did you have a problem out there today, Two-four?" he asked me.

"No, sir," I replied. "I didn't have any problem at all."

"Then can you explain why you didn't get the insertion mission completed?"

"I didn't get the insertion completed because there was no mission, sir. I am not going to put the Blues on the ground unless I have a pretty good idea what they're up against. Operations don't tell us squat and—"

He interrupted me. "That is not your call, Mr. Zahn." When you are given a mission, you complete it to the best of your ability and you do it without question. Is that understood?"

"No, sir, it is not," I answered. "Since when do we put the Blues on the ground for the sake of putting them on the ground? What do we do if somebody gets shot down while the Blues are out on some goat-fuck mission? And since when do ops call the shots? They give us the assets we need when we need them."

"Since now, Mr. Zahn, I am the commanding officer, not you," he asserted. "You do as you are told or I'll pull your AC orders. Is that understood?"

"You don't have to pull them. You can have them!" I told him.

Major Nelson knew how close Larry and I were so Larry was next: "I don't expect I will have the same trouble with you, will I Mr. Edeal?"

"No, sir," Larry smiled. "No trouble at all. You can have my AC orders too."

There was dead silence in the bunker except for Mauser chomping on a cockroach.

"Sir, before you start pulling AC orders, you had better go on over to the scout meeting and see how many of the scouts will be flying tomorrow when they hear that Larry and I won't be covering them," I smiled.

I did not mean for that to sound arrogant, but there is a great deal of trust and mutual respect between the scout crew, when they are hanging their lives on the line, and the Cobra AC, who is there to protect them.

The major walked out in a huff, but not before giving Dick a look that could kill.

Larry and I were both flying the following day and we still had our AC orders. We learned later that most of the scouts refused to fly if we weren't covering them. Once again I was given a bullshit mission. Assets were bounced that I did not require, did not want, and could not use. We flew our fuel load and went back to Phuoc Vinh and shut down. I walked into the TOC and this time I fired the first shots. "Mike! You want to run the fucking missions? You run them. You are welcome to take my aircraft and run them however you see fit," I told him in as controlled a voice as I could muster.

"You have another mission," Captain LaChance spat.

"What is it?" I asked

"Division wants a recon of an area southwest of Odin," he told me.

"Why? What's out there?"

"Goddamnit! Will you for once just do as you're told?" he yelled.

I just stood there. "What is out there that they want us to look for?" I asked as calmly as I could.

"You don't have a need to know!"

That said it all.

"If I don't have a need to know, I don't have a need to go. I am not putting my little bird on the deck until I know what's out there. Why all of a sudden are you giving me a specific grid coordinate? Who is out there? What size force are we up against and what kind of weapons do they have?" I asked. "Damn it, Mike, the scout's job is dangerous enough without our own people withholding intelligence information from us. You get somebody else to do your mission. I'm not flying anymore today. You got that?" I announced and walked out.

I went back to the bunker and grabbed a coke. I had expected an invitation to the CO's office but it never came. What did come was Special Orders Number 322. Under the authority of Paragraph 15-3, Army Regulation 37-103, I was appointed as Class A Agent to the Finance Officer. In other words, I was the paymaster for that month. Funds would be entrusted to me from the finance office at Bién Hoa and I would have to go around and pay all of the soldiers assigned to Charlie Troop. If they were in a hospital, I had to go to the hospital, if they were attending a school I had to go to the school, wherever they were in-country. I had a whole list of regulations, field manuals, and instructions that I had to comply with to be the Class A agent. It was perceived to be another shit detail. There was no question why it was assigned to me.

That night Dick didn't say much at the meeting about my refusal to fly that afternoon. He agreed with what I had done but he couldn't say so. What he did tell us was that the major told him to make himself an aircraft commander and to take control of his pilots. Dick refused to make himself an AC. He knew he wasn't ready and we all admired him greatly for his refusal. He, above all, knew what it took to become an aircraft commander in Charlie Troop and he had no delusions of grandeur. After the meeting the others headed back to their hooches or over to the club. Mauser curled up on my flight suit and Dick got a drink for Larry and me.

"The old man told me I should take disciplinary action against you two," Dick told us. "I told him I would talk to you, but I am not going to order you to do something that you know is unsafe and could put lives in jeopardy. Hell, if I did that I would have a platoon full of pilots with Article 15s or a file full of 1049s!"

We sat and talked until close to ten o'clock when John came in.

"Guess what?" he asked with a big smile on his face.

"What?" we asked in unison.

"Some of the guys just had a blanket party with the ops officer," he said, turning both palms up in the air.

A blanket party is when some unsuspecting soul has a blanket thrown over him so he can't see who is around while they proceed to beat the shit out of him.

"Pity!" Larry exclaimed, as we all laughed.

It was obvious we weren't the only ones he was pissing off. The party took place unbeknown to those of us in the bunker that night, but if I had known about it there is no doubt that I would have been a willing accomplice.

We talked for a while longer and then I retired to my room to finish my tape. I was really upset about how things were going and all the bullshit being caused by a gung-ho operations officer and a CO who didn't seem to care whether or not we came back from a mission. Just before I switched off the light Dick came in and grabbed Mauser.

"Hey, what are you doing to the cat?" I asked him.

Dick had a sheepish look on his face as, heading for the door, he said in a child-like voice, "It's my turn to sleep with the cat tonight!"

On November 8 I woke up late. The water bowser filled the showers as I watched while relieving myself at the piss tube. Still half asleep, I went back to the bunker and grabbed a towel and a bar of soap. As ever, the water was cold, but in this environment it was welcome and refreshing.

I had to go to Bién Hoa to get briefed by the finance officer for my up-and-coming assignment as Class A Agent. After a snack and a can of apple juice, I dressed and headed in the direction of the transient pad to catch a ride to Bién Hoa. As I passed the orderly room, the clerk called me. "Mr. Zahn! The CO would like to see you, sir."

In resignation I entered through the front door. Major Nelson was in his office. I knocked on the doorjamb and the major looked up.

"You want to see me, sir?" I asked.

"Yes, Mr. Zahn. I do. Come in and close the door behind you," he ordered.

Even with the door closed there was no privacy. The walls were made of thin plywood and almost half of the exterior walls were screen.

"Mr. Zahn. We seem to have a problem," Major Nelson began. "Is there any particular reason why you are so adverse to doing things my way?" he asked.

"Sir, when I am in the AO, when I am running a mission, I run it one way and one way only, and that's my way," I told him. "I learned my job from guys like Grover Wright and Ed McDerby, Felix Poindexter and Larry Grover. I had the best teachers that anybody could hope to have, sir. The reason I do things my way is because it's the way I was taught. It's the best way that I know how to do it. Now if you, or anybody else, can show me a better way, a safer way, then I'll give it a try. Until then, I will continue to do things my way, sir."

He didn't respond.

"If there is nothing else, sir, I have to get a lift down to Bién Hoa."

"Good day," he wished me.

I saluted and left.

The trip to Bién Hoa was anticlimactic. I got my briefing and was told to report back on the fourteenth to collect the money and all of the paperwork. By the time I got back Larry was done flying for the day. Neither of us was happy about how things were going so we went down to see the headquarters troop commander, Capt. Al DeMailo. Al had been a gun pilot and knew what we did and what role the Cobra AC played in the overall scheme of things. We told him what was going on and, like us, he was dismayed.

"If things really turn to shit, Al, do you have any slots in headquarters for aviators?" we asked.

"Hell, yes," he said. "I'd love to have you guys. You'd be flying UH-1s on strap runs, but heck yeah, come on over."

We thanked him for his time and promised to keep him in the picture.

"Lar, if we can find a way, we really have to stay in Guns," I told him. "You and I are two of the senior ACs in the troop. If we go, who is going to train the x-rays? Who is going to cover the scouts?"

We agreed to hang in for as long as we could. Being short of ACs, we had to fly most days and November 10 was no different. Larry and I and our little birds took off at first light and flew over to Fire Support Base Odin east of Phuoc Vinh. We landed at Odin and shut down to get briefed. The Brigade S-2 gave us a thorough brief on the area and the tactical situation, where the friendlies were, and the location of suspected enemy troop concentrations. The brief took about fifteen minutes, after which we updated our maps with the new information. Larry and I had decided that from now on we would land and get briefed by brigade since our own operations never briefed us adequately, if at all.

It was a long day, 9.3 hours of flying. That evening in the club Major Nelson stopped at our table and asked how things went that day.

"No problems, sir," I offered.

"Fine and dandy," and through clenched teeth and glaring eyes he said, "From now on, you will NOT land at fire bases . . . unless you have an emergency or get my permission. Is that understood?"

"We landed to get briefed on the tactical situation in the AO," I replied.

"You should learn to trust our ops people," he retorted.

"Sir, speaking of ops, why don't you let us alternate working in ops with the ops officer?"

"And why would I do that?" he asked.

"Because we know how things work in the AO. We know how to run a mission. We know how long an arty prep takes, we know how to back plan to have the assets where they are needed and when," I offered. "We think we can make a contribution by better utilization of the assets and things will run more efficiently."

"Thank you, gentlemen," he responded with a sarcastic air. "Your job is in the AO." And he walked away.

"At least we still have a job!" Larry said before he started laughing.

Things really came to a head after that. Major Nelson called Dick down to his office and told him if he wouldn't discipline us, he would get somebody who would. Capt. Dick Skaaden, being the officer and gentleman that he was, refused to discipline us when he agreed with what we were doing. Major Nelson made him the sacrificial lamb and relieved him of his command of the Weapons Platoon. Dick came back to the bunker and told us what had happened. He was upset at having been relieved, but not half as upset as we were. In spite of his disappointment, Dick was also relieved that he didn't have to put up with the bullshit anymore. He was re-assigned to the Squadron S-2 shop, Intelligence.

It wasn't long before we found out who our new platoon leader would be. Capt. Richard Sides would be taking over. Tall and slender, and very military, he would have to attend the in-country AH-1 Transition Course at Vung Tau. In his infinite wisdom, the CO had given us a new platoon leader who wasn't even qualified in Cobras!

On the eleventh I had a 7:00 A.M. pitch pull. My x-ray for the day had only just arrived in-country. This would be Capt. Ross Rainwater's first mission. Flying with new guys was fun if not challenging. Everything was new to them and there were lots of "oohs and aahs." Ross was excited about his first mission, albeit apprehensive. He was keen to learn and asked lots of questions. The day went well even if it was relatively uneventful. The LOH found a hooch that had been built in a deserted LZ. Our two aircrafts destroyed it and left it in flames.

The CO came up on frequency, "Two-four. This is Six. Why don't you—"

I interrupted him before he could finish his sentence. "Six, you want to run the mission?"

There were no further communications, but I knew this wouldn't be the end of the conversation. By the time we got back and shut down it was raining heavily. Never one to miss an opportunity, I ran back to the bunker, got undressed, and went out to take my shower in the rain.

On the morning of the fourteenth my alarm clock went off early. A UH-1 crew was waiting at the TOC to fly an armed escort and me to Bién Hoa to pick up the payroll. The only good thing about that job was that the UH-1 was mine for as long as it took to get everybody paid. They dropped me off at the transient pad and I walked to the Finance and Accounting Office. After counting the money twice, I signed for the total amount. I was accountable for $13,186 in Military Payment

Certificates (MPC). For three days we flew from Phuoc Vinh to Biến Hoa, over to Lai Khe, across to Long Binh, and to the coast to Vung Tau. Getting to the bases was the easy part. Locating our people once we got there was not always as simple. On the sixteenth I reported back to Biến Hoa with an empty pay box and a balanced ledger sheet.

I hadn't been around much the last three days and got back to the bunker after the meetings, but the stories about our new platoon leader and the changes that he was attempting to make were already proliferating. I was at the meeting the next day.

"Gentlemen, Headquarters Troop has acquired a Nighthawk bird and we will be covering it on its mission," he began.

"Excuse me?"

"We will be covering the Nighthawk mission," Captain Sides reiterated. "I told the CO we would handle it."

"Dick," I couldn't bring myself to call him Red, "We already have problems keeping aircraft in the air and we are all high on hours. Our mission is not to fly around at night in VFR-equipped aircraft!"

"Is there a problem, Mr. Zahn?" he asked rather emphatically.

"Yes, sir, there is," I protested. "It's a waste of blade time. In case you haven't noticed, there are no lights in the AO. Once you leave the perimeter, it's like flying through a bottle of ink. How the hell are we supposed to navigate? How do we find the area we're supposed to VR? Has anybody thought this through?" I asked him.

"I'm sure you'll find a way, Mr. Zahn. The mission begins tonight and since you are well rested and have lots of experience, you will fly it. You can choose an x-ray for the mission. Pitch pull is at 9 o'clock," he told me.

"9 o'clock?" I confirmed.

"That is correct."

"Fine," I smiled. "YOU have the aircraft pre-flighted and ready to go by a quarter to nine. I'll see you at the TOC."

"Me?" he asked in amazement.

"Yes, sir, you! You told me to pick an x-ray and you are an x-ray. You volunteered us for this shit, so you can come along and see what you've committed us to," I told him. "I'll see you at the TOC at 2045."

There was stifled laughter, smiles, and sneers in the bunker as he stormed out the door. I grabbed my flight gear and walked down to the TOC. I was actually feeling pretty good. I walked in and greeted the Huey crew. Captain Sides had just come through the back door.

"Okay, gang. Here it is," I began. "When we crank up, I am going to give radar the coordinates for the box that division wants us to search. It's up by Bunard," I said pointing to the area on the map on the wall. "They'll vector us into the area. We'll check our weapons systems before you let down to your mission altitude. If at any point GCA loses us on radar, or we lose commo or visual contact, we terminate the mission and come home. Understood? We won't be able to navigate out there at night. If either of us gets shot down there will be no rescue attempt tonight so make sure you have survival gear. I want a commo check on the assault strip before we lift. Any questions?" I asked.

Everybody seemed happy enough, so with the mission brief complete, we walked out to our aircraft. There was no conversation between Captain Sides and myself. Bones, as ever, was at the aircraft. He untied the blades and rolled his eyes as I yelled, "Clear."

"Clear!" Bones replied and I pulled the start trigger.

As the engine came up to operating RPM, the blades beat the otherwise quiet air with a steady WHOP WHOP WHOP. Commo check complete, I called the tower, "Phuoc Vinh Tower, this is Cavalier Two-four. Flight of two on the Pine Ridge assault strip for hover departure to the north."

"Two-four, Phuoc Vinh. You are cleared to depart runway two seven with a right turnout."

"Roger."

"Dick, call arty and make sure they aren't shooting," I requested.

Lifting into the hover I waited for the UH-1 to depart before me. The same rules applied. If we can't see him, we can't protect him.

"Phuoc Vinh GCA, Cavalier Two-four," I called.

"Good evening Two-four, this is GCA. Go ahead."

"Roger. Can you give us vectors to center of mass two seven eight nine?"

"Two seven eight nine. Roger. Turn right radar heading zero five eight degrees. That's right at the edge of our cover," he informed me.

"Yeah, I know. If you lose either one of us on radar would you give me a heads up?"

"Roger that Two-four," the controller responded.

It was as black as black could be with a barely visible horizon. I concentrated on the flight instruments and keeping the aircraft right side up as we flew northeast. We had been airborne for about fifteen minutes when I looked to our right where the Nighthawk bird had been. I didn't see anything. I looked left.

"Hey, Dick, where's the Nighthawk bird?" I asked.

Silence.

"Dick? Where is the Nighthawk bird?"

"I don't know," he told me.

"You don't know? What in the hell do you mean you don't know?" I ranted.

"I lost him?" he said sheepishly.

"When?"

"About five minutes ago," he said.

"You lost him five minutes ago? Why the fuck didn't you say something?" I asked.

I began looking frantically right and left. I called the Nighthawk bird on our internal frequency. There was no response. I tried again and again and still nothing. At one point I looked back over the right stubby wing and in the glow of the position light it looked as if we were flying through a river!

"Phuoc Vinh GCA, Cavalier Two-four. Are you showing any weather on your radar?" I asked.

"Roger that, Two-four, there are big build-ups out there. Heavy rain showers. You are about four miles from the largest one."

"Well, thanks for telling me," I said. "Do you still have the Nighthawk bird on radar?" I asked him.

"Negative. He's already landed." Now I was genuinely dumbfounded and really pissed off.

"Son of a bitch. Give me a vector back to base," I said. "Dick, you have the aircraft. Take us home," I said relinquishing control to Captain Sides.

"I cannot fucking believe this!" I said into the intercom. "You lose the Nighthawk bird and don't say anything. GCA damn near flies us into a monsoon and they don't say anything, and then those fuckers in the Nighthawk turn around and go home and they don't even bother telling us! What in the hell is going on around here?"

Captain Sides knew I was really angry.

"Cavalier Two-four, turn right radar heading two-four-zero," GCA advised.

"Roger, two-four zero."

As the aircraft turned, a light came on in the lower left corner of my instrument panel. It was the SCAS control panel.

"Shit! We've just lost the pitch channel," I told Dick.

"You'd better take it back," he said.

"No, you're doing fine. Just maintain two-four-zero."

A few minutes later Dick called me over the intercom again. "You'd better take it back. My wrist is getting sore."

I sat there in silence thinking, "Tough shit. You're the one who got us into this."

"Two-four. You want to take it back? My wrist really hurts," he repeated.

After a few seconds I said, "Are you talking to me? I can't hear anything. My intercom must be tits up."

"Yeah. Take the aircraft. My wrist really hurts," he said again.

"I'm sorry, Dick. I can't hear a word you're saying. Just take us home and we'll talk when we get back on the ground."

He began to yell at me, thinking I would hear him over the noise of the aircraft. I did.

"Dick, I can't understand what you're saying. We'll talk on the ground."

GCA vectored us home and as we approached the airfield I yelled, "I have control!" The controls in the front seat of the Cobra are space capsule controls and the cyclic stick is four times as hard to move from the front as it is from the back. Unless you have a lot of time in the aircraft and are used to flying it from the front, your wrist gets very tired and very sore rather quickly.

As I hovered into the revetment I put the aircraft down with a small jolt.

"Oh!" I said. "My intercoms, back now. What were you saying back there?" I asked.

"Nothing," Captain Sides fumed as he unbuckled and climbed out.

I stayed behind to talk to Bones and by the time I got back to the TOC, there was nobody there but the radio operator. I walked back to the bunker in the dark enjoying the cooler air that led the approaching storm. I walked in and Larry, Dick Skaaden, John, Blue, and Barney were there talking. "Get me a cold one," I said.

"That was quick," Larry commented. "How did it go?"

I sat down, cross-legged, on the floor and told them the story from start to finish. By the time I finished they were in hysterics.

"Serves him right," somebody said. "That'll teach him to volunteer us for some dumbass mission!"

Chapter 20

Keeping Your Head

Later that evening somebody set off a tear gas grenade and as the cloud of gas drifted through the area, it permeated the hooches, the bunkers, the O Club, everything. A gas attack was usually somebody's way of saying, "You guys pissed me off!" Tear gas stings the eyes and the throat. Once the direction of the wind carrying the gas is ascertained, the best thing to do is go back through the cloud upwind until finding uncontaminated air. Gas masks help, but they must be put on before the gas reaches the victim. Most of us viewed this as nothing more than an annoyance. We gathered on the corner across from division headquarters and waited for the gas to subside before going back to the bunker. Gas lingers longer in confined areas such as buildings but it was tolerable, and besides we were tired. We lit a mosquito coil and turned in.

I flew with a new guy to the troop the next morning. Brian Holcomb was an experienced combat pilot who had come to Charlie Troop when his former unit stood down. He knew the ropes, but being new to the troop he had to learn our methods of operation. Brian was from northern California and we hit it off immediately.

Not much went on that morning. My aircraft had developed a strange vibration and I spent much of that morning trying to diagnose what had produced it. Helicopters are finely tuned and balanced pieces of machinery. With so many moving and rotating parts they are very susceptible to vibration. If the main rotors fly outside of the same plane, you get a vertical vibration and if the blades aren't balanced chordwise, you get a lateral vibration. A worn engine mount or oil cooler fan induces a high frequency vibration, and an out-of-track tail rotor can cause a harmonic vibration that manifests itself as a vertical or rumbling vibration. Most experienced helicopter pilots feel every vibration and hear every sound that is out of the norm. The vibration I was feeling that morning was not normal but I couldn't diagnose the cause. We went back to Phuoc Vinh and shut down for lunch. Larry was in the mess hall.

"Hey, Lar, do me a favor, will you?" I asked him.

"Sure, what?"

"Take my bird after lunch and fly a fuel load for me. I have a weird vibration and I can't figure out what it is," I told him. "Will you see what you think?"

Larry and I had developed an unwritten rule. Once a week we would fly each other's aircraft for a day. Very often when flying the same aircraft day after day and it begins to develop a vibration or noise, it is difficult to identify because a pilot becomes used to it in its development. By flying each other's aircraft, anything out of the ordinary is almost always immediately apparent. After lunch I took Larry's aircraft, seven nine seven, and he took mine.

We had been airborne for less than half an hour when Larry called, "Two-four, Two-three on fox. Come up channel three," he requested.

I complied. "Two-three, Two-four, go ahead."

"How have you been flying this thing?" he asked me. "I can hardly keep it right side up," he said.

"Yeah, I knew something wasn't right, but I can't put my finger on it. Take it home and let my Charlie Echo look her over while it's still light," I told him.

"Roger that."

By the time I got back to Phuoc Vinh, Bones had towed the aircraft into the hanger. I walked over to see whether he had found anything.

"Not yet, Sir. She's due a periodic inspection in a few hours. I'm going to move it up and do it now," he told me.

"Sounds good. Let me know whether you find anything or need any help with anything. Yeah?" I asked.

"Roger that, sir."

At the meeting that evening, nothing was said about the mission the previous night. All I know is I never had to fly it again. I don't think anybody did. As fast as it landed in our laps, it went away. Captain Sides announced a new policy that USARV had just put in place. It had to do with leave and R&R. Effective November 16, we were authorized one seven-day R&R, one seven-day leave, and if we were between the first day of our fourth month and the last day of our eighth month in-country, we could take a two-week leave and go home! Everybody began to make calculations. It didn't take me long to figure out that the closing date for the two-week leave was one day past the end of my eighth month in-country, the effective date of the policy. I got screwed by one day. Following on from that, Captain Sides continued, in lieu of going home we could also take a two-week leave at an R&R site or two separate one-week leaves to an R&R site. Travel would be on a stand-by basis. In actual fact, I wasn't too disappointed. I wouldn't have wanted to go home in any case. There is no way I would've got on the plane to come back, and one of the other requirements for this leave was that the serviceman would have to pay his own way back to Vietnam. Fat chance!

After the discussion about the new policy, the assignments for the next day's crews were announced. I didn't feature in any of the crews because my aircraft was still in the hangar. We were in our room that evening, me making a tape, and Larry writing to his wife, Patricia, when the XO walked in, ever so slightly intoxicated.

"Hey, did you hear that your aircraft lost its head?" he asked.

"What are you talking about?" I asked.

"Our prolific maintenance platoon took the head off today during the inspection and the Teflon trunnion bearings in the head disintegrated. If you would have flown that thing another four or five hours there is a good chance that the head would have separated from the aircraft," Fred muttered.

Larry and I looked at each other with eyes wide open.

"No shit?"

"No shit," he repeated. "You would have been a statistic."

After that bit of information I needed a drink. I went to the club and Steve Beene was there. He was going home on the first. "Hey Steve, before you split I want to buy you dinner," I told him.

"When?" Steve asked.

"You name it."

"How about tomorrow if I don't get called out on a mission?" he asked.

"You got it. I'll see you tomorrow night," I told him.

Zero six eight was back up with a brand new head and ready for a test flight on the morning of the twentieth. After Bones signed it off as fit for return to service, I went out and flew for almost ten hours. When I got back I found Steve. "Where do you want to go?" I asked.

"There's a good movie on at DIVARTY tonight. What say we go have dinner and stay for the movie?" Steve suggested.

Divarty wasn't far so we decided to walk. As we passed by division headquarters we walked straight into a cloud of tear gas.

"Shit!" Steve coughed.

My eyes stung as the flood of saliva began to flow in my now-stinging esophagus. We began to run to get out of the gas cloud and by the time we cleared it we were in front of the post library.

"Let's stop at the guard shack by the main gate," Steve suggested, "they may have some water so we can rinse our eyes."

We went up to the guard on duty, still coughing and tearing.

"Good evening, sir," he saluted.

"Good evening. You wouldn't have a canteen we could borrow, would you? Somebody gassed division and we'd like to rinse our eyes," I told him.

Handing us his canteen, we poured water into our hands and rinsed our eyes out. The water was refreshing and soon the stinging had ceased.

"Thanks a lot," we said as we handing the guard back his canteen.

"Do you know who popped the gas?" he asked us.

"No, we're going to DIVARTY and walked into the cloud," Steve explained.

"Okay. Thank you, sir." He saluted and we left.

I bought Steve a steak dinner and we sat and chatted about his pending departure. We spoke of when we first met, when we got lost in Cambodia, of Tom and Kevin. We had been through a lot together and I was going to miss him. When we finished dinner, we crossed the room and took our seats for the movie.

KAWHOMPH!

"Oh shit!" I had been more jumpy than normal about incoming since I got wounded.

KAWHOMPH!

"Must be 122s," I said to Steve. "Nothing else makes that sound."

"I really don't fucking need this, man," Steve replied. "I'm going home next week."

The siren began to sound on post and the movie came to an abrupt halt. The club sergeant announced that the base was on Red Alert. We were under threat of imminent attack and anybody outside had to have on their flak jackets and steel pot. The incoming ceased. "We better get back to the squadron area," I said to Steve.

As we approached the guard shack that we had stopped at earlier, the same guard came out. "We're on Red Alert. You are required to have your flak jacket and steel pot on," he said matter-of-factly.

"Yes, we know," I responded. "We're on our way back to our troop area to get them."

"If you are out of doors you have to have them on. Why are you out here without them?" he demanded. About that time a jeep pulled up. It was the sergeant of the guard.

"Hey, Sarge," the guard called out. "I caught these guys without their alert gear. I also have reason to believe that these guys gassed division earlier tonight," he told the sergeant. I couldn't believe my ears.

"What in the hell are you talking about?" I exclaimed.

"You guys gassed division," he said.

Steve was livid.

The sergeant came over and barked at us, "Why aren't you wearing your alert gear?"

"That's why aren't you wearing your alert gear, SIR, Sergeant. These are bars we have on our lapels and we expect to be shown the respect we are due," Steve yelled.

"Never mind that," the guard said. "These guys gassed division."

It was my turn. "What in the hell led you to that conclusion?" I asked.

"Where is your alert gear?" the sergeant repeated.

"Our alert gear is back in our squadron area," I said. "We were at DIVARTY when the siren went off and we were on the way back to get it when this guy stopped us."

He asked again, "Why don't you have your alert gear on?"

"What the hell are we supposed to do, shit it?" Steve yelled. "You get on your radio and get the officer of the guard down here. NOW!" A few minutes later another jeep pulled up. A lieutenant climbed out and both the sergeant and the guard saluted.

"What's going on?" he asked.

The guard repeated his story. "These guy's gassed division earlier and now I caught them without their alert gear."

The lieutenant looked at us and then walked over to the guard. "These GUYS are officers," he stated, "And you will address them as such!"

"Yes, sir" the guard replied. "These officers came by earlier asking for a canteen to wash the gas out of their eyes and now they are out walking around without flak jackets and steel pots on."

The lieutenant came to us. "Excuse my guard for his insubordination. Will you tell me what is going on please?" he asked.

I began, "Lieutenant Beene is going home in a few days. We're with the First of the Ninth and we were at DIVARTY for dinner and the movie. On the way over, we walked into a gas cloud in front of division. We stopped here to ask the guard for a canteen so we could rinse our eyes. End of that story. While we were at DIVARTY, we got hit, the alert siren went off, and we were on our way back to get our gear when the guard stopped us. We tried to explain to him that we were on the way back to get our gear when the sergeant pulled up. Next thing we know we're being accused of gassing division."

The lieutenant turned to the guard, "What makes you think these officers gassed division," he asked him.

"I just think they did, sir!" he responded.

Steve was still mad. "I want this guy's name, rank, and serial number," he told the lieutenant. "I don't like being accused of something I didn't do."

The lieutenant told the sergeant to call for the guard's relief and when he arrived for them both to meet us at their office. We got into the jeep with the lieutenant and went to the Headquarters of the 545th Military Police Company. We walked into their orderly room and their CO was waiting for us. He was a black captain. He welcomed us and offered us both seats and a drink.

"Thank you very much, sir," we both saluted.

"Can you tell me what is going on please?" he asked.

We repeated the entire story once again, everything, from start to finish. He was clearly dismayed by the lack of respect the guard had afforded us and was no less pleased with the sergeant of the guard. After we finished our story, he asked several questions before the sergeant and the guard walked in. They were pretty laid back. They dropped their flak jackets onto a chair and placed their steel pots on top of them.

The captain stood up and glared at them. "I am going to tell you a story and I want to know if the facts are correct!" he said to them. "And while I am telling this story I want you both to stand at attention."

They both just looked at him.

"ATTENTION, NOW!" he yelled.

They both came to attention and he repeated the story we had told him. He had all of the facts correct. When he finished he asked the guard, "Are those the facts of this matter?"

The guard corroborated what the captain had stated.

Then the captain looked at his two people, "I believe you owe these two officers an apology," he suggested.

The guard protested. "But sir, these—"

"Private," the captain addressed him, "I told you a story and you told me the story I told was correct. Did you not?"

"Well, yes, sir, but—"

"BUT NOTHING!" the captain admonished him. "Apologize and apologize now!" he ordered.

Both the private and the sergeant offered apologies but their sincerity was questionable. The captain asked the lieutenant to drive us back to our area. He offered his hand and he too apologized for the actions of his soldiers. "This isn't the end of this," he told us. "I will be in touch and let you know the outcome."

"Thank you very much, sir," we both said. Steve and I saluted him and left.

As we walked out the door Steve said, "Man, I wish we had a CO like him!"

"We did have once," I told him. "His name was Galen Rosher!"

"Dig it," Steve smiled as we got into the jeep for the ride home.

On the twenty-fifth I was flying with Lt. Ronald "Dexter" Evans. We had a late pitch pull and had flown for about six hours when fuel ran short and we broke station for the last time that day. We landed at Phuoc Vinh and refueled before shutting down.

Departing north POL to reposition to the revetments the fox-mike beckoned. "Two-four, this is Three." It was operations.

"Go ahead, Three. This is Two-four."

"Roger. I'd like you to go and do a lima lima for me." A last light mission.

"What and where?" I asked.

"We'd like you and your little bird to go and have a look around the area east of Rang Rang," he said

"What are we looking for?"

I was very skeptical of these impromptu last-light missions after what had happened with Bill Cahill in October.

"Nothing in particular. Just have a look around," I was told.

"Shit, Dexter. I don't like these goat-fuck missions."

I called my little bird as we turned to the east. "Hey One-nine, we have another mission," I said. The little bird was being flown by one of our newest scout pilots, WO1 Mel Sheldon, whom we had affectionately nicknamed "Red Cloud" because of his full-blooded American Indian heritage.

"We have a last light recon around Rang Rang," I briefed. "Ops says there is no known target but I would take that with a pinch of salt. You be careful and keep your eyes peeled when we get there."

"Roger that, Two-four."

Dexter called arty to get a clearance while I briefed Red Cloud. Arriving on station we tested the turret and I cleared the little bird out of altitude. We had been working for about fifteen minutes when a light came on on my instrument panel. It was the master caution. A light illuminated on Dexter's panel too.

"Shit! It's the number one hydraulic system," I announced to Dexter. "Tell Red Cloud to get up here and escort us home. I'll call ops."

"Three, this is Two-four," I called.

"Go ahead, Two-four. This is Three."

"Be advised we are heading for home. I've lost my number one hydraulic system."

There are two hydraulic systems on the Cobra. It may sound as if two represent one too many, but both are essential. Without hydraulics the aircraft would be uncontrollable. The rotor blades are so massive and the aerodynamic forces acting upon them so great, that without hydraulics it would be physically impossible to overcome the forces manually.

"One-nine is escorting me. We should be there in about one-five," I continued.

"Two-four, this is Three. Isn't a fuel load normally about an hour forty-five?" he questioned.

"Fuel is not the problem, Three. I've lost the number one hydraulic system," I repeated.

"Oh, I think you can fly another hour, can't you?" he asked.

"Do you understand what I am telling you? I have lost my number one hydraulics and we are RTB," I stated.

"Do you believe that asshole?" Dexter asked.

"Fuck him!" I said, "That guy is a complete idiot!"

"Phuoc Vinh, this is Cavalier Two-four, AH-1 about twenty to your east. I need the runway for an emergency landing. I've lost one of my hydraulic systems."

"Roger, Cavalier Two-four. Phuoc Vinh. You're cleared for a straight in approach to runway two seven. I'll alert the crash rescue unit. Do you have an ETA?" he asked.

"Yeah, we should be with you in eight to ten minutes."

"Roger that, Two-four. Do you require any additional assistance?"

"Negative. My little bird is escorting me. His call sign is One-nine."

"Roger. Good luck."

The number one hydraulic system provides hydraulic power to both the cyclic and collective controls, the yaw channel of the stability system, and charges the emergency collective accumulator. The pedals were now very stiff and required a great deal of pressure to have any effect on the tail rotor controls.

"Right, Dexter. Let's go through the emergency check list," I told him.

"Okay, emergency collective hydraulic switches?"

"Mine is off," I verified.

"Mine too," he responded.

"Hydraulic control circuit breaker?"

"It's in."

"SAS?"

"The yaw channel is disengaged," I confirmed.

"Master arm switch?"

"Damn, I hate to make the guns cold. It's off," I said. "Wait one!"

"One-nine, Two-four. Be advised we are weapons cold. I say again we're going cold on the guns," I told him.

"Roger that, Two-four. You just worry about getting that thing on the ground. We'll cover you for a change," Red Cloud said.

"God help us," we laughed. "Okay, Dexter, let's finish the checks."

"Rog. All that's left is to land as soon as practicable. Do you want me to turn on the accumulator switch on final?" he asked.

"Yeah, but wait till I call for it. It'll only give us four strokes max," I told him. "You might just want to follow me through on the pedals. If the nose starts to wander, help me keep her straight."

"Roger that!" Dexter said.

"Phuoc Vinh, Cavalier Two-four. We are one mile final for two seven," I announced.

"Roger that, Two-four, you are clear to land. Crash rescue is holding abeam the threshold."

"Roger. Copy all that . . . and thanks."

We came over the green line in a very shallow approach while maintaining about seventy knots. The recommended speed to touch down was fifty knots. As we approached the threshold of the runway I allowed the speed to come back and at sixty knots I told Dexter to turn on the accumulator switch.

"It's on," he told me.

"Roger. Fasten your shoulder harness!"

We touched down traveling about sixty knots. I gradually lowered the collective to increase the weight on the skids. We skidded and scraped along the runway for about three hundred feet before the aircraft came to a stop.

Taking a deep breath I announced to whomsoever cared, "Cavalier Two-four, shutting down."

"Good job, Two-four," Dexter said.

"Two-four, this is tower. Can you move the aircraft over to the assault strip for me? I have a C-130 waiting to land," the tower asked.

"I wish I could Phuoc Vinh. He'll just have to hold until they tow the aircraft off the runway," I replied.

"Roger. Understood."

Dexter and I walked back to the TOC. Nobody said anything when we walked in. Nobody dared.

After the meeting that evening, Captain Sides stayed behind. "Mr. Zahn. Can I have a word?" he asked.

"Sure."

"Six isn't too happy with your attitude," he began.

"My attitude? What are you talking about?" I asked, genuinely confused.

"He was monitoring the radio today when you had your hydraulic problem. He thought you were very sarcastic to operations."

"Sarcastic? Fucking typical," I raised my voice. "No well done! No thanks! No, gee Two-four, good job getting the aircraft down! He doesn't give a damn about the troops. All he is concerned about is that I might have been sarcastic to his ops officer. I had an emergency situation, sir, and I didn't need that little jerk in ops making insinuations about how long he thinks a fuel load lasts. I don't give a shit what he thinks and I don't care what the CO thinks. I was concerned about getting my aircraft on the ground in one piece and keeping Dexter and me alive!" I stopped and took a breath. "Unfuckingbelievable!" I yelled as I stormed out the door, slamming it behind me.

Thanksgiving Day meant many different things to different people. Most of us were used to spending the holiday with our families and loved ones. Thanksgiving 1970 would be spent with family, too—our Charlie Troop family. The Armed Forces Vietnam Network played oldies on the radio, which just served to make us think of home and what we were missing, and depressed us even more. It is hard to believe that a song could bring back a memory that would trigger a thought and make you feel so lousy, but it did.

Larry had two wisdom teeth pulled in the morning and spent part of the day doped up on morphine. The rest of his day he spent in agony.

The mess hall put on the best meal I had had since arriving in-country, a full-blown Thanksgiving supper. After lunch I went back to the bunker. It rained most of the day so I sat around reading old letters. Another new policy had gone into effect: we had to put all of our letters from the States into a burn can within seventy-two hours after receiving them. Evidently some of the hooch maids had either been stealing letters or copying down return addresses and allegedly some families in the States had begun to receive letters saying their sons or husbands had been captured or killed, causing them a great deal of distress. While it was understandable, it was another blow to our already waning morale.

The Hail and Farewell on the twenty-ninth would be an especially sad one for me. I tried not to think about it too much as I flew that day. Steve had already left and tonight we would be saying farewell to Harvey Lee Hopkins. Blue and I had become very close over the past several months and saying good-bye to him was not something I was looking forward to.

The missions over the past week were tedious and uncomfortable. The First Cav was going to be forming the Ninth Air Cavalry Brigade (Provisional) soon and we were given the task of training the pilots who would form the new troops. We were told that the frag order would be issued during the first week of December, which gave us about four days to teach them what it had taken most of us five months to learn. The days were becoming longer and longer and the missions less and less meaningful. All they wanted us to do was to get hours on these guys, but flying around in circles hour after hour, doing nothing, didn't teach anybody anything. After seven hours of flying and doing not a lot, I looked forward to getting down and, I hoped, getting a shower in before the festivities began that evening.

The Hail and Farewell was held in the officers' club at Phuoc Vinh, as usual. The other troops flew in for the event as we hailed and farewelled their troopers as well as our own. Before the farewells we were introduced to the new guys who had just joined us. We met our new CO that evening, Maj. Eldon "Keith" Ball.

Ed McDerby was the first to be recognized from our ranks. Ed had been a good friend, my former section leader, and our platoon instructor pilot. He had taught me a lot and was always available when I needed somebody to talk to. Next on Charlie Troop's list was Maj. Turner Nelson, who was leaving the week after Ed. His departure marked the first time that we had ever collectively hailed somebody's farewell. Major Nelson never had the support of his troops. He had tried to demand our respect rather than earn it. It is fair to say that following on the heels of Major Rosher, he had a tough act to follow, but he never even made an effort. Next came Blue, along with a lump in my throat. First came the not-unexpected harassment he was due for getting a twenty-five-day drop, which would allow him to be home for Christmas. Then came the stories about Blue's crowning as "King of the Donut Dollies," before I got a chance to get up and say something. I told the story of the night I got wounded when Blue was in the field.

"Lieutenant Hopkins hadn't been told about the incoming," I began. "He walked around the aid station toward our hooch, saw the rubble and the burned out shell of our quarters, and apparently asked somebody where I was. He was told that I had been wounded."

I couldn't look at him as I spoke. I tried to suppress my own tears at this point before I continued, "Then our big six-foot-two-inch Blue platoon leader, a combat veteran of ten months . . . cried."

Through blurry eyes I looked straight into Harvey's face and noticed that he was crying again. Saying nothing he came up and hugged me. And there we stood in front of the officers of the most elite fighting force in Vietnam hugging and crying.

"Shit, Jewish," Harvey sobbed, "I'm going to miss you."

"I'm gonna miss you too, Blue," I told him.

When we returned to our seats, I noticed for the first time that others also had tears in their eyes. Emotions were displayed at odd and varied times in Vietnam. I wasn't the least bit embarrassed about my public display. I remembered what my father had told me before I had got on that aircraft to San Francisco almost nine months ago: "The friends you make in combat will be your best friends for the rest of your life. The guys whom you depend on to keep you alive, and the ones who depend on you, there is nothing that will ever break that bond. You will share experiences that will be personal and private and you will continue to share them for the rest of your lives, and don't you forget it." Wise man, my father.

One of the other topics at that Hail and Farewell was the never-ending rumor of troop moves, drops, and stand-downs. President Nixon had begun the Vietnamization program and most of the ground troops were being sent home while the bulk of the fighting was left to the aviation units. Harvey had indeed got a drop, as had many of the enlisted troops, but it was becoming more and more apparent that there would be no drops for aviators.

Larry was still grounded following the removal of his wisdom teeth. He had developed an infection and remained on antibiotics and in pain.

On the thirtieth I woke up with an itchy neck. Looking in the mirror I saw a large red raised area around my neck. Unable to resist the temptation, I scratched at it and almost immediately it began to bleed. I went to the aid station. Doc took one look at it and diagnosed a severe case of heat rash. The area affected was where the chinstrap of my helmet rested and rubbed. I was given an antibiotic ointment to put on it, along with orders not to shave for five days, and I was also grounded because I couldn't wear my helmet.

As expected, on December 5, a frag order was issued authorizing the division to form F Troop, First of the Ninth—using Company D of the 229th Aviation Battalion as the bulk of the new troop. At the same time, the First Aviation Brigade formed Echo Troop, Third of the Seventeenth Cav using the 334th Assault Helicopter Company as the nucleus of that organization. With the new troops in place, an additional frag order was issued on the same date forming the Ninth Air Cavalry Brigade (Provisional). The new brigade had under its operational control the entire First of the Ninth. HQ, A, B, C, D, E, and F Troops along with HQ, A, B, and E Troops of the Third of the Seventeenth. Following the formation of the new brigade, an operations order was issued: OPORD 1-70, which task organized the brigade and assigned each troop their new missions. Bottom line was that the new brigade was now responsible for approximately 5,976 square miles.

The following day a major milestone occurred for me. I became a two-digit midget with only ninety-nine days left to go of my tour.

I wrote Mom and Dad, *"I am now officially a two-digit midget. The year is drawing to a close, my tour is drawing to a close, the war . . . they say is drawing to a close, too, but I don't know. Once I go home, I embark on a whole new way of life I guess."*

One thing that always happened in the formation of a new troop was that they took experienced aviators from the existing troops in order to train pilots in Air Cav tactics. We were about to undergo some major changes in our bunker. Dick was ordered to move out of the Charlie Troop area into the squadron hooches and Uncle John was moving to Lai Khe to join F Troop. Fred Joles and my former next-door neighbor, Van Joyce, would be moving into the bunker.

Larry's infection had moved to his ear so he continued to be grounded. He was given an additional duty as scheduling officer for the platoon. He had to make sure that no one was getting too high on hours and would schedule the crews to ensure that everybody carried an equal load. We were running short of parts and because of that we weren't able to field as many Cobras as division wanted, but it was a situation that we had no control over. Larry's solution to the problem was to triple-crew each aircraft every day. Each crew would fly two fuel loads, or three hours, and it worked out well.

We also got a new assistant ops officer, Capt. Joel Hageman. Joel was a retread warrant officer, a big man with only six months left in the Army. Captain LaChance did his best to get Captain Hageman to adopt his attitude toward everybody, but Joel was smarter than that. He was a personable guy who made his own decisions, often the opposite of his boss's, and was immediately liked by most everyone.

Larry and I were down at the TOC one day while we were grounded. Joel asked us an operational question about the running of a Pink team, when Mike interrupted him, telling him it was no use asking us because we didn't know what we were talking about.

"I don't think the question was directed at you, sir," I told him.

He looked at us through venomous eyes. "You are both immature and you continue to make all the wrong decisions," he told us.

"When we are in the AO, the only decisions that count are ours, Mike, and you can't handle that, can you?" I asked. I was in the mood for a good argument.

"You haven't got enough information to make decisions," he retorted.

Larry jumped in "And whose fault is that?" he asked. "You are the one who withholds the information. Information that could get us or our little birds killed."

"It isn't your responsibility where the little bird goes to VR. All you have to do is cover him."

"That just shows how little you know," I interjected. "Our job isn't to cover the little bird. Our job is to keep them alive. Our job is to brief him so he has all the information that is available on the enemy situation, the tactical situation. He needs to know that and if you can't figure that out, you're dumber than I thought."

Larry grabbed my arm as I was getting out of control.

Larry glared at Mike challenging him, "When we get back in the air, unless we get briefed on the enemy situation, we will NOT put our little birds on the deck."

We turned to leave and as we approached the door I couldn't resist the urge, "He's a real douche bag!" I said in a voice loud enough to make sure he heard me. We stopped by the mailroom on the way back to the bunker. There was a large package for me and one for Larry, too. Mine was a care package from all the girls in my mother's office and Larry's was from his sister, Anita. She had sent us a small artificial Christmas tree for the bunker. On our way back we bumped into Major Ball, our new CO.

"Can you two meet me at the club in ten minutes? I'd like to have a chat with you," he told us.

"Sure, sir. We'll be there as soon as we drop these packages off," we told him.

"I wonder what this is about?" I asked Larry after we were out of earshot.

We dropped off our packages and went straight to the club. The major wasn't there yet. I went and got us each a coke while Larry grabbed a table. I had just got to the table when Major Ball walked in. "Can I get you something to drink, sir?" I asked him.

"I'll have whatever you're having," he said with a smile. "Thank you."

After getting another coke, I returned to the table and sat down.

Major Ball began the conversation. "I know that you two are the most senior ACs in the Gun Platoon. How much time do you have left in-country?" he asked.

"I just became a two-digit midget," I told him.

"And I go two weeks after Randy," Larry said.

"I hear that you have been having some problems with the ops officer . . . um, let me rephrase that," he said. "I hear the ops officer has been having problems with you two. I am interested to know what those problems are and how to resolve them. You two have a great deal of experience and I need to be sure that that experience doesn't get wasted."

I began by telling him how much time and effort went into making AC. "Sir, first of all, being a Red AC in Charlie Troop is more than shooting rockets and flying a helicopter. This may sound funny but our job is to save lives."

"Haw!" he chuckled. "You fly a helicopter armed to the teeth with enough firepower to destroy damn near anything and you tell me your job is to save lives!"

"Yes, sir," Larry interjected. "Our scouts. The LOH crew, the Blues, ground troops . . . those are the lives we're talking about."

Major Ball listened more intently.

"The little birds don't carry maps, sir," I told him. "We have to navigate and we have to know where we are at all times. We have to get arty clearances and we have to know how to employ artillery. We have to know how to put in air strikes and conduct BDAs. We have to insert and extract the Blues from single-ship hover-downs to a combat assault. We copy down and pass spot reports and, before anything else, we protect our little bird. We vector them around open areas, we vector them to the AO, and we vector them back to base. We provide cover for dustoff when we need them and we employ the ready reaction force when they are needed. Sir, basically we are the guys on the spot. We run the mission because usually we are on station as the situation develops. I don't mean we as in Larry and I, but whoever the Red AC is who happens to be on station. We know what assets we need and when we need them and once we get them we know how to use them."

"My, oh my," Major Ball said tentatively.

"The last thing we need, sir, is a non-rated guy sitting in the TOC, miles away from the contact, trying to second-guess and then question everything we do," I said in summary.

"Yes. I can understand that."

Larry continued, "Sir, we are not trying to make waves or cause anybody any trouble. Randy and I do what we do because it's the best way we know how to do it. We haven't made it this long by making dumb decisions or because we're lucky, but the ops officer won't listen to us. You have the best damn scout crews in Vietnam and I'd like to think that they think they have the best Red pilots covering them. They couldn't do their jobs if they didn't trust us. They know that we will do everything in our power to protect them."

My turn. "Sir, we might not be in the LOH with those guys, but we are very much a part of their crew. They have the toughest damn job in-country. Those three guys in those LOHs have brass balls, sir. I am not going to start changing the way I do things now, with three months left in-country, just because some captain in ops wants to do things his way."

"I understand," Major Ball said looking me in the eyes.

"So what do you guys want to do for the rest of your tour?" he asked.

"Sir, I would like a job that would keep me on the ground a bit more," I said. "I just got a copy of a letter that our family doctor just sent to our Congressman. My Dad hasn't been too well, sir. He's sixty-three years old and he's a very emotional man. He almost had a breakdown a few months back. In fact, he was hospitalized. Being over here has been harder on my dad than it's been on me. If I could do something that would keep me on the ground a bit more, I would be very grateful and I know it would ease some of his stress and anxiety."

"Do you have any admin experience?" the CO asked. "The admin officer's slot is open."

"But isn't that a full-time job, sir? I don't want to quit flying. That's not what I went to flight school for," I stated.

"We could probably work out a schedule where you fly two or three days a week and do admin for the remaining days," he told me.

"That would be great, sir. That would be really great. Thanks."

I went to get some more drinks as Larry had his discussion with the major. We finished our drinks over small talk before the major excused himself to leave.

"Wow!" Larry said. "He's not a bad guy."

"You can say that again!" I replied.

Eager to start my new job, I went to the orderly room and sat at my new desk. I shared the front office with the enlisted clerk-typist while the CO and the XO, Capt. Judson "Pappy" Dukes, occupied the back office. Pappy was a black man who had transferred in from the 229th Assault Helicopter Battalion. He was big and jovial and all business that day.

"So you hung up your wings, huh, Two-four?" he asked.

"No Pappy, I'll be in the office three days a week and flying the others," I told him.

"I don't think so," he replied shaking his head.

"Yeah, the CO and I agreed to that the other day," I confirmed.

"Well, the CO told me to tell you that the admin job is full-time and there will be no flying."

"Shit, Pappy. Who the hell can you believe any more?" I asked.

I was Charlie Troop's administration officer for two days and I performed as such for one. In the short time since the CO and I spoke, admin was deemed a full-time job and my flying would virtually have ended. Sitting in the orderly room all day drove me nuts. I did the job to the best of my ability, but my heart wasn't in it. Effectively I was out of the Red Platoon and the only ones happy about that were Captain Sides and my new section leader, Lt. Jim Williams. Being out of the platoon didn't keep me out of the meeting though, since they were held in my living room. I couldn't stand sitting there and listening to the guys talking about flying and what had happened in the AO and not being a part of it.

"Lar, I can't do this damn admin job," I said.

"I know," he replied.

"What do you mean you know?"

"You love flying too much and if you don't fly, you'll go crazy! Besides, we need you in the AO. The scouts need you," Larry said. He knew me too well.

"I'll tell the old man in the morning. I'm going to sleep," I told him. My mind was made up.

I didn't sleep much that night. I had never been a quitter and I felt like I was quitting.

After breakfast the next morning I went to the orderly room. "Good morning, sir!" I greeted the CO as I walked in. "May I have a word please?"

"Sure, Mr. Zahn! What's on your mind?" he asked sitting back in his chair, hands crossed behind his head.

"Flying, sir. I thought we had agreed that I could fly a few days a week and now the goal posts have changed and effectively, I've been grounded. I'm an aviator, sir. I'm not cut out to sit behind a desk all day every day. I need to be out in the AO," I told him.

"Are you quitting?" he asked me.

"If that's the only way for me to keep flying, yes, sir." I told him despising the label he had just put on me.

"What about your father?" he asked.

"Sir, I know my dad. If there is one thing he has always wanted it's for me to be happy. If he knows I am doing what I enjoy doing, what I'm good at, then he'll be okay. I'm a lot more use to the troop in the AO than I am sitting here, sir."

"Well, that's one point I can't argue," Major Ball told me. "I'll talk to Red when he gets down. Go fly!"

"Yes, sir!" I saluted and left, double-timing it back to the bunker. The meeting went on as usual that evening until the crew assignments were given out for the next day. Larry had scheduled me to fly and Captain Sides announced, "Two-four will be back in the air tomorrow. He couldn't cut the mustard as the admin officer."

"Pardon me?" I asked.

"I heard you quit today," he said. "Too much hassle."

"No sir, that isn't exactly how it happened," I defended myself.

"You don't need to explain, Mr. Zahn. I know the truth," he said giving me a challenging glare out of the corner of his eye.

I thought it best not to respond. Most of the guys stayed after the meeting. Sides and Williams left.

Larry looked at me. "Wow!"

John snickered, "He knows the truth. That asshole doesn't know shit!"

In fact it was a good thing I left the admin post. The monsoon season was ending and the change of weather brought on a lot of illness. More than half of the Cobra platoon was grounded with colds, intestinal bugs, and viruses.

I wasn't left out. On Saturday morning, I took off on a first-light mission. Things were uneventful in the AO but as the morning wore on I broke out in a sweat. I lowered the temperature on the ECU until ice was coming out of the vents, but I continued to sweat and began to feel pretty awful. By the time we flew off our second load of fuel I was having severe stomach cramps. I couldn't continue. I went straight back to the revetment to shut down, which was a no-no. We always refueled before shutting down in case we had to scramble on a down bird, but I just didn't have the energy. Having shut down, it took ages for me to climb out of the aircraft. I was cramping so bad I couldn't walk upright or for any distance. Bypassing the TOC, I went directly to the aid station where one of the medics helped me to a cot.

Our flight surgeon came out and took one look at me.

"You're grounded," he told me.

"No shit!" I would have laughed but it hurt too much.

Doc Eckert gave me some medication and told me to get some rest. I was asleep within an hour.

John Craig left to go to F Troop on the thirteenth. As per regulations, his departure required the completion of an efficiency report for all of us who were in his section.

Mine read:

Chief Warrant Officer Zahn during this period has displayed the highest standards of performance as a weapons aircraft commander. He has accomplished his mission in a professional manner. Chief Warrant Officer Zahn has been instrumental in the training of newly assigned pilots in relation to Air Cavalry tactics. I would welcome the opportunity to serve with this officer again.

Captain Sides, being the platoon leader, was the endorser. His comments weren't so complimentary.

Chief Warrant Officer Zahn has performed his duties as a Weapons Platoon pilot in a satisfactory manner. Chief Warrant Officer Zahn has a sound knowledge of the aircraft he flies and the mission it performs in an Air Cavalry Troop.

By Monday morning I was feeling a lot better, but I still wasn't feeling well enough to fly. Larry had the day off too and went to retrieve the mail. A few minutes later he ran back into the room hooping and hollering.

"What the hell is the matter with you?" I asked. "Is the war over?"

"A letter just came down from DA," he began. "All Warrant Officers who DEROS after March 1, 1971 will ETS simultaneously. Can you believe it? When we go home, we'll be out of the Army!"

"Are you sure that applies to us, Lar? I mean, we are voluntary indefinite."

"Well sure it does!" he exclaimed. "Doesn't it?" he asked, now not quite so sure.

"We'll just have to wait and see, I guess."

I had mixed emotions about this issue. Despite being in Vietnam, I liked the Army. The military suited me and I thought about staying in. That was one issue.

The next thing that bothered me was we had answered our country's call and now that the war was supposedly winding down I felt that we were being discarded like so much old garbage, and that really pissed me off.

The fifteenth was a big day for Larry and me. There was going to be a party in the club that night and we were paying the bill. For me the day marked the completion of my ninth month in-country and it was also the day that we were promoted to CW2, Chief Warrant Officer. Officially we were promoted in the afternoon when a formation was called, the orders read out, and Major Ball pinned our new bars on.

Special Orders Number 349 Extract. 15 December 1970. By direction of the Secretary of the Army, following Warrant Officers PROMOTED in the Army of the United States.

Larry went first only because it was done alphabetically. Unofficially we didn't get promoted until we bought the bar and drank our bars that evening. The tradition of buying the bar upon promotion had long been established and I had no problem with that. Drinking our bar was something else. The bartender took a tall glass and put shots in it—rum, vodka, tequila, bourbon, Scotch—and anything else he could fit in the glass. Once it was full my CW2 bar was dropped into the cocktail. The idea was to down the cocktail in one gulp ending up with the bar in the drinker's mouth. Larry and I decided this one we would do together. At the count of three we both raised our glasses and began to drink. It was, without a doubt, the foulest-tasting concoction I had ever experienced. Having successfully completed this rite of pas-sage I removed the bar from my mouth, excused myself, and went outside and stuck my finger down my throat. It seemed like it took a lot longer for the alcohol to come up than it did to go down, but I knew what I would feel like in the morning if I had-n't done this, especially since I was scheduled to fly.

Larry got to the bunker shortly after I did. "What is this?" he asked when he came in and saw me in my bed.

"This is 'I feel like shit and I am going to sleep.'"

Even after voiding most of the alcohol from the drink, I was still feeling light headed and sick.

"Why you candy ass," Larry said, having difficulty standing up. "I'm going back to the club."

"Be my guest. Just don't wake me up when you come back. I'm on first light," I told him.

"Well, so am I," he told me slurring his words. "So am I."

Larry wasn't a pretty sight in the morning. He felt even worse than he looked and I left him in his bed when I went to fly. When I got back that afternoon, Larry was awake but still in bed.

I smiled. "Hey Lar, how ya doing?"

"Oh, man! What happened last night?" he asked.

"We got promoted! Remember?"

"I feel like I got hit by a truck," Larry told me.

I laughed.

"Oh, so you can go out and play with the boys, but you can't get up and go to work with the men, huh? What a candy ass."

AFVN was playing a lot of Christmas music on the radio as the holiday was fast approaching. Decorations had been going up around the area for the past few weeks and as I walked by them, it made me very melancholy.

I couldn't help but think what everyone would be doing at home, and here I was in Vietnam, where Christmas Day would undoubtedly be close to a hundred degrees. I, along with everybody else, was starting to become pretty depressed.

There had been a lot of talk of a Christmas Day cease-fire, but we were still going to be expected to field three teams on the holiday.

There was also talk about the NVA launching a big offensive over the holiday period. December 20 would mark the fourth anniversary of the National Liberation Front (NLF), and the intelligence folks were expecting an increase in enemy activity.

Larry and I were making plans to take another R&R. We were getting "short" and every day out of country would be one less day exposed to the inherent dangers of war. We had planned to go to Bangkok but the tactical situation was not conducive to two ACs being gone at the same time.

Captain Sides had got his allocation to go to Vung Tau for an in-country Cobra transition. He was already gone and would be away for several weeks. Having been our platoon leader for almost a month he was finally going to become qualified in the aircraft. Ross Rainwater would take the platoon over as the acting Red because he outranked everybody else.

When the mail arrived on the morning of the seventeenth I received a letter from the Department of the Army. Was this confirmation about the ETS thing or something else? I tore open the envelope to find a sheet of thin blue paper. It was a copy of the request for orders for my new assignment. After I DEROSed and took thirty days leave I was to report to the Army Aviation School at Fort Rucker, Alabama. No doubt to be an instructor pilot. The concurrent ETS did not apply to me because I had signed a contract for Voluntary Indefinite status as payment for Cobra school. I was not disappointed.

The closer we got to the holiday, our workload and commitments in the AO increased tenfold. The crew chiefs and maintenance people were working around the clock to keep the aircraft in the air. Parts were getting harder and harder to acquire.

WO1 Barney Vestal, who had been shot down the day after Bill Cahill's death, had completed his six months as a scout and was now a Cobra AC. He was flying on the twenty-first with Captain Rainwater in the front seat. While Barney was inserting the Blues they heard a loud popping sound and the aircraft began to yaw. The compressor in the engine was stalling, causing severe engine vibrations and a rapid increase in the internal engine temperature. If allowed to continue, the engine could flame out or sling a compressor blade. An uncontained failure of that sort could be catastrophic. Barney landed in an opening and shut down. One of the lift ships landed simultaneously to evacuate him and Ross. The Blues were extracted from their original landing area and reinserted on the downed Snake to secure it and prepare it to be lifted out. A tandem-rotor CH-47 would have to come in and sling it back to Phuoc Vinh where the engine would have to be changed. The aircraft were getting tired, and flying as much as we were with all of our new commitments, the preventative maintenance that is so crucial to keeping the aircraft flying just wasn't getting done.

The following day was a sign of the times. Two LOHs landed with chip detector lights illuminated. The chip detector is a magnetic plug in the oil system. It attracts pieces of metal that have become suspended in the oil. When a piece or accumulation big enough is caught on the plug it closes a gap and completes a circuit, illuminating a light on the caution panel. There are chip detectors in the engine oil system and in all of the gearboxes. Metal floating around in the system is usually an indication that something is coming apart internally. A short while later Larry was refueling when he noticed fuel leaking from the belly of his aircraft. He shut down and waited for his crew chief to come across and look at it.

In less than thirty minutes we had three aircraft taken out of action.

Chapter 21

On Christmas Day

"Good evening, men!" Major Ball greeted us as he entered the bunker during our meeting. It was Wednesday, December 23. We were having the meeting early because it was Hail and Farewell night.

"I'd like to get your opinion on something," he began. "We're having a tough time giving division the number of Pink teams they want each day. Spare parts are getting hard to come by. We've just inherited a minigun kit for a LOH. What do you think about putting a White team in the AO?" he asked.

"A White team?" I asked. "What exactly is a White team?"

"Two LOHs," the CO replied. "They will both VR but the aircraft with the minigun will provide cover for the other LOH," he stated confidently. "It won't have the capabilities of an AH-1 and he won't be able to carry a third crew member because of the weight of the gun and ammo."

"Bad idea," I piped up.

"Why do you say that?" the major asked.

"Sir, it's asking for trouble. You put a scout pilot in a LOH; it doesn't matter what it has on it. He's going to fly it like a scout. Scouts are used to having a Cobra above them. We're their security blanket. They don't know anything about flying guns. They don't get arty clearances, they don't know about getting clearances—"

Van interjected, "They don't even know how to read a damn map, sir. I flew scouts in my old unit and I couldn't find shit on a map. They never use them. That's our job."

"Sir," Larry joined in, "It would just be too much to expect of them without lots of additional training."

"Something as simple as the direction they fly their orbits is going to be a problem. They fly right-hand circles because that's the side the pilot's seat is on," I told the CO. "We fly left-hand orbits. We have equally good visibility out both sides so it doesn't really matter which direction we fly except if we fly in the opposite direction to the little bird, it's a lot easier to keep him in sight. You tell a scout to fly left-hand orbits and he is unsighted. He'll have a hell of a time just trying to keep the other bird in sight. They're not used to flying at altitude. They don't have a turret. They roll in and they have to point the aircraft at the target.

Most of our scouts have never flown the tactics that we employ. Sir, with all due respect, this is the craziest damn idea I have ever heard of. Somebody is going to get killed."

"So what exactly are you saying, gentlemen?" Major Ball asked.

Almost in unison, we all said without reservation, "Don't do it!"

"Well, thank you for that, gentlemen. I appreciate your opinions. We'll be putting a White team in the AO tomorrow," he told us before turning and leaving the bunker.

"I do NOT fucking believe he just said that!" Van said in exasperation.

"What was there about 'don't do it' that he didn't understand?" I asked.

"Well, fuck it. He asked our opinion and we gave it. Let's go to the club," Van said, leading the way.

We awoke early on Christmas Eve. We went to the TOC before sunrise to get briefed on our first light mission. I was to take a Pink team to VR an area northeast of Phuoc Vinh. My scout pilot for the day was WO1 Bruce Campbell.

The White teams' crews showed up at about the same time. Lt. Art Harmon was flying the low bird, with WO1 Gary Buchanan as his observer. Gary was training to be a scout pilot. Their gunner that day was Jerry Cameron. WO1 Barry Sipple flew the high LOH.

As my team headed for the door of the TOC, Barry said, "Hey Two-four, help. We haven't got a fucking clue what we're supposed to be doing out there today."

I told the crews about our chat with the major the night before. To say they were all a bit apprehensive would be a gross understatement.

"Just don't let Art out of your sight, Barry" I told him. "If you can't see him you can't protect him and if you can't protect him you may as well stay home. Make sure your minigun is operational before you let him descend and make sure you know where the hell you are at all times. If you get in any trouble, call one of us."

"Yeah right, know where you are. Who the hell is supposed to do the navigating?" he asked in frustration.

"Well, according to the old man, you are!" I said before taking my leave.

The morning was pretty uneventful. The White team didn't launch until after lunch. One of the aircraft was in maintenance and they had to wait for it to be released. This OH-6 had had a history of engine-related problems with fluctuating rpm. As a matter of fact, Barry had had an engine failure in that aircraft earlier that morning while he was refueling.

We had flown one fuel load after lunch and landed at the POL point to refuel shortly before 2 o'clock. I had just climbed back in and strapped into my harness before plugging my helmet in to the avionics chord.

"Three, this is One-four," an obviously distressed Barry Sipple called. "I can't find my little bird!"

"Son of a bitch," I said, "I knew it. Two-zero, Two-four, you up?"

"Roger that," Bruce replied.

"Follow me, we may have a down bird," I told him.

"Phuoc Vinh, Cavalier Two-four," I called as I rolled the throttle up to operating rpm. "Pink team at north POL, scramble departure to the east."

Lifting into the hover, I pushed the cyclic forward before tower responded.

"Roger, Two-four. You're clear to depart."

I don't remember who was in my front seat that day, but I asked him to get on to arty and get us a clearance.

"Three, this is Two-four. We're on the way. Break. One-four, Two-four, where you at?" I asked.

"Two-four, One-four. I'm not real sure. Head about one three zero out of Phuoc Vinh," Barry said.

"Roger, come up uniform channel two," I instructed.

"Two-four, One-four, channel two," Barry called, checking in.

"Okay, tell me what happened."

"What do you mean what happened? I can't find the little bird," Barry told me.

"Tell me exactly what happened from the time you left Phuoc Vinh. Did you get an arty clearance?" I asked.

"Arty clearance?" he responded sounding perplexed.

"Yeah, an arty clearance. Did you call Phuoc Vinh arty and make sure they weren't shooting in your direction?" I asked. I was getting really angry.

"No, I've never done that before," Barry said.

"Oh, that's just fucking wonderful!" I yelled into the intercom. "So he could have been blown out of the sky by arty."

"Did you call Brigade and get clearance for the box you were going to VR?"

"Two-four, One-four," Barry called.

He was really upset and I wasn't helping the matter any. I was livid, but not at Barry. I was mad at the CO, I was mad at myself for not being more assertive the night before, and I was mad at the whole world for allowing this to happen on Christmas Eve.

"Doesn't the high bird normally do all of that?" he asked.

"You ARE the high bird damn it," I emphasized.

To my x-ray: "Get on to ops and tell them to get some more teams out here. We'll send him a grid as soon as we find One-four. Better tell him to crank up the Blues too."

"One-four, Two-four. Pop a Willie Pete," I requested.

"A Willie Pete?" he asked.

"I say again, pop a Willie Pete. It'll help us find you quicker."

White phosphorus is a nasty, deadly weapon. The grenades were used for two purposes, first and foremost as a marking means, and second to burn. White phosphorous is a chemical that burns on contact. It will burn a hole right through skin. That said, a Willie Pete airburst produces a beautiful billowy brilliant white cloud that is visible in clear skies for miles.

"Roger that, Two-four. Willie Pete is out," Barry called.

"Okay, we have you. We'll be there in about zero three. Now, when and where did you last see the little bird?" I asked.

"We came out together and then he started to descend when we got out here. Last time I saw him was when he crossed under my tail. I was waiting for him to come out the other side but he never did," he explained.

I was at boiling point by this time. "What do you mean when he passed under your tail? How the hell are you supposed to see him when he's behind you?" I continued to admonish him. "SHIT!"

WO1 Gary Buchanan died that day, his third day flying scouts, leaving behind a wife pregnant with the baby daughter whom he would never know.

Apparently when the aircraft had descended out of altitude and arrived at treetop level, Lieutenant Harmon pulled in power to arrest the descent and nothing happened. The engine had either failed in the descent or as he applied power. The aircraft continued down into the trees where it later blew up. Mercifully, Gary Buchanan died on impact. Lieutenant Harmon suffered a left eye injury and had several broken bones. Jerry Cameron suffered a dislocated hip and second-degree burns on his legs and stomach.

I wrote home that night: *"Hard as it is to comprehend, from what they tell us it's Christmas Eve. Huh! Christmas Eve at 97 degrees with no lights, no carols, no family, and no possible perception that it's even that time of year. Just another lousy day in Vietnam! Well, I can't even say it was a typical day. I can hardly wait to hear the Army's greeting to one of our friend's wife, "Merry Christmas, P.S. Your husband is dead."*

Yes, that was our Christmas Eve, watching another friend die in this stinking shitty country, and for what? For nothing, not a goddamn thing.

If you think I have a lousy attitude, you're right! I am sick and tired of the lifers playing their silly stupid games at the cost of other people's lives. It stinks. It really, really stinks."

After I finished my letter I went to the club. I needed a drink. I was already depressed and Gary's death left me feeling really low. It only took one drink to make me call it a night and go back to the bunker and my bed.

Leaving the club, I passed the CO on his way in. I said nothing. After I passed him I heard a loud "Ah hem," as if he were clearing his throat.

"Excuse me," Major Ball stopped.

Turning around where I stood I asked, "Are you talking to me?"

He walked back to me. "I don't know what they taught you in flight school, Mr. Zahn, but I'd like to think they taught you that it's military courtesy to salute a superior, especially your commanding officer!" he emphasized.

"No, sir, they didn't," I told him. "They taught me that a salute is a symbol of respect, and what respect I had for you I lost today."

"Everybody is entitled to a mistake, Mr. Zahn," the major stated.

"That's good, sir. That's real good. When you go down to your office tonight to write that letter . . . 'Dear Mrs. Buchanan, your husband is dead because I made a mistake. Oh, by the way, Merry Christmas' . . . you tell me if that's going to make a difference to her and her daughter, sir. The one who'll never know her father."

I walked away leaving the CO standing there. I didn't salute nor did I envy him his duty.

Things began to pop that night. A runner from the TOC told us we had a brief in the TOC at 6 o'clock Christmas morning.

"What's up?" Larry asked.

"I don't know all the details, sir," the runner said. "But the word is that an NVA regiment is getting ready to cross the border up by Tay Ninh. If you were planning to have tomorrow off, you can forget it."

We were already depressed just being in Vietnam at Christmas. The talk of drops had died a death and Buchanan's death that day was just about the last straw. What could be so important that we needed to be up for a 6:00 A.M. brief? Morning came sooner than we had wanted it to. There was no Santa, no snow, and no gaiety.

"Two-four, you and Two-three will be flying a heavy Red team today. One-six will be your little bird," we were briefed.

"What's going on?" I asked.

We had never routinely flown a heavy Red team, two Cobras and a LOH, unless a little bird had been shot down. Something big had to be going on to warrant the need for that much firepower.

"S-2 got word that an NVA regiment came across the border from Cambodia. We'll be laagering out of Tay Ninh for a few days. We'll be flying in support of the Second ARVN Airborne Brigade," we were briefed. "And by the way, gentlemen, the cease-fire *is* in effect. I say again, *is* in effect. You will have no clearance to fire on anything unless you're shot at."

I turned to look at Major Ball who was standing quietly behind us listening to the briefing. Our eyes met before I turned back around.

"What kind of shit is this?" Van asked.

"What the hell are we supposed to do, wave at them and wish them a Merry Christmas?" I asked sarcastically.

"There is a cease-fire in effect, gentlemen. There will be no shooting."

"You mean to tell me that every swinging dick out in the jungle knows that today is Christmas and we're not supposed to shoot at each other?" Van asked.

"What if we get shot at?" One-six asked.

From the back of the room Major Ball spoke up. "You get shot at, you return fire. Just make sure they shoot first," he said.

I turned to look at the CO. Our eyes met and he nodded and smiled.

"I thought Tay Ninh was closed," Mother said.

"There is one U.S. unit still there, the 187th Assault Helicopter Company; the Crusaders," we were told.

"Is that it?" I asked.

"That's it!"

"What do we do for arty support?" Larry asked.

"There is arty at Thien Ngon."

"Man, this whole thing stinks out loud," Van voiced his displeasure.

We headed out to the aircraft in the ninety-seven-degree Christmas heat. On the way to Tay Ninh, the situation continued to develop back at Phuoc Vinh. At 8:25 A.M. the Task Force 1-9 commander informed Major Ball that the troop was being committed in support of the Second ARVN and he was to move the combat elements of the troop to Tay Ninh. By 10:45, every available aircraft had launched and was en route to Tay Ninh. We were on the border looking for signs of a crossing. One-six was reporting trails with heavy recent use, water puddles that had been muddied from people walking through them, broken branches and other telltale signs. The one thing he hadn't reported was the sighting of any people . . . yet.

At about 2 o'clock, that changed.

"Okay, I think we have gooks down here," Chuck reported.

"Roger that. Keep your eyes peeled and as much as I hate to remind you, make sure your Charlie Echo doesn't shoot," I told him.

"Roger that. But I think we're going to take fire," Chuck said instinctively.

"You take fire, you return it," Larry said.

"I think we're about to take fire," he repeated. "I think we're going to take fire. I think we're going to take fire right about . . . now. TAKING FIRE!" he yelled.

"I'm in hot, get the fuck out of there!" I called as the first rockets left their tubes.

"Holy shit!" Van yelled from my front seat as the trees where the LOH had just been exploded. "They're shooting fucking artillery. RPGs!"

"I'll cover your break," Larry said. "Which way you turning?"

"I'll break left," I said.

"Hold to the south, One-six," Larry instructed the LOH. "I'm in hot!"

"Okay guns," Chuck called. "There's gooks all over down there."

Larry and I made repeated rocket runs on the area before I called Chuck back, "Okay One-six, you don't have to go back in there," I told him.

"Bullshit!" Chuck replied as expected.

"Okay One-six," Larry called. "I have you in sight. You're cleared back in, but watch out."

"Oh yeah," Chuck called. "Give me a vector."

The LOH approached the area at speed. Nothing happened. Chuck Frazier, the ultimate scout pilot, put the aircraft through its paces before settling back to a hover over the area where the NVA had just shot at him.

"Hey guys," Chuck called. "Merry Christmas. You got three KBHs."

"Wonderful," Larry said sadly.

"Yeah good, huh?" I said. "Just what I wanted to do on Christmas Day. Go out and kill somebody."

That evening Larry was really upset and didn't want to talk on the tape. This was very unlike him, but I understood his feelings. Finally, he relented. *"Hi Mr. and Mrs. Zahn. It's me, Larry. How are you? I hope you had a nice Christmas. I hope you had a nicer Christmas than I had and I hope you'll have a happier New Year than I will have. As you will probably notice in my voice, there is a sound of sarcasm and there is a sound of sorrow I guess you could say.*

I'm sick. I have a cold and a cough.

"And I just got sick today" [I interjected].

"My ears hurt and I'm grounded for three days" [Larry continued].

Let me tell you what has been happening the last three or four days. Christmas Eve . . . let me start out with Christmas Eve. Christmas Eve I thought was going to turn out to be a pretty nice Christmas Eve until about two o'clock in the afternoon when one of our LOHs crashed, and one of our good friends died.

And, uh, I don't know, Christmas is something about rejoice, and the birth of the Savior, and everybody is supposed to be happy, wishing everybody peace, Merry Christmas, joy to the world, peace on Earth and good will to men.

But yet, one of our good friends dies on Christmas Eve, and it just doesn't seem right that the spirit of Christmas should allow a friend to die on Christmas Eve. He crashed in a LOH. He was VRing, and I guess he had a transmission failure [we thought at the time], *and he went down in the trees and he burned.*

I don't know. Maybe I'm kind of weird, or old-fashioned. I don't care what people tell me but I have some pretty strong feelings for this man. He might not have been a really good friend, but he was a friend, he was a GI, and most of all, he was a human being. Some of the people over here have seen a lot of deaths and they say you get used to them, that if a person dies, you should just thank your lucky stars that you're not dead.

Christmas Eve for a lot of people is just a joyous, happy drunken brawl that a lot of people got drunk at, but I just couldn't bring myself to be happy this Christmas Eve and I couldn't bring myself to get drunk or stay merry or anything like that.

I just couldn't help thinking about Mrs. Buchanan and how she must feel when she gets a telegram saying her husband is dead . . . on Christmas Day, or how his parents feel when they get their telegram."

Larry was grounded for three days because his ears were blocked and as a consolation for flying on Christmas, they gave me the next day off. Chuck got the day off too.

We slept in and had an early lunch. About 3 o'clock somebody came into the bunker and asked, "Are you guys Cavalier Two-three and Two-four?"

"Yeah, why?" I answered.

"I'm from the *Stars and Stripes*. I'd like to interview the two of you and ah, Mr. Frazier," he replied.

"For what?" Larry asked.

"It's about the action that took place yesterday. I hear you ran into some trouble up north of Tay Ninh."

"No," Larry said. "Trouble ran into us!"

The guy smiled and started asking all sorts of questions.

"I'm sorry," I told him. "For answers to some of your questions, you'll have to go to the S-2 shop. I don't know how much they want us to say."

"Do you realize that you guys got the only kills in the division on Christmas Day?" he asked.

"No, we didn't," Larry replied not amused at the question.

"You sure did. Do you want to tell me about it?" he asked.

"No, we don't," I stated emphatically.

"It'll make a great story," he said.

Larry stood up and pointed to the door. Glaring at the reporter, he demanded, "No! It won't, so fuck off!"

Sensing our mood, he did.

Chapter 22

To Tay Ninh

More "good news" was delivered on the twenty-sixth of December. Captain Rainwater, who was still the acting Red, was the messenger. "Gentlemen, I've just come from the daily briefing. On the twenty-eighth we're moving to Tay Ninh," he told us.

The response came in the form of everybody talking at once with a tirade of profanity.

"At ease!" Ross commanded. "I don't like it any more than you do, but the bottom line is, like it or not, we're moving. I suggest you pack your stuff and have it ready tomorrow night. A Chinook has been laid on to carry our personal gear to Tay Ninh."

"Where the hell are we going to live?" somebody asked.

"We're going to play Army," Ross told us. Our accommodation will be GP medium tents that we will erect in vacant Chinook revetments on the Manchu pad."

More protests.

"We are going to have to build our own bunkers. There's no water and no electricity. We'll have to fill our own sandbags and pull our own security. The only other U.S. unit at Tay Ninh, as you know, is the 187th. We'll be messing with them and using their showers. There aren't enough cots to go around right now, so some of us might be sleeping on empty sandbags for a while."

"Our security force is eighty-six Regional Force ARVNs who man the green line. The next closest friendlies are about fifty clicks away in Lai Khe. And with that happy thought gentlemen, this meeting is adjourned."

Ross stayed behind to share our bitches and moans. He wasn't at all happy either.

Activity in the new AO picked up rapidly. With three more KBH on the twenty-sixth, we got six kills in two days, more than we'd got since Bill Cahill was killed in October.

We had a fairly quiet day on the twenty-seventh, but not so the 187th. They sent some aircraft out into the Dog's Head area and got several slicks shot up and one of their door gunners was killed. They were feeling pretty low when they got back at the end of the day.

When I got back from flying I found fresh blood on my chinstrap. The rash that I had been previously grounded for was back with a vengeance. Raw and extremely itchy, it bled at the touch. I had an appointment with the dentist the morning of the twenty-eighth and he told me to go straight to our flight surgeon and get it treated. Our new flight surgeon, Capt. Marty Kaplan, cleaned the area with an antiseptic disinfectant of some sort that almost sent me through the ceiling. It burned till I was almost in tears. Next, he coated it with an ointment and told me to be sure to reapply it at least twice a day. The ointment was cold and soothing. Doc Kaplan grounded me for the rest of the year . . . all four days of it, and I was given a profile that prohibited me from shaving for two weeks.

To say I was disappointed about being grounded would be a lie. With our new situation, most of the guys were looking for reasons to get grounded. Phuoc Vinh, with all of its inadequacies, seemed like the Ritz compared with Tay Ninh. At Phuoc Vinh, I spent the day trying to organize my R&R. I was entitled to two and I fully intended to take them. Larry and I made plans to go to Bangkok together. Some of the others had been there and had fallen in love with the place, or at least with the Thai women. After being wounded and going to Hawaii to see my folks, this R&R was going to be my chance to let go of some frustrations and have some real fun. The allocations were in and we got a reporting date of January 20 to be at Camp Alpha at Tan Son Nhut.

We also stocked up on ammo for our time in Tay Ninh. Larry and I acquired sixteen hundred rounds of ammo for our CAR-15s and a box of fragmentation grenades. We wanted to be well prepared for all events.

The S-2 insisted that the intelligence they had received clearly indicated that an NVA battalion was preparing to cross the border north of Tay Ninh. While our Pink teams kept finding trails that showed recent use and other indicators, the enemy itself remained elusive. We all worried about the reports. No friendlies were anywhere close to us and if this phantom battalion made its way across the border undetected and launched an offensive against Tay Ninh, there wasn't a lot to counter their attack. We continued to work the border in hopes of finding the enemy before it found us.

On New Year's Eve my melancholy showed in my words. *"It's New Year's Eve they tell us! It's kind of hard for us to comprehend it is anything but another day.*

We watched the Bob Hope Christmas Special from Long Binh on TV, which I'm sure will be on TV there shortly. I wish I could tell you how it feels to sit and watch and then look to your side to your friends all sitting with tears in their eyes. If only I could make you realize how lonely and depressing it is over here. It just seems to me like I should be home with the family at this time of the year.

Yeah, you'll probably watch Bob Hope's show when it comes on TV and say how great it is. But then you can't understand all of the side comments he makes that mean so much to us.

One thing he said was really great. He said that all the politicians in Washington, D.C., sit over their paperwork and say they want peace. Then he looked at all of us and said, 'But you're the ones fighting and watching your friends die. What the hell do they think you want?'

You should have heard the response.

Yeah, its New Year's . . . at home!

All I can say is thank God I've only got seventy-two more days to go. I'd go absolutely batshit if it were any longer. Won't it be fun trying to readapt to civilization? It'll be just great, but what about guys like Tommy Whiddon, or Kevin Frye, or Bill Cahill? Guys who died playing our older, knowledgeable world leader's Southeast Asia war games.

You're going to have to bear with me when I get home because I'm afraid I have changed in a lot of ways. There is a lot of stuff I used to tolerate before I got here and found out what living and dying is all about. You remember when Bobby and I were waiting at Lockheed for our plane when those guys he knew started making cracks about our uniforms and being warmongers?

Anyway, let it happen again, from anybody, even as a joke and I guarantee you it will only happen once!

Wow! You should see this place. Nobody has any firecrackers or pyrotechnics but the sky just came alive. Have you ever seen a sky full of parachute flares, hand flares, star clusters, M-16 tracers, M-60 tracers, etc.? It is really wild!

No fireworks, so the next best thing is machine guns and assault rifles. What a year 1970 has been!"

We had champagne at the club that night, but nobody was jovial. There were only a few Charlie Troopers left in Phuoc Vinh, mostly admin types and those of us that, for one reason or another, either weren't required at Tay Ninh or were grounded. With the shortage of cots and amenities, it made sense for non-essential troops to stay in Phuoc Vinh. We had aircraft in maintenance and although I wasn't supposed to fly I could do ground runs and leak checks without fastening my chinstrap.

We kept one of the Snakes airworthy and fully armed in the event the troop got hit at night and the guys couldn't get to the aircraft. Rash or not, grounded or not, chinstrap fastened or not, if the troop got hit I would be airborne without question.

The first day of 1971 was as big a fiasco as Christmas Day. A truce had been declared for the day, another cease-fire, and another day that the enemy could take the first shot. True to his word, Doc released me on New Year's Day. My involvement in the war that day was to move myself to Tay Ninh. My gear had gone on the Chinook with the rest of the troops a few days back. With Bones in the front seat, I lifted off shortly after lunch for the thirty-minute flight to Tay Ninh. I flew over the base before landing and located our tents in the revetments next to the green line on the northern perimeter of Tay Ninh. It looked pretty Spartan and once I shut down and found our tent I realized just how Spartan it really was. There were cots crammed together in every direction imaginable with barely enough room to fit between them. Everything was covered with dirt and dust. And as Song Be had gargantuan rats, Tay Ninh had mosquitoes the size of hummingbirds, and they were everywhere! The guys saved me a cot and my dufflebag was there waiting for me. The first thing I did was erect my mosquito net and tuck it in under my bedding. Then I took a can of Raid and sprayed the whole cot until it became invisible under a cloud. Leaving the area until it aired out, I went over to the makeshift TOC in the next tent over.

Joel Hageman was in ops and I asked him to brief me on what had been going on. The story was the same: we were expecting an NVA battalion to cross the border and our mission was to find and neutralize them.

While I was talking to Joel one of the LOHs was shot at by a B-40. No one had been spotted and even after the Cobra had expended some rockets on the area from where the rocket had been fired, no bodies or blood trails could be found. B-40s were indicative of a hard-core enemy element. We hadn't found anything to indicate the size of the element so we didn't know if we were making contact with a lead element, a recon patrol, or folks who were creating a diversion while the main body of their force circumnavigated the area we were working.

January 2 was my first full day flying in the AO since the move. Our teams worked the border so that we almost overlapped. If the NVA were contemplating a border crossing we were bound and determined to catch them in the act. My team had been out for thirty minutes when we got our first kills. We stayed in contact throughout the day. The enemy was definitely in the area, but the main body continued to elude us.

During the night of the third we took our first incoming. The rounds impacted in an area where some engineers were and five of them were wounded. We grew increasingly jumpy. We didn't have the luxury of our bunkers. Across from the revetments that we called home were a few derelict bunkers left from the unit that used to occupy our area previously. They weren't the best, but they were a damn sight better than nothing.

Since being wounded I was particularly uncomfortable during incoming and the fact that now all I had over my head was a piece of canvas didn't help matters. After what turned out to be a sleepless night, I had a first light pitch pull. My team was assigned an area east of Thien Ngon. Brian Holcomb was in my front seat and our scout was Capt. Rudy Gutierrez. Rudy was the new scout platoon leader and a by-the-book new guy who hadn't gained the trust or respect of his platoon yet. In actual fact, he was about as popular with his troops as Captain Sides was with us.

I liked Rudy and I liked working with him. He didn't take the chances that most of the experienced scouts would take, but he knew what he was doing and, true to the Charlie Troop ethos, he was always up for a good fight. We worked the area the entire day and kept turning up trails and eventually a bunker complex. One-six had taken fire out of this area the day before and after several of our Snakes had worked the area over, we got one KBH and uncovered a few bunkers. Our mission that day was to exploit the area to try to determine exactly what we had. Rudy and his crew found a few blood trials in the area, but to our frustration, we still couldn't find the elusive battalion.

Each day in the new AO we got a few kills, but they were widespread and all we were finding were small pockets of NVA troops. We were beginning to pooh-pooh the intelligence information about the border crossing, but the AO was very active. Once again we were flying long hours and word had come down that division had requested us to overfly periodic and scheduled inspections on the aircraft just to keep teams in the AO. It seemed to me that the Army's needs changed when it suited them. Standing units down and releasing soldiers from active duty upon DEROS was at one extreme. At the other was moving us to Tay Ninh to live in tents and asking us to ignore required inspections.

Had my aircraft not been inspected when it was the last time, the disintegrating trunnion bearings in the head would not have been found and chances were high that I might have been nothing more than a memory and another statistic by this time. Suffice it to say that we refused to accept any aircraft that was overdue anything.

On Tuesday, January 5, Rudy and I went back into the same area. It made sense for the same team to go back to the same area. It provided continuity and avoided covering the same ground. It was also easy for the same scout to notice whether anything had been moved during the night.

"Two-four, White, there's been a lot of movement down here over night," Rudy announced.

"How do you know?" I asked him for confirmation.

"Lots of footprints and some wheel tracks. Smoke still coming from camp-fires too," Rudy told me. "They're down here and they were here only a short time ago. They just put the fires out."

"Roger. Keep the eyes peeled," I told him.

"Brian, make sure we have a good accurate grid on his location and keep the turret ready," I instructed through the intercom.

"Roger that," he replied.

We flew our first fuel load without finding anything moving. "I'm down to bingo fuel, White," I announced on the radio. "Climb out to the north and let's go get some gas."

"Okay, but mark our location. I want to start in the same spot when we get back," Rudy told us.

We refueled and before I climbed back into my seat I walked over to the LOH. Rudy was still strapped in as his crew chief filled the fuel tank with JP4. I didn't have that luxury.

"What do you think you've got down there?" I asked having plugged into the CE's avionics chord.

"There are gooks down there," Rudy said as I stood next to him. "Lots of footprints, lots of use. They're there and we're going to find the little bastards."

"Okay. Just be careful when we get back there and keep talking to me. I want to know what the hell is going on down there," I told him.

"Count on it," he said as he winked at me.

I patted Rudy on the shoulder and said, "Watch yourself, bud," before unplugging and going back to my aircraft. As I approached I gave Brian a circling finger signal and he began to roll the throttle up to 6,600 rpm.

Rudy took off with me on his left wing. We approached the area and reconfirmed that we had a free fire clearance in the area. "Okay, White," I called, "You have clearance to recon by fire. We're going to test out the turret again before you descend. My x-ray will vector you back into the area. Let's find these assholes."

"Roger that."

Brian tested the twin miniguns in the turret on the first detent. Each gun spat out a short burst at a rate of two thousand rounds per minute.

"Okay, White, the turret is fully functional. Go get them," I told him.

Brian gave Rudy vectors back into the area and the LOH descended to treetop level and began to reduce its forward speed.

"TAKING FIRE!" Rudy called as he flew along the side of an open area.

Instinctively we reacted. Brian had rounds impacting the area as I slammed the left pedal. The Cobra rolled onto its left side as I eased the cyclic forward. I selected the 35 mm Vulcan and started spraying the tree line.

"We're going down," Rudy called. "Cover us, we're going for the hole in the trees!"

"Down bird! Down bird!" Brian called over the fox mike.

I hauled back on the cyclic as the Cobra rocketed back into the air. As the airspeed approached forty knots I kicked the pedal and instantaneously we fell to the left in a hammerhead turn that resulted in a ninety-degree dive. I selected outboard on the wing store arm switch and both on the rocket pair selector switch. We were diving straight down at the area the LOH was headed for as I punched the button on my cyclic stick.

Seven pairs of rockets impacted the area just before Rudy descended into it. His engine flamed out as he was making his approach and they hit pretty hard. The aircraft stayed upright as it came to a stop about thirty feet from the trees. Rudy and his crew scrambled out the right side, away from the tree line.

"Fuck me!" yelled Brian. "Look at that tree line!"

There were NVA soldiers in full combat gear running along the treeline toward the downed LOH. I switched to guard on the radio as the beeper came alive.

"Walk the minis in from the south away from the LOH!" I instructed Brian.

BEEP BEEP BEEP

"Beeper, beeper, come up voice!" I called.

"Get on to ops. Launch the Blues and get us some help out here," I told Brian.

"Already done that!" he said. I should have known.

"Two-four, this is White," Rudy called. "What the hell are you shooting at?" he yelled. "That was pretty close!"

"You okay?" I asked.

"Roger that. We're all okay," he told me.

"Okay, listen up White. We've got gooks in the tree line to your west. Take up a defensive position away from the aircraft and hug the ground. I'm going to have to shoot over your heads if I'm going to get these fuckers. I can only get them if we run east to west. I'm not happy about it but I don't have a choice. Now get moving!"

Brian continued to hose the area with the miniguns. "Okay, Brian. I'm going to walk the Vulcan in from the south too. Once I'm on target I'll switch to rockets."

"Man, don't miss," Brian pleaded. "Our guys are right in the line of fire."

"I know, but I don't have any choice," I said.

I pulled the trigger as the gun spat to life shooting flames out the front. Every fifth 20mm round was a tracer so I could see where the rounds were impacting. The first rounds impacted wide to the left.

"Okay White," I yelled, "Kiss the ground!"

Turning slightly to the right, the rounds walked on to the target. I switched to inboard and held the button down as rockets left the tube. Some of the NVA were killed immediately, some disappeared in a cloud of blood and human flesh, and others reversed their course and ran back in the direction from which they came.

"All right!" Brian yelled as he chased those retreating with the miniguns.

"Two-four, Four-one," WO1 Sammy Hinch called.

"Hey Four-one, get your ass out here man. We need to get these guys out of here," I told him.

Before long, the air was full of Charlie Troop aircraft. I refused to let the lift recovery ship go in until we were sure that the LZ was secure.

"Okay White, the Cavalry is here. Can you see or hear anything down there now?" I asked.

"Yeah, we hear helicopters. Lots of them and it's the best sound in the world," he said.

"Save it, man!" I told Rudy. "Can you guys cover the lift in before the Blues get on the ground?"

"Yeah, just tell us where to concentrate our fire," Rudy said.

"Okay, stand by," I told him.

"Brian, I don't like this," I said into the intercom. "The only clear shot we have is to the southeast. Sammy's going to have to approach south to north and that means we have to run in in the opposite direction or worse, across his flight path."

"I know," Brian said. "But we haven't got any choice."

"Okay Four-one, come up guard and listen out. Have you got the LOH?" I asked.

"Rog," he replied keeping radio traffic to a minimum.

"Good. Now listen up gang. White and his crew are about fifty feet east of the aircraft. They're hunkered down. Your approach will be south to north along the east side of the LZ. We've got gooks on the west, okay? We've engaged them but I have no way of knowing how effective we were," I briefed.

Another Pink team approached the area. The scout was WO1 Bruce Campbell. Bruce hadn't even got down to the treetops when we yelled "Taking fire!" He was still at seven hundred feet when the 51-cals found their target. Campbell's LOH took hits through the vertical stabilizer.

"Shit!" I yelled. "Okay guys we have to move fast or we're not going to get them out."

Bruce took his damaged LOH back to Thien Ngon.

"Okay, guns, follow my lead and watch where you're shooting. We have friendlies on the ground. Four-one, we're going to be shooting across the nose of your aircraft. Hug the east tree line. White, when I say 'now' I want you to pop a smoke and then open up with everything you have on the tree line on the southwest corner. Let me know when you're ready, Four-one," I told him.

So many things were going through my mind at that point. "What haven't we thought of, Brian?" I asked. I was so grateful to have an experienced x-ray in my front seat.

"I think we've covered all the bases," he replied. "Now all we have to do is pray it works!"

"Two-four, Four-one, I am one mile final. Give me vectors," Sammy called.

"Handle that," I told Brian over the intercom.

"White, pop smoke. I say again pop smoke and get ready for extraction. I don't want the lift ship on the ground any longer than they have to be. Pop smoke and open fire . . . NOW! I'm in hot!" I called.

A red smoke appeared in the LZ. It was closer to the LOH than I had expected.

"I have the smoke," Sammy announced.

Rockets impacted the area from where the scout ships had taken fire. The tree line erupted as rockets from the three Cobras on station kept pounded away until the rescue operation had been completed.

Sammy Hinch's UH-1 was on the ground for about five seconds. White and his crew scrambled on board. "I'm coming out!" Sammy yelled.

The whole operation went like clockwork.

I escorted Four-one and my downed scout crew back to Thien Ngon.

I landed just behind the UH-1. As I was climbing out, Capt. Rudy Gutierrez and his crew ran back to the Cobra and in the bright sunshine of the afternoon and with the noise of the running helicopters, the four of us embraced one another. We danced around hugging and laughing while Brian sat in the front seat of the Snake holding the controls.

Over all the noise and in the excitement of a successful rescue came the bellowing voice of Brian Holcomb. "ALL RIGHT!" Brian yelled. "ALL RIGHT!" Sitting in the front seat of the Cobra, he gave us all a big thumbs up and a smile as tears rolled down his cheeks.

We were very lucky to get White and his crew out without injury. The aircraft was recovered and written off as a combat loss. Most of us who had been involved in the contact the previous day were given the day off on the sixth. It had been an intense day and we were mentally fatigued. We spent the day in the 187th's O club and enjoyed the cool air provided by the air conditioner.

Larry and I discussed our up-and-coming R&R. Pappy was with us and told us that because of the current tactical situation it was very doubtful that two Red ACs would be allowed to go at the same time. The troop simply couldn't afford to lose us both at once.

Brian piped up, "Hey Two-four, if they'll let me, I'll take Larry's slot and go with you!"

"That's up to the XO, but it sounds good to me."

Pappy said he'd fix it and Larry could go as soon as we got back. Larry was happy with the arrangement and decided that, since we weren't going together, he would try to get an allocation for Hawaii and fly Trish over again.

The conversation turned to the AO and all of the activity. There was a lot of talk and speculation that all of the activity we had been encountering was a build-up for the approaching Tet holiday. After what had happened in 1968, I think everybody was on edge and I was very thankful that during Tet my young ass was going to be in Thailand.

Brian and I flew together again on the seventh. Red Cloud was our little bird pilot. One-six was flying as Larry's little bird. We were in a relatively quiet area when the down-bird call came, 12.7mm anti-aircraft guns had hit One-six. The NVA were getting serious. Fortunately no one was injured and Chuck and his crew were extracted within minutes. Larry escorted them home while my team stayed on station. He briefed me on his way back to Thien Ngon.

"There are fifty-ones down there, Two-four, one for sure and maybe two. Make sure Red Cloud keeps his speed up," Larry suggested.

"I have a solid copy, Two-three," I replied in our jargon. "Why don't you re-arm and re-fuel and come on back out here? I have a feeling I can use some help. In the mean time, I'm going to get Tac Air to nape this place."

"BREAK LEFT!" Brian yelled.

I immediately rolled into a diving left turn and headed for the treetops as 51-cal tracers raced down our right side.

"Shit, that was close!" I told Brian.

"Hey man," Brian said as I looked at him through his rearview mirror. "There are two guns down there, maybe three."

"Okay, let's not fuck with them. We'll get a section of fighters out here. Three, this is Two-four."

"Go ahead, Two-four," Joel Hageman replied.

"Okay, the area where One-six got hit is hot. We've got two fifty-ones for sure and possibly three. Keep the lift birds and others out of the area and crank me up a section of fast movers, will ya?" I requested.

"Roger that, Two-four."

A short while later Rash Two-six checked in. George Lamperti worked with us in Cambodia when the OV-10s were part of our team. It had been a long time since I'd seen or spoken to him.

"Cavalier Two-four, this is Rash Two-six," he called.

"Hey Two-six, how the hell are you?" I asked.

"You still here?" George asked. "I thought you'd gone home already."

"Yeah, well I almost did a few months back. In a bag! I'm still here, but not for much longer," I told him.

"Me too. I'm getting short," he claimed.

"Listen old friend, this area is hotter than shit. We've had one little bird shot down already and they've been taking pot shots at us at altitude. We've confirmed two fifty-ones, but I think there may be more. My little bird is on the deck, but I have him holding well clear of the guns," I briefed. "Can we get a flight of fast movers out here with some nape?" I inquired.

"They're on their way," George told me. "I expect them to be checking in any minute."

More tracers raced into the sky and for the first time we were able to confirm three guns. They were set up in a triangle so no matter which way an aircraft broke, one of the guns would have it in their field of fire.

"Okay Two-six, these guys are playing for keeps. There are three guns down there. I say again, three guns."

"Good copy. Stand by. The fighters are checking in," George reported.

"Hey Two-four, Two-three, I am back en route to the party," Larry called.

"Okay. Rash Two-six is on station. These gook bastards are shooting at us so watch yourself," I told him.

"Well, well, well," Larry responded. "Did I hear you say there are three guns down there?"

"You did. These guys aren't screwing around."

"Okay Two-four. Rash Two-six, I have a flight of F-100s on top. Who is going to mark the target for me?" he asked.

Under normal circumstances, the LOH would drop a smoke to identify the target. The Rash bird would then roll in with marking rounds that the fighters would use as their target. Three 51-caliber anti-aircraft guns, however, were anything but normal circumstances.

"Two-three, Two-four. If you'll cover me I'll mark the center of mass. I don't want my little bird going into that hornet's nest. We've already had one LOH shot down."

"I know," Larry stated. "And he'll be back out here as soon as he can get a ride to Tay Ninh and get another aircraft."

"You've got to be shitting me!" I exclaimed. "Doesn't One-six know when to call it a day?"

"Nah. All getting shot down did was piss him off. You know One-six, he doesn't quit until he gets even," Larry said.

"Right. Rash Two-six, this is Two-four. I'm in for the mark," I announced over the radio.

"Cover our break with the miniguns, Brian. I'm going to break low and early and try to stay out of their sights," I told him. "Man, I am getting too short for this shit!"

"Son of a bitch!" Larry said as I began my dive.

All three guns were shooting at us. "Breaking right!" I called after punching off a couple of rockets.

"Two-six is in," George called. "Cover me!"

Larry and I both covered his break as the guns were now directed at the OV-10. Below us, his white phosphorus rockets exploded in billowy clouds of white.

We all moved off to the north to wait for the fighters, but nothing happened.

"Hey, Two-six, Two-four. What happened to your boys?" I asked.

A few minutes passed before I got a response.

"Uh, Two-four, this is Two-six, the Sabers are RTB, I say again, RTB. They're going home!"

"Going home?" I asked. "What do you mean they're going home?"

"If you want to know the truth," he began, "Lead says that the ground to air is too intense for them to risk their aircraft."

"Too intense!" I yelled. "Chickenshit motherfuckers. It isn't any less intense for us. Somebody has to take these guns out!" I pleaded.

"I'm really sorry," George said, obviously embarrassed.

Brian muttered, "Air Force. More like the Air Farce!"

In actual fact, two airstrikes were aborted that morning.

"Well, Two-four," Larry interjected, "I guess it's up to you and me."

We went back and re-armed with nails and after two more loads of fuel and another three plus hours of flying, the 51s were no more. Neither Larry nor I took any hits during the shoot-out. When it was all over the Blues were inserted to check out the area. We were all surprised to find out that the tripods that the 51s were mounted on were fitted with leg shackles. The gunners were shackled to the guns so they wouldn't run. I wondered who they had pissed off to draw that duty.

The rash on my neck was acting up again so I went back to Phuoc Vinh on the briefing bird to see the doctor on the seventh.

On Friday morning, January 8, I was asleep in my bunk when the orderly room clerk came and woke me up.

"They need you up at Tay Ninh, sir," he said as I rubbed the sleep from my eyes.

"What for?" I questioned. "I can't fly. Doc grounded me again."

"I don't know, sir. I was just told to get you on an aircraft back there ASAP." I got dressed and went down to the flight line where a UH-1 was just cranking up.

General Putnam arrived from Phuoc Vinh shortly after we did. We stood in formation in front of our tents. I received my second DFC that morning and many others were decorated too. My orders were to follow, complete with mistakes.

General Orders number 2279. Award of the Distinguished Flying Cross.

The following award is announced.

Zahn, Randy R. Chief Warrant Officer CW2, United States Army. Troop C, 1st Squadron (Airmobile) 9th Cavalry.

Awarded: Distinguished Flying Cross (1st Oak Leaf Cluster)

Date of Action: 10 January 1971.

Theater: Republic of Vietnam.

Authority: By direction of the President, under the provisions of the Act of Congress, approved 2 July 1926.

Reason: For heroism while participating in aerial flight evidenced by voluntary actions above and beyond the call of duty in the Republic of Vietnam. Chief Warrant Officer Zahn distinguished himself by exceptionally valorous action on 10 January 1971 in the Republic of Vietnam. While on a visual reconnaissance mission, Chief Warrant Officer Zahn's aircraft began taking intense antiaircraft fire from several enemy emplacements. Realizing that these positions must be destroyed, Chief Warrant Officer Zahn with complete disregard for his own safety attacked the hostile fortifications. His courageous actions resulted in complete destruction of dangerous antiaircraft sites. Chief Warrant Officer Zahn's outstanding flying ability and devotion to duty were in keeping with the highest traditions of the military service and reflect great credit upon himself, his unit, and the United States Army.

Signed G.E. Newman, Colonel, GS, Chief of Staff.

This action actually took place on January 7, 1971. Another big contact followed on the tenth for which I was put in for another award. I never got it. The reason on this award is correct, but the date is that of the subsequent action.

After all of the awards had been pinned on and citations read out, General Putnam addressed the entire troop: "Gentlemen, you may have heard that the Cav may be standing down soon. That means many of you will be going home. Some of you may be re-assigned to other units and for that I am sorry.

"Having served with Charlie Troop you are elite. As a matter of fact you are in one of the most elite and highly decorated units in the history of the United States Army.

"When those of you who will be going home depart you wear those Stetson Cavalry hats and you wear them proudly. There are some that will tell you they are not authorized headgear and they may ask you to remove them.

"Bullshit! Until you sign in to your new unit, you are still assigned to Charlie Troop, First Squadron, Ninth Cavalry of the First Cavalry Division and you *are* authorized to wear them and gentlemen, wear them proudly.

"If any MP has the audacity or the balls to ask you to remove them and they threaten you with a DR, you tell them to send it to me."

Showing not a lot of military discipline, we cheered as we stood in formation.

On the tenth Red Cloud was on the deck VRing the area where the anti-aircraft guns had been. There were still things to be found, and we didn't have a reputation for leaving anything behind. We were checking the area out prior to inserting a recon platoon. In another area not far away, WO1 Al Sellers and Captain Williams had just caught seven NVA in the open. They were now nailed to the ground. As we flew overhead the LOH, Brian and I were chatting inconsequentially. Looking south toward Tay Ninh we saw a plume of black smoke rising into the air.

"What the hell is that?" I asked.

"I don't know," Brian replied. "But it looks pretty close to Tay Ninh."

From where we were we couldn't actually see the base camp, but we knew its location with respect to Nui Ba Den, the Black Virgin Mountain, that dominated the terrain.

"Three, this is Two-four," I called.

"Go ahead, Two-four."

"We have a plume of black smoke somewhere down in your area. Is everything okay there at base?" I inquired.

"Roger that, Two-four, we're fine here," Joel told me.

"OK, I'm going to go and check it out then," I told him. "One-nine, Two-four, come on up to altitude and follow me. We need to check out some smoke in the vicinity of tango November."

"Roger that, Two-four!"

I waited for Mel to come up to altitude before heading south. From two thousand feet we had a pretty good vantage point, but what we found when we arrived at the scene was totally unexpected. From about ten miles out we could see several fires along Highway 22. Located between Tay Ninh and Thien Ngon was an abandoned Special Forces camp at the unused Trai Bi airstrip. An ARVN convoy, on their way to Thien Ngon, was just passing the deserted airstrip when all hell broke loose.

The area around the camp consisted of mostly elephant grass and low scrub. About two hundred meters west of the road was a wooded area, quite apart from the main jungle. Getting to or from the wooded area was impossible without being completely exposed.

I dove down to see what was happening as we approached the fires. The convoy had been ambushed and there were three deuce and a halfs and a V-100 Duck on fire. ARVN soldiers were shooting to the west and some still on the road did their best to keep their heads down. One soldier, hiding behind the northernmost vehicle, stood up as we passed over and pointed to the west.

"Brian, lay down some minigun along the west edge of the road. Keep it wide in case there are any friendlies in there," I told him.

The miniguns spat to life and we were confronted with the most unbelievable sight I had seen since arriving in-country. The entire grassy area between the road and the wooded area came to life as NVA soldiers got up in an attempt to run back to the cover of the woods.

"Holy shit!" I yelled. "Three, this is Two-four, divert all the teams down to the Trai Bi airstrip. We've got gooks in the open, lots of them. They've hit an ARVN convoy!"

Flying low level to keep my exposure to a minimum and maximize the effectiveness of the fleshettes, the NVA began to fall. The 20mm shot flames as it roared into action. Gently kicking the pedals as I strafed the area got incredible results. People fell like bowling pins. I couldn't tell whether they had been hit or were diving for cover. It looked as if the entire field just picked up the grass around their waists and started running.

More teams joined in the turkey shoot as we rotated back to Thien Ngon to re-arm. Two heavy fire teams of Blue Max Cobras were called in and even the Air Force decided to play that day. In all we spent close to six hours fighting it out with the NVA and when it was all over, the wooded area no longer existed. It had been leveled. We were officially credited with fifty-two kills. At the end of the fight, we had captured a complete 51-caliber anti-aircraft gun, six POWs, a 75 mm recoilless rifle, and an 81mm mortar. Chuck Frazier and his crew captured a POW by themselves as well.

We were all elated when we shut down back at Tay Ninh for the night. Everyone was still buzzing from the day's contact and the adrenaline rush. We were like a bunch of kids when we got to the tents. A short while after we arrived Captain Sides walked in, having just returned from his Vung Tau Cobra transition. He had heard all of the activity as he monitored the radio from the TOC during the afternoon. He didn't say anything to anyone when he walked in. He went and sat down on a bunk that had been added to the melee, and listened.

Finally, he spoke. "Did you lose your razor blade, Two-four?"

Because of my profile from the doctor, I hadn't shaved in two weeks. Larry nicknamed me "the Rabbi" because of the short beard that had attached itself to my face.

"I'm fine, sir. Thanks for asking, and welcome back," I replied to his asinine comment.

"We aren't in the Navy, Mr. Zahn! I suggest you go and shave that thing off your face . . . now," he commanded.

"Wrong again, sir. I am on a medical profile due to a severe case of heat rash on my neck. According to Doc Kaplan I am not supposed to shave. Would you like to see my FL 89?" I asked.

"The only thing I want to see is that growth off of your face," he said.

"Then I suggest you talk to Doc Kaplan, Captain, because until he gives me an all-clear you're just going to have to get used to it."

"Fine!" Captain Sides barked as he stood up. "You go and see the Doc right now!"

"Yes, sir! Anything you say, sir," I mocked. "But he happens to be in Phuoc Vinh. Gee, I'm so glad you're back."

"I want you on the next aircraft to Phuoc Vinh. Do you understand?" he ordered.

Van butted in, "Hey Dick, lighten up. Who the hell put a bee in your bonnet?"

"You stay out of this, lieutenant. This is none of your concern!" Captain Sides yelled at Van. "And to you guys it's either Red, Captain Sides, or sir. You got that!"

Not knowing what provoked the outburst I eased off. The captain was obviously upset about something and our continued counterattack wasn't helping the situation. Captain Sides just stood glaring at me and all I could do was smile. He stormed out of the tent.

"Bye Dick . . . head," somebody said from behind me, and we burst out laughing.

The tech supply Huey was leaving shortly for Phuoc Vinh and not being one to disobey an order I was on it.

Doc Kaplan examined my neck when I got back.

"Is there something fundamentally wrong with you, Mr. Zahn?" Doc asked. "Your neck is infected. What the hell are you doing wearing your helmet? You are only exacerbating the problem. You are grounded. Do you understand? You are *not* to wear a helmet and you are *not* to shave, and if your platoon leader has a problem with that, then that's his problem."

Doc grounded me for two days initially, January 11 and 12, with instructions to come to see him before I went back to Tay Ninh. I went over to division headquarters that evening and had the first hot shower I had had since returning from R&R in September, and it was wonderful. That night I went to the club and was surprised at my luck. There was a floor show on and I proceeded to get shitfaced.

I made a tape to the folks before retiring that night . . . one I would later have to apologize for.

"I'd had a real bad few days. I'd flown over 16 hours in three days, got no sleep the night before, we got into a big contact and we killed a lot of people that day. I had been shot at a lot and two of my friends got shot down.

That night after returning to Phuoc Vinh, we had a floor show and I got drunk.

There are times that you just have to say, "fuck it" and let it all hang out to maintain some sense of sanity.

My platoon leader has a hard-on for me for some reason that I can't explain. Maybe it's because I know more about his job than he does. I don't know.

All I do know is that I am getting too short to put up with his shit."

I went back to see Doc Kaplan on the morning of the thirteenth.

"When do you go on R&R?" he asked.

"I'm supposed to be at Bién Hoa on the seventeenth and I go on the twentieth," I answered. "Why?"

"I'm grounding you until the sixteenth. You leave on the seventeenth, which means you won't be back until when?"

"All things being equal, I should be back here on the twenty-eighth, depending on transportation from Bién Hoa," I told Doc.

"Good! That should give you plenty of time to get rid of this damn infection. You can shave before you leave. Actually you better shave before you leave," he winked.

"Why?" I asked him.

"I hear that Thai women don't like facial hair," he said.

Most of us had been recommended for awards for the ambush on the tenth and most people got them. I didn't, despite being the first Cobra on station and despite the fact that I had been recommended for a Silver Star. I was beyond caring. I didn't have to go back to Tay Ninh before R&R and I didn't have to put up with Captain Side's bullshit. Brian returned to Phuoc Vinh on the sixteenth and the following morning we caught a ride down to Cav Rear.

Chapter 23

Routine, Rancor, Resolve

Our week in Bangkok went far quicker than either of us would have liked, but on January 28 we arrived back in-country and back in Phuoc Vinh. The troop was still up at Tay Ninh. The bunker was quiet compared with what it had been before we moved. Larry had been back and left me a note before going on R&R. He was off to Hawaii to see Trish again. I unpacked my gear and cleaned up the place a bit before going to the club for dinner. Doc Kaplan was there, "Hey Randy, welcome back. How's the neck?"

"To be honest with you Doc, I just got back from Bangkok and I haven't paid much attention to it," I told him.

"Well, after you eat come by and let me have a look at it."

At 8:30 I walked into Doc Kaplan's bunker. "Come with me," he said leading the way to the aid station.

He poked and prodded and hemmed and hawed before announcing, "You're grounded!"

"What do you mean I'm grounded?" I asked.

"Yep. Forty-eight hours . . . and you are not to shave anymore. Do you understand?" he asked.

"Oh, that will thrill Captain Sides," I replied.

"Screw him," Doc stated. "If he has a problem with it, you tell him to come and see me."

I wasn't real enthused about returning to Tay Ninh, but return I did. There had been another big contact the day after the ambush and the troop had been credited with another twenty kills to make our total seventy-two for January 10 and 11. We didn't really know what was going on. We were not sure whether they were using the 51s as a diversion to infiltrate their troops around our AO, or they had simply stepped on their dicks. Later in the month we captured a POW who helped us piece together the puzzle. The 271st NVA Battalion came across the border as Intelligence predicted, only they came across a few days before we had arrived. They originally had orders to launch an offensive on Tay Ninh in preparation for Tet, the Lunar New Year, but that had been changed at the last minute. They were within striking distance when they got orders to abort their mission.

Hanoi had received word that U.S. troops were starting to stand-down and they felt that by launching another Tet offensive we would reverse ourselves and start throwing more troops back into the country. That was the last thing they wanted. While they were waiting further orders the convoy came by and the temptation was too great, so they ambushed it.

Officially we were credited with fifty-two kills but the POW told us that we had, in fact, annihilated the entire battalion, more than two hundred men including some very high-ranking officers.

In the contact on the eleventh, the Troop had come into contact with a company-sized element of NVA from the Seventh NVA Division. Credited with the twenty kills that we could actually count, we had really wiped out the entire company.

NVA intelligence was often as bad as ours. They had known that the 187th and a few ARVN soldiers were at Tay Ninh, but they had not been told that Charlie Troop had moved to Tay Ninh. According to the POW remaining NVA and VC units in the area were pulling back across the Cambodian border to await replacements and reinforcement. We caught them totally off guard and they didn't know what had hit them.

The two contacts not only cost the NVA dearly in lives, but also in intelligence. We had captured a lot of documents on anti-aircraft training as well as proposed enemy ambushes and operations plans. Now we knew what we were up against. The contacts we had made were with elements of the Seventh NVA Division. The documents made reference to the fact that major enemy units including the Fifth and Ninth VC and the Seventh NVA Divisions were spread out from Kampong Cham to Snoal, just across the border from us. With this new information we were forced to reevaluate the enemy ground-to-air capabilities and modify our tactics accordingly.

There was some controversy to deal with at the same time. Many of the guys were upset. At the last impact awards ceremony the CO had been awarded a DFC.

"Why is everybody so upset about that?" I asked.

"Because he wasn't even in the air that day," Van told me. "It's a fucking joke!"

Box ticking was still the order of the day.

"Forget your razor on R&R, Mr. Zahn?" asked Capt. Jim Williams, my section leader, on our first meeting after my return.

"Jim, don't start. You know I've had a rash," I told him. "I just got back and I don't want any hassles with you or Dick, so don't give me any shit, okay? If you have a problem, talk to Doc Kaplan."

"I have a problem all right. You're the problem!" he continued. Others intervened before the conversation cum confrontation got too explosive. With forty-four days left in-country this is what I had come back to.

On the morning of February 2, I took off at first light. It was great to be back in the air. I always derived a sense of comfort from flying, and even under the circumstances that sense of comfort prevailed. We were supporting the Eighteenth ARVN Division now but nothing else had changed. I felt strangely at ease in the hostile skies over western South Vietnam.

Not a lot happened my first day back in the air. The potential was there as we located another area showing signs of recent use and we were prepared to insert the Blues to do a ground recon. The only thing that stopped us was that the ARVNs claimed they were over-committed and unable to provide a ready reaction force if the Blues got into contact. It was the shape of things to come.

Fog and haze blanketed the AO on the morning of the third. It was the NVA's free ticket. They moved freely throughout the night and mainly hid during the day. Fog, however, provided them with a natural phenomenon that tied our hands.

That day was significant in another way. President Thieu was due to visit Tay Ninh that day and we were tasked to provide security. Tensions were high that the NVA would send an assassination squad and the fact that we were unable to fly only made those tensions worse. There was a lot of pressure on us to fly that morning.

I pulled pitch as soon as the weather improved enough to do a weather check but the AO was still below limits.

"Is there a problem with the weather, Two-four?" Major Ball asked through Captain Sides.

"The cloud is still on the trees in most of the AO. Give it another hour or two to burn off. There's no way we can VR now," I reported.

"Is there any reason why we can't fly?" he asked.

"Is there any reason why we can't fly with the cloud on the trees?" I repeated not believing he had asked the question.

"Yes. There is. For one thing the little birds won't be able to VR and we wouldn't be able to get high enough to cover them even if they could. We'll be in small arms range; navigation will be impossible from that altitude—"

"So what is there to prevent us from flying?" he interrupted.

"Dick, it's pretty damn hard to cover a little bird when we can't see him. How effective do you think rockets will be from low level?" I asked him raising my voice. "We have no control over the weather. If it's below limits, it's below limits. What is the big deal?"

"The big deal is we've been tasked with a mission to provide security for the president."

"Has anyone stopped to consider that with the fog he probably won't get here anyway?" I asked. "When are you going to start backing up the decisions your aircraft commanders make? When are you going to become part of this platoon? When are you going to stop trying to score brownie points?" I asked in total frustration.

"I am not *part* of this platoon, Mr. Zahn. I am *the leader* of this platoon!" he shouted at me.

"Oh, yes, sir! So when the hell are you going to start leading?" I walked away in disgust.

The weather broke a few hours later and we took to the air. We did provide some visual reconnaissance around the city of Tay Ninh for the president, who arrived long after the fog lifted. There was no assassination squad and what started out as an unnecessarily confrontational day turned out to be a total bore.

February 5 was my first day off since getting back and the XO summoned me that afternoon.

"Pappy, what's up?" I asked curiously.

"You're out of here on the eighteenth," he told me.

"What do you mean out of here?"

"Leave," he told me stone faced.

"Leave? Where am I going?" I asked him.

"You know, leave, R&R, women, out of this hole?" he said as he broke out with an ear to ear smile.

"Leave? On the eighteenth?"

"No! Leave on the twentieth, but you'll be out of here on the eighteenth," he told me.

"Thanks, Pappy!"

I was elated. Another ten days had just been removed from my tour. Brian came by to see me when he got back from flying. He, too, had had his leave approved.

Larry got back to the troop on the sixth. I had missed talking with him. We stayed up half the night just talking about Bangkok, Hawaii, and home.

I brought him up-to-date on what had been happening in the AO. Things had got quiet again after the big contacts in January and the word being spread was that we would be moving back to Phuoc Vinh on February 24 and standing down on March 11.

The rash on my neck continued to get worse and once again I had to go to Phuoc Vinh for Doc Kaplan to examine it. "I can make it so you won't have to fly for the rest of your tour," he told me. "Despite your not shaving it is still infected. Does it bother you?"

"Only when I think about it. But I am not going to end my tour like this, Marty. I won't shave, but I am not going to stop flying. That's what I do."

When I got back to the bunker I was overcome with feelings at this proposal to stop flying. I was twenty years old, I had seen a lot of good friends die horrible deaths, and I had killed enough people to qualify me as a mass murderer back at home. Now I was being offered, on a silver platter, the opportunity not to have to face death again . . . and I turned it down. I had fought my war and survived. So why couldn't I quit?

I went back to Tay Ninh on the eleventh and the answer presented itself. I walked into our tent and sat on the side of my bed, looking and listening to the faces of friends I had shared the experience of combat with. I looked at my scout buddies, Barry and Bruce, Rudy and Chuck, Red Cloud and all the others. I felt a sense of responsibility to these guys; these guys who were bigger than life and put their lives on the line every day of their existence in Vietnam. And I thought about Tommy and Bill and Gary. I looked at my Cobra buddies, Larry and Brian, Walker and Van, Barney and Al, and I thought about Kevin. I couldn't walk out on them just because I was short. I had experience and knowledge, and I had to share it with those that would remain after I went home in five more weeks. And I was scared again. Not about losing my own life, but about my friends losing theirs when, perhaps, just maybe, I could have made the difference between their living and dying. So many others had passed under Charlie Troop's arch back at Phuoc Vinh and I owed it to them. I owed it to Grover Wright who placed so much hope and responsibility in my hands. No, I wouldn't quit! I couldn't quit!

The emotions were overwhelming. I looked forward to going home and yet, I was afraid. I had changed so much over the past ten and a half months that I wasn't sure how I would reintegrate with society. Rumors persisted that the troop would be standing down soon and the colors returned to the States. Should I extend and stay until the end?

"Hey kiddo, don't be stupid. You've fought your war. You got wounded. You were almost killed. Don't you think you've done your share? Go home. You don't need to put up with this shit anymore," he told me genuinely concerned, as one would expect a true friend to be. "Go on leave. Go back to Bangkok and clear your head . . . and your tubes," Larry told me before winking his eye.

"You're right," I told him.

Chapter 24

Good-bye to a Good Friend

In the morning we were on the first flight back to Tay Ninh. We checked in with ops to let them know that we were back. I was scheduled to fly as soon as my aircraft came out of maintenance. Mail was waiting on my bed when I got back to the tent and the first one I read made me angry. My brother had taken exception to a statement I had made in a tape to my parents. I had commented how close I was to Larry and Harvey and said that I loved them like brothers. He had taken offense and commented to my dad that he didn't understand how I could compare and have feelings for people that I knew for less than a year.

I couldn't believe his naïveté. I wrote to my dad, *"I have never had to depend on Steve for my life like I do my friends in Vietnam. We've established bonds that are stronger than blood. We've had to. I have to depend on them to keep me alive and they depend on me to do the same. We are willing to put our own life on the line for each other. If he can't understand that and doesn't like it, tough shit!"*

News of my second DFC had been published in articles in the paper at home, and unexpected but welcome letters arrived from friends I had gone to school with.

Barney came in and mentioned that something was up, but nobody seemed to know what. The troop had been assigned a Brown platoon and they were in training with the Blues. The Browns were ARVN soldiers who were training as an Aero Rifle Platoon. But why?

As American forces withdrew from Vietnam, it had become necessary to back up our Blues with an ARVN quick reaction force. The use of ARVNs as an RRF or a QRF had been established when we first moved into the AO, so why now were we training them to replace the Blues? At the same time the Blues had been put on a strict down-bird standby status. The arrival of fifteen new soldiers from the States was given as the reason, but even this made no sense. The Blues had always picked experienced cream of the crop infantry troops, experienced combat foot soldiers, and now we were getting FNGs. A lot of things were beginning not to make sense any more.

The ARVN Browns created problems for us. They were not known for the same ferocity in battle that we were and some of us questioned whether or not they would fight or run when the shit hit the fan. There was also the language problem. The difference in language caused some confusion on the ground during operations and even more so when we were trying to shoot for them. They didn't use the same terminology that we did and in the middle of a firefight is not the time for confusion. To overcome the problem a U.S. advisor was put on the ground with the Browns and one of the lift ships had to act as a Command and Control aircraft with an ARVN officer sitting next to our CO to try to resolve the problem. The end result was a waste of an aircraft asset and a far less proficient and effective fighting force on the ground.

But nobody was able or willing to answer the big question. Why?

We thought we knew but it was pure supposition. With the intelligence information that we had acquired from the firefights in January we had learned of new NVA buildups in Cambodia. When we officially ended our Cambodian incursion in 1970, the president stated that we would not employ the use of ground forces in Cambodia again. Nothing was stated about the use of aviation assets. We couldn't be *in* Cambodia but there had been no commitment not to be *over* Cambodia. Were the Browns being trained to go in on down aircraft recovery and exploit targets in Cambodia? Nobody knew for sure or, at least, nobody was telling us.

The Lam Son operations were launched into Laos about this time. U.S. aviation assets were spearheading the drive. Was Cambodia next? The areas we were working since my return to Tay Ninh were closer and closer to the border north and west of Tay Ninh. The weather was very hot and uncomfortable, between 96 and 105 degrees, and a thick haze blanketed the jungle.

The way things were shaping up I couldn't wait to go on leave; the sixteenth couldn't come soon enough. I was averaging about six and a half hours of flying per day until the sixteenth when I was scheduled and given additional missions. After a long and arduous 10.3-hour day, I shut down long after my scheduled down time, missing the flight back to Phuoc Vinh.

"Don't worry," Joel Hageman told me. "I'll get you on a flight in the morning. The tech supply aircraft is coming up."

The plan changed in the morning. Somebody had got sick and my services were required in the AO.

"You can fly a fuel load in the AO before you go," Captain Williams told me.

I was beyond arguing, despite the fact that I knew that if we ran into any NVA that the one fuel load would automatically become two or three. I packed my gear in preparation to leave before I went flying. I was actually happy to be flying that morning. This would be my last flight in-country, my last combat mission, and it would be bittersweet. I was flooded with emotion and thoughts as the aircraft went through translational lift. I climbed out over the perimeter fence as my mind raced.

I had been through so much in the past eleven months. I remembered how I felt being told I was going to be assigned to Charlie Troop and I remembered Major Rosher's words, and he was right. There was not another unit in-theater that I would rather have served with. I thought about that mission with Jake when we weren't able to get to the LRRP in time, and they died. I thought about Tommy and Gary, Bill and Kevin—I always thought about Kevin—and I thought about all the guys who I had looked up to and admired as I prepared to be an aircraft commander—Grover Wright, Felix Poindexter, Ed McDerby, and Hubert. I thought about those that I would be leaving behind: Larry and Brian, Walker and Mel, Red Cloud and Sammy, and Smitty and Farrell.

My mind continued to work and as I flew I relived those moments and saw the faces of the dead looking at me from outside of my aircraft, and before I knew it, it was time to break station for fuel.

What seemed like the fastest fuel load I had ever flown was gone and I was shutting down in the revetment. It took me longer to unstrap that morning, and the climb out of the cockpit was like climbing Mt. Everest. Something was holding me in. I stepped down and walked around the aircraft in the post-flight ritual that I had learned in flight school. I touched its skin, and opening the engine cowls I looked over the Lycoming engine, and the guns . . . I touched the rocket pods and ran my fingers along the barrels of the Vulcan cannon.

The turret was in its stowed position and I pushed the miniguns down to lock them in place. As I did so, I thought about the lives of my friends and fellow Americans these guns had saved and about the deaths, the hundreds of deaths these now cold steel barrels had inflicted on the enemy.

And at the same time I thought about the families of those whose deaths I was responsible for and how my dedication to duty would affect them for the rest of their lives.

Lost in my thoughts, I stayed with the aircraft longer than usual. Having completed the logbook I grabbed my helmet and began the walk back to the tent when I stopped. I turned back and touched AH-1G, 68-15068 for one last time.

"Thanks, old girl. You've been a good friend," I whispered hoarsely.

Three hours later I was on my way back to Phuoc Vinh.

Most of the troop was still up at Tay Ninh when we arrived back at Phuoc Vinh. The troop area was deserted except for a few guys on day off and those out-processing to go home. Larry had finagled another trip to Hawaii.

The note he left me said he'd be back on March 1. I looked at the calendar. There were no more pages to tear off. I was closer to Larry than anybody else and I looked forward to his return.

Major Ball was at Phuoc Vinh that day and stopped by to say hello at lunchtime.

"Welcome back, Two-four. Did you have a good leave?" he asked.

"It was incredible, sir. Just amazing," I told him.

"I'm afraid I have some bad news for you," he began.

I had an incredible feeling of dread and I thought to myself, "Please don't tell me somebody else has been killed." I didn't know if I could handle that.

"Sir?"

"We are down on our strength. We are authorized two hundred thirty-three people and we are down to a hundred and sixty. The area we are weakest in are warrant officers," he stated. "As a matter of fact we're down by eleven. Mr. Edeal is due back tomorrow and I'm going to need you both to fly."

My heart sank. "Fly, sir? But I only have fifteen more days until I go home."

"I know that but the Cambodian situation is getting out of hand. I need to field four Cobras a day and I need your butt in a seat. I need your experience!" he pleaded.

To say I wasn't happy would be a gross understatement, but I was still in the Army and I was subject to orders. Although Major Ball didn't order me to fly, there was no doubt he would have done so if I put up an argument.

Almost as an afterthought he added, "I will do my best to get you back here as soon as I can release you, but I really need you. The scouts need you." He knew how to get to me.

Larry got back the next day as planned. We hadn't seen each other in several weeks and we had some catching up to do. The biggest news was that Larry was going to be a father. I waited until the good news had been exchanged before I told him about my encounter with Major Ball the previous day.

"No fucking way," Larry said adamantly. "I already told Trish I've quit flying. She's going to have a baby. Damn it, we've fought our war. We've done our bit. Why do we always get fucked around just because of other people's screwups? Is it our fault the troop is under strength?"

I sympathized with him. "Yeah. I hear you. None of our plans have worked out, have they? We didn't get to go on R&R together because of the tactical situation and now we have to keep flying because of the tactical situation. This really sucks! Man, this is going to be a long two weeks."

We were given a reprieve a few hours before we were scheduled to return to Tay Ninh. Word had come down that the troop would be standing down soon, and we were asked to do various tasks around the troop area in preparation.

First Cavalry Division Operations Order 183-70 had been issued and the whole of the First of the Ninth was in chaos. Echo Troop had reverted to D Company of the 227th, Alpha Troop had orders to move from Fire Support Base Buttons at Song Be to Phuoc Vinh in preparation for the planned stand-down of the squadron. The Sixty-second Combat Tracker Platoon, who had been opcon to us, entered stand-down and Delta Troop was ordered to make preparations to stand-down on March 8. It finally looked as if the war was coming to an end for the squadron.

One of our tasks was to dismantle our bunker. We were told not to leave anything behind that the VC or NVA could use tactically. The bunker that we had called home, where we had laughed together so often—and cried all too many times—was being stripped of our identities. In a few short weeks nobody would know we had ever been there. It was becoming bare as we proceeded in our task and it was sad to see.

On February 28 I went to Tay Ninh, not to fly, but to collect all of my personal belongings and to say my good-byes. I was not looking forward to it. It felt different this time when we landed. I climbed out of the UH-1 and headed for the tents. Zero six eight was sitting in the revetment and it brought a smile to my face. But as I passed her I froze. For the past seven months, below the rear canopy, it had white lettering, AC ZAHN; below that CE MARING; and in the center of the yellow circle that designated the aircraft as belonging to Charlie Troop was my call sign, 24. All that was there now was AC and a blank spot; the circle was empty. My name and call sign had already been painted out and for some reason that I still can't explain it hurt. It hurt so much that it almost brought tears to my eyes.

Collecting myself I carried on to the tent and packed all of my gear into my duffel bag. Most of the guys were flying so the good-byes were few.

One hour after we landed, I threw my duffel bag in the back of the Huey and took a seat by the pinned back sliding door. Dave Farrell was the AC. Dave was going home too. As he lifted into the hover the ever-present red dirt that Tay Ninh was noted for swirled into a great cloud below us. And then we were gone—clear of the dust cloud, clear of the green line, clear of Tay Ninh—and for the first time I felt like I was really going home. I watched Tay Ninh as it disappeared behind us. Closing my eyes in thought and hope and prayer I said my good-byes to those I didn't get to see. "Good luck guys. Hurry home and Godspeed."

Over the next few days I was running back and forth between Phuoc Vinh and Bién Hoa clearing troop. All of my government-issue field equipment had to be turned in, as well as my flight gear; I had to get a medical clearance and pack all of my personal belongings to be shipped back.

On March 6 we went to the club and got drunk. I had entered an elite group known as the single-digit midgets. I had only nine days left in-country. The worse for drink, Larry and I went back to the bunker and began to play with a piece of exercise equipment that had been left behind. It had two handles that were connected by three springs and could be used in various ways to strengthen different muscle groups of the body. Larry slipped one handle under his foot and standing on it proceeded to do arm curls by pulling up on the opposite handle. After four or five curls the handle under his foot slipped out and sprang up hitting him in the eye. Blood poured from his face. His eyelid looked badly lacerated and he couldn't see. Sobering up in record time I rushed him over to see Doc Kaplan.

"Marty, Marty!" I yelled as we approached the aid station.

Doc Kaplan met us in the receiving area.

"Holy shit!" he said looking at Larry. "What in the hell happened to you?"

We explained what had happened and Marty proceeded to clean up Larry's eye. His inability to see was because his eye was full of blood. Once cleaned up his vision returned.

"You are a lucky guy," Marty told Larry. "If that had hit you half an inch lower, you would have lost your eye."

Larry gave me one of those "oh shit" looks as Doc Kaplan finished patching him up. He would have to wear an eye patch for four days and it went without saying that Larry was grounded. On the way back to the bunker Larry put his arm around me. "Hey kiddo," he said.

And before he could go any further I answered the question that I knew would follow. "No Lar, this doesn't qualify you for a Purple Heart."

"Shit!" and we walked back to the bunker in tears of laughter.

The next day the family car returned from Tay Ninh and an envelope for me arrived with it. It was my last OER. I began to read the report and my blood began to boil. Larry could see my rage.

"Wow! What the heck did they write?" he asked me.

I didn't speak. I just handed it to him.

Captain Williams wrote: *"CW2 Zahn performed his duties as an aircraft commander in a satisfactory manner."*

"Satisfactory manner?" Larry questioned, "Two DFCs, a Bronze Star, the Vietnamese Cross of Gallantry with a silver star, Two ArComs for valor, two Air Medals for valor, forty-three regular Air Medals plus all the other crap they give away. And that's just satisfactory? Is this guy for real?"

He was almost as mad as I was as he continued reading. *"He has an adequate amount of knowledge about his aircraft, and the mission he performs."*

"Adequate knowledge," Larry laughed. "You taught him every damn thing he knows. Shit, you've forgotten more about the Cobra and our mission than he's ever known!"

"His performance was hampered by his immature attitude and his excessive concern for his own feelings."

"What the hell is he talking about?" Larry asked incredulously.

"He wanted to stop flying when he still had two months left on his tour in Vietnam. Since that time he has continually made excuses for not flying, or for doing any extra duties. He was offered the job of Administration Officer and quit after three days saying it was too much of a hassle. CW2 Zahn will have to make considerable improvement to become a good all around pilot and officer."

"I have never read such a crock of shit in my life," Larry said. "Excuses? Your neck was bleeding. Your dad was in the hospital. The goalposts changed on the admin job. What in the fuck is this guy talking about?"

"Shit Lar, read it again," I said to him. "The admin job was too much hassle. Whose words are those? That's what Sides said that night. He can't even come up with his own words. Those guys are two peas out of the same pod. I guess when you consider the source it don't matter Lar. I'm going home in a few days and they just don't matter. Read what the dickhead wrote."

"CW2 Zahn has a sound knowledge of the aircraft he flies and aviation in general. He has performed his duties as an AH1G aircraft commander in a satisfactory manner. CW2 Zahn's lack of maturity detracts from his overall performance. He shows great concern for his own personal comfort and relegates his mission to a secondary role. Mr. Zahn has considerable potential but until he develops a more mature attitude his success in the military will be only marginal."

"What a bunch of flaming assholes!" Larry said. "I cannot believe this."

"You can't believe it?" I asked him. I couldn't say any more. I was speechless and really pissed off.

Most of my spare time I spent lying around, reading and trying to come to terms with my thoughts and feelings.

On the eighth, the Army reversed itself again. It was announced that the remaining troops of the First of the Ninth would not enter stand-down, but they would continue with their previous commitment to support the ARVN in Military Region Three in its Cambodian operations.

Headquarters at Phuoc Vinh, along with Alpha and Charlie Troop, would be moving to Di An. I was beside myself with anger and compassion. I knew what a disappointment this new news would be to the guys.

And on March 10 I left Phuoc Vinh for the last time. Larry walked out to the aircraft with me. "Well kiddo, here it is. You're out of this place," he said offering me his hand. I shook his hand and instinctively we gave each other a big hug.

"Listen Edeal, you're out of here in a few more weeks. Keep your head down and call me as soon as you get home."

"You know as well as I do that two weeks is a long time over here. A lot can happen in two weeks."

"Larry, it'll be over before you know it," I told him.

"Yeah, I know. Besides I'm going to Hawaii again so I don't have much time left at all," he reminded me.

"You take care of yourself and say so long to the guys," I told him, as the UH-1's rotors began to turn.

"I wish they had left your call sign on zero six eight," Larry smiled. "I was looking forward to painting 'retired' after it."

I waved as we lifted off. Larry just stood there watching as the helicopter got smaller and smaller. The Huey departed on runway zero nine and as we climbed out over the rubber plantation where I had almost shot one of our own troops that night, I felt 360 days of pressure lifted from my shoulders.

I was elated and I was drained. After saying my farewells to Dave Farrell and Jack Schwarz, who flew me down, I walked from the transient pad to Cav Rear where I had arrived a year ago, nineteen and scared. My good friend, Bobby James, was there and we took up where we had left off as though no time had passed. We had both been through a year of hell and neither of us wanted to speak about it.

Having finally completed the out-processing procedure, we were transferred by bus back to Long Binh to the Ninetieth Replacement Battalion, where I had arrived one year ago. The buses still had the chicken wire over the windows but I wasn't scared any more. When it's your time, it's your time, chicken wire or no chicken wire. We arrived at the Ninetieth unscathed, signed in, and were given our military transport authorization (MTA)—the military's equivalent of a plane ticket—and I was amazed to find my departure had been moved forward to March 13. I looked at my MTA . . . McGuire Air Force Base, New Jersey?

"Hey Bobby, where the hell is your MTA to?" I asked him.

"To Travis. Where do you think?"

I went back to the office from where I got the MTA. "Excuse me," I interrupted the clerk from his paperwork. "I have a problem. My MTA is to McGuire
and I think that is a mistake."

"Why is that, sir?" he asked.

"Because I live in California. I don't want to go to the East Coast. I want to
go to Travis." I was really exasperated. With only hours to go the Army was still
fucking with me! The clerk checked with one of his officers and after a few minutes he came out to speak to me.

"Mr. Zahn? Is there a problem?" the lieutenant asked.

"Yes, sir. I live in California and I have been allocated a flight to McGuire. I
left from Travis and that's where I want to go back to," I told him.

"We allocate flights not by your home of residence, Mr. Zahn," he said sym-
pathetically. "If it's your DEROS date, we put you on the first available flight.
We're getting you out two days early."

"That's all well and good, sir. But going to McGuire is ridiculous. The flight
time is four hours longer and then when I arrive I'll have to pay my own way up
to New York and fly all the way back across the country at my own expense.
Surely there has to be somebody on the Travis flight that lives on the East Coast
that would like to go to McGuire."

"I'm afraid it doesn't work that way," he said. "If you don't want to go to
McGuire, that's fine. I can reallocate your seat, but you may have to wait three or
four days to get seated on another flight."

"But my DEROS date is the fifteenth," I pleaded.

"I'm sorry," he said. "If you want to be home on the fifteenth, then I suggest
you take the McGuire flight and make whatever arrangements are necessary to
get to your home."

Bobby was waiting when I got back and I told him what had happened.

"Man, that really sucks!" he said.

"The whole fucking Army sucks," I said, defeated. I had no more fight left in
me, no emotion. I couldn't bear the thought of staying in Vietnam for one more
minute than I had to, much less four days. I just wanted to go home.

Epilogue

"Hi Kiddo, I'm Home!"

The chartered MAC flight lifted from Bién Hoa on time, March 13, 1971. I had been in Vietnam two days shy of a year. As the wheels of the aircraft lifted from the runway, the roar and cheers from within the aircraft were deafening. People were patting one another on the back and giving high-fives. I participated in the cheers and after the noise died out I sat in reflection.

An infantry sergeant sitting next to me noticed my Cav hat.

"Excuse me, sir. What unit did you fly with?" he asked.

"Charlie Troop, First of the Ninth Guns," I told him.

His response was "Wow. Right on. Can I shake your hand, sir?"

I was only too glad to comply.

The flight ahead was going to be long. Our route would take us to Guam to refuel, then to Hawaii, and then over the top of the world arcing down over Canada into McGuire. Total flying time was estimated to be twenty-six hours. Most of the time I slept.

Approaching the West Coast of the United States, the captain of the aircraft came on the intercom. "Gentlemen, I'm afraid I have some disappointing news. The East Coast is covered in fog and it's not forecast to lift for quite some time. We'll be diverting to Seattle to refuel and wait on an improvement. I'm truly sorry. I know you're anxious to get home and I know there are a lot of anxious people waiting for you." The intercom clicked off.

We touched down at SEATAC, the airport that serves Seattle, shortly after midnight. It was a cool evening and the fact that we had just spent a year in temperatures that rarely got below 90 degrees made it feel all that much colder. The aircraft taxied to the ramp and came to a halt on the apron across from the main terminal. We walked across the dew-covered ramp into the terminal building. It was teeming with activity, which surprised me at that time of the morning. My fellow passengers raced to the telephones and within minutes there were queues at every telephone to be found. I went to the Western Airlines counter.

"Good morning," a male agent greeted me, "Can I help you?"

"Yes, sir," I answered. "When is your next flight to Los Angeles?"

251

"We have a flight leaving at 2:55 A.M. arriving in Los Angeles at 6:10," he told me.

"Can I get a ticket," I asked?

A few minutes later I had a ticket in hand and then found a phone. I called my friend, Mike Rosenthal, who had come to Hawaii with my parents. His father answered the phone with a sleepy "Hello!"

"Sid. Hi, I'm sorry to wake you up. This is Randy. Can I speak to Mike please?"

"Randy? Where are you? Do you know what time it is? Michael's asleep," he told me.

"I'm in Seattle. Yes I know what time it is and go wake his ass up!" I requested.

Mike answered the phone and plans were made for him to pick me up when I arrived at LA.

As I was going back to the Military Affairs desk an MP stopped me. "Excuse me, sir. You're not in Vietnam any more. You'll have to remove that cowboy hat and wear authorized headgear."

"Corporal, I know that I'm not in Vietnam any more. No one knows that better than I do. My hat is not a cowboy hat. You got that? Now, my Cavalry hat is authorized to be worn as long as I'm still a member of my unit and I will be until I sign in to my new unit after leave. And until then not you or anybody else is going to tell me I can't wear it. You got that?" I asked him. "And before you threaten me with a DR, if you're going to make one out, make it out to Major General George Putnam, commanding general of the First Cavalry Division, and when he gets it, God help you."

That issue resolved I proceeded to Military Affairs. "I need my gear off the airplane," I told him.

"Why, sir?" he asked me.

"Because I live here on the West Coast and I am not flying back to McGuire just to turn around and fly all the way back."

"But, sir—"

"But, sir, nothing. I have a ticket in hand. My flight leaves in an hour and a half and I will be home in my bed before this flight even leaves for New Jersey. My leave starts when I get to the States, so officially, I am on leave. Now either you can get somebody to take me back to the airplane to get my gear, or the military can worry about getting it delivered to my house. I don't really care. But either way I am leaving on a Western Airlines flight to Los Angeles at 2:55." I stood my ground.

The Western Airlines 737 touched down at LAX on time. Mike was nowhere to be found. I called again, and his dad woke him up for the second time. Within an hour he pulled up in his 911 Porsche.

"Sorry," he offered climbing out of the sleek car.

"Sorry shit," I chided him. "Some friend you are, leaving me standing on the sidewalk."

Mike walked over and gave me a big hug. "Welcome home, Randy!"

The drive to my house took about thirty-five minutes. We didn't talk about Vietnam. Mike talked about friends and cars and he acted as if Vietnam had never existed. I took in the familiar sights, but thought about Larry and all of my friends still over there. Part of me was still there with them.

I hadn't called my parents when I arrived. I wanted to surprise them. At 7:45 in the morning of March 15, 1971, I grabbed the door handle and twisted it. My folks were eating their breakfast as I walked through the door. I startled them, and we had an emotional reunion.

Both of my folks called in to their respective places of employment and took the day off.

I needed some sleep and for the first time in a year I slept in my own bed.

I woke up at about 2 o'clock and Mom began to tell me about all the plans she had made for my homecoming. People were coming over and a big party was planned.

"Mom, Dad, you may not be able to understand this, but I don't want a party now. I don't want to be around people now. I don't want to answer a lot of questions. I need time to myself. I still have a lot of very close friends in Vietnam. Larry is still there and until he's home, part of me is still there with him," I tried to explain. "I have nothing to celebrate."

I am not sure they understood, and Mom was insistent on the party.

"When Larry's home I'll party, okay? If you have a party before then, I will not be there," I told her. I know that I sounded ungrateful, but nothing could have been farther from the truth. My emotions were being pulled in so many different directions. I was elated to be home but I wasn't really there. I was there in body, but I was still living each day in Vietnam with Larry.

I didn't want a party; I didn't want to see anybody. I just wanted to be left alone.

I spent many hours walking the streets of my hometown. With my hands in my pockets and stuck in another world, I walked.

On the twenty-second of March, a tape arrived. It was from Larry. I couldn't open it fast enough. Mom and Dad sat down to listen to it with me. He began, *"Hi ya kiddo. I'm back from leave. I went to Hawaii again. Trish came over and we had a wonderful time."*

Then there was a long pause.

"This tape has some good news on it and, Randy, this tape has some bad news on it."

Larry proceeded with the good news. He was done flying and doing odd jobs around Phuoc Vinh waiting to go home. I dreaded what was coming next and Mom and Dad sensed that feeling of dread. They looked at each other and said nothing.

"Now for the bad news and if you're not sitting down I would advise you to sit down. I just heard this yesterday and I'm still kind of shaken up. On March 12 one of our Snakes went down and both the co-pilot and pilot were killed and Van got

killed and so did Hageman. Joel was in the front seat and Van was in the backseat, naturally. The story is they were flying around and the little bird dropped a pete and they were going to make a gun run and the helicopter flew apart. The observer said that first he saw the tail boom fall off or part of the tail boom fall off. Then he saw the rotorhead come off, and the engine doors came off. It didn't burst into flames or anything but when he hit the ground, well, there's nothing you can do if you lose your rotor head. I'll tell you more about it when I get back but I thought at least you should know."

The tears welled in my eyes. I didn't hear the rest of the tape. I just sat there and cried. Van Joyce's death hit me really hard. It made me realize that no matter how short you were, you could not relax until you were actually home. Van Joyce, who was so full of life and fun, young and energetic and good looking. Van Joyce, who had been in Vietnam for over two years and who had only three weeks left in Vietnam, was dead. Joel Hageman, with a wife and young children, who had only two months left in the Army, was dead. It all seemed so senseless and so unfair. So very unfair that I should be sitting here in our den and my friends were still over there dying.

Wiping my eyes I realized that my mom and dad were no longer there. I hadn't seen them leave. They understood.

The following day I listened to the rest of Larry's tape.

"Well, I'm back and I have something to say. This part of the tape is rated X. Any female personnel not wishing to hear obscenities, cussing, or bad words; I'll give you exactly five seconds to leave the room or plug your ears.

One, two, three, four, five . . . Hi fucko, how are you ya sack of shit! Boy, am I happy. Guess what today is?

Today is the twenty-fourth and I'm not short anymore, I'm next! Yep, Dave and Schwarzy left yesterday but I didn't tape you anything yesterday. I just sat around and didn't do jack shit. But they left and that means that Dale and I are next.

In exactly four more days I leave fucking Phuoc Vinh and I get out of this hole. I am done. Fini, not to fly in this shithole again.

We had a floorshow on the twentieth. Alpha Troop lives here now and they got pretty rowdy so Farrell and Schwarz told them to cool it and then, well, Schwarzy got drunk and yelled the First of the Ninth sucks! The Alpha Troop CO told the colonel and then he ordered him to be in his office at 0700 the next day. Well, Jack got up and showered and shaved and all that crap and with fifteen minutes left he decided to lie down for a few minutes and woke up after 0900. He missed the meeting altogether."

Larry was laughing and I was laughing with him. I could just see it unfolding and I laughed hysterically.

"Phuoc Vinh really sucks now and so does Vietnam!

This'll be my last tape so I'll call you as soon as I get home, okay? Well, maybe not as soon as but soon after. Take care kiddo and I'll see you real soon. Bye."

Days and night merged into one. My circadian rhythm was still messed up and night was still day for me and vice versa. I often went out walking at night. I walked by Donna's house. I walked around my old schools and I froze. The temperature was in the low sixties, but that was thirty to forty degrees colder than what I had become accustomed to.

People asked questions about Vietnam. They asked the same questions. It became obvious to me that many of the people asking the questions didn't understand our involvement in Vietnam. But did I? I had been there for a year and now I wasn't sure why. What had we achieved? What were we trying to accomplish? What were our goals? We lost more than fifty-eight thousand lives and the Vietnamese over two million. And for what?

The telephone rang early in the morning on April 6. Mom called from her room and said it was for me. I got out of bed and went to the phone.

"Hello."

"Hi, kiddo. It's me, Lar. I'm home!"

He didn't have to say anything else. That was all I needed to hear. Larry was home from the war, and so was I.

Glossary

AA anti-aircraft.

AAFSS (a-fis) advanced aerial fire support system.

AC aircraft commander, normally left seat in the UH-1, right seat in the OH-6, and rearseat in the AH-1.

ADF automatic direction finder, a navigational aid with an AM radio incorporated into it.

AFA aerial field artillery, *see* ARA.

AFVN Armed Forces Viet Nam, Saigon-based military radio station.

AI advanced instruments.

AK or AK-47 assault rifle used by the enemy.

AO area of operations.

AR Army Regulation.

ARA aerial rocket artillery, AH-1 Cobra in the hog configuration armed with 76 2.75-inch rockets.

arc light carpet-bombing raid conducted by B-52s.

ArCom Army commendation medal.

ARP aero rifle platoon, the Blues.

arty artillery.

ARVN (Arvin) Army of the Republic of Vietnam, soldiers of the South Vietnamese Army.

B-40 rocket-propelled grenade, used by the NVA. Also RPG7.

B-52 USAF Stratofortress heavy bomber.

base camp a semi-permanent administrative and logistical center for a given unit, usually within the unit's area of operation. Depending on the unit's tactical mission it could operate within, outside of, or totally away from the base camp.

battalion military unit, in Vietnam could be fixed or flexible. A fixed battalion had assigned lettered companies, usually four or five with a headquarters company. A flexible battalion was in effect only a headquarters detachment that controlled any number of attached separate companies. Fixed battalions usually consisted of between 500 and 920 personnel. A flexible battalion varied greatly in number.

BCT basic combat training.

BDA bomb damage assessment.

BI basic instruments.

bingo term used to identify friendly forces when they didn't want to give their position away by popping a smoke. When an aircraft was directly overhead their position, they would call "bingo" over the radio.

bleeding, bled off, or to bleed term used by helicopter pilots to describe when they are losing rotor rpm in the main rotor.

blood trail a trail of blood on the ground left by a fleeing person who has been wounded.

Blue birds troop UH-1 Huey helicopters. The Blue platoon.

blue line (or blue) water feature on a tactical map, i.e., a river, creek, or stream.

Blues internal infantry platoon assigned to the Air Cav Troop to conduct ground reconnaissance, downed bird recovery, and evacuation and recovery of downed crews.

BOQ bachelor officer quarters.

brigade military unit of which divisions are made up.

BUFF big ugly fat fuckers, the USAF B-52 Stratofortress bomber.

C and C command and control.

C's C rations or combat rations. Canned army meals used in field conditions.

CAR 15 Colt automatic rifle; early version of the M-16. Usually carried by Cobra crews due to its shorter length.

Cav cavalry, either ground or aerial reconnaissance. Short for 1st Air Cavalry Division (Airmobile).

Cayuse Army designation of the Hughes OH-6A light observation helicopter (LOH).

CE charlie echo. Phonetic initialing for Chief Engineer, or the crew chief of an aircraft.

Charlie Viet Cong. Short form of "Victor Charlie," the phonetic initialing of VC.

chicken plate armored vest worn by pilots and aircrew.

Chinook cargo helicopter manufactured by Boeing Aircraft. The CH-47 is a large tandem-rotor helicopter.

claymore (mine) remote detonated antipersonnel mine, used in ambushes and on defensive perimeters.

click one kilometer, .621 mile.

CO commanding officer.

Cobra Bell AH-1G Huey Cobra Attack Helicopter—also referred to as the Snake.

collective the control stick to the left of the helicopter pilot used to control the "collective" pitch of the main rotor blades. A twist grip throttle is incorporated into the collective allowing the pilot to control the engine rpm's.

company assigned to a battalion with a lettered designation, or separate with its own numbered sequence. Companies were called batteries by the artillery and troops by the cavalry.

concertina wire barbed wire that is rolled out along the ground around perimeters of fire support bases or base camps to delay the enemy in penetrating the defenses.

COSVN Communist Office of South Vietnam.

CSM command sergeant major.

cut donuts flying around in circles, what the Cobra did while watching the LOH.

CW2 Chief Warrant Officer 2; warrant officer, grade 2.

CW3 Chief Warrant Officer 3; warrant officer, grade 3.

cyclic the control stick the helicopter pilot holds in his right hand, between his legs; controls the cyclical pitch of the main rotor blades and allows the aircraft to fly forward, sideward, or backward.

delta bravo phonetic for down bird.

DEROS date eligible for return from overseas.

deuce and a half two-and-a-half-ton utility truck.

di di mau Vietnamese for "get out of here" or "leave."

dink the enemy.

DIVARTY division artillery.

division the main military unit of combined arms and service support.

DO duty officer.

"down bird" the alarm given when an aircraft has gone down as a result of enemy activity.

DR disposition report.

dustoff medical evacuation helicopters; originally the call sign of Major Charles L. Kelley, KIA July 1, 1964.

E & E escape and evasion, to avoid capture by using one's own resources.

ECU environmental control unit, AH-1 air-conditioning system.

EM enlisted man.

EOD explosives, ordnance, and demolition.

ETA estimated time of arrival.

ETS estimated termination of service; the date of scheduled release from active military service.

F-4 McDonnell Douglas Phantom all-weather jet multi-role fighter-interceptor.

FAC forward air controllers usually assigned to ground elements to coordinate air strikes.

family fox internal troop FM radio frequency.

fastmovers jet aircraft.

firebase artillery-firing positions established to support ground elements and often secured by infantry.

"fire for effect" command given to artillery batteries when they are to open fire on a given target.

first sergeant the senior non-commissioned officer at company level.

flak shrapnel caused by an air burst artillery round or anti-aircraft weapons.

flak vest a vest worn by personnel to protect them from shrapnel.

flechette a warhead that contained 2,200 twenty-grain flechettes, or nails. The nails were about an inch and a half long. The nose of the nail was as sharp as a pin and at the back were four small razor sharp fins to aid its aerodynamics in flight. The flechette rocket was an airburst weapon. It exploded at about 200 feet and dispersed tiny, lethal missiles over a wide area. One pair of rockets provided coverage of approximately fourteen nails per square yard over an area the size of a football field.

FM frequency modulation; low-frequency radios used for ground-to-ground and ground-to-air communications.

FNG most common reference to new arrivals in Vietnam; literally a "fucking new guy."

fox four phonetic for F-4, the Phantom fighter-bomber.

fox-mike FM radio.

frag common term for any grenade, but specifically the fragmentation grenade.

free fire zone an area usually designated by grid references where a Pink team could shoot at anything that moved.

FSB fire support base, firebase.

FTA First Team Academy, the 1st Cav's in-country indoctrination course at Bién Hoa.

GAF ground-to-air fire.

GCA ground-controlled approach, a non-precision radar approach for landing in poor weather.

gook the enemy, Viet Cong or NVA; derogatory generic term for all Vietnamese.

GP general purpose.

ground probe an enemy tactic to *probe,* or test, the ground defenses of a base camp or firebase.

grunts foot soldiers, the infantry.

guard emergency radio frequency.

gunship a heavily armed attack helicopter.

HE high-explosive artillery round.

heavy Red team two Cobras and a LOH.

heavy White team two LOHs and a Cobra.

higher higher command, usually meaning brigade or division.

H-model latest version of the UH-1 Huey helicopter.

hooch a primitive dwelling of any type that afforded protection from the elements.

hot dangerous, such as a hot LZ (a landing zone where aircraft are taking ground-to-air fire).

Huey popular name for the Bell UH-1 utility helicopter.

humping marching with a heavy load.

hunter-killer team a Pink team consisting of a LOH, the hunter, and a Cobra, the killer.

IFR instrument flight rules.

IG Inspector General; an inspection conducted by the office of the IG.

III Corps military region 3, the geographical area around Saigon, one of four so designated for military command and control.

IMC instrument meteorological conditions, flying in the clouds.

incoming receiving enemy rocket or mortar fire.

IP instructor pilot.

ITO instrument takeoff. A takeoff under instrument meteorological conditions by sole reference to the aircraft instruments.

JP jungle penetrator, a metal device lowered by search and rescue or medevac aircraft with fold-down seats to extract personnel vertically.

JP4 refined kerosene used in turbine-powered military aircraft, jet fuel.

KBH killed by helicopter.

KIA killed in action.

laager positioning of helicopters, usually to a secure forward area so that flight time is reduced to re-arm and re-fuel facilities from the AO.

LARA Light Armed Recon Aircraft.

loach *see* LOH

LOH (Loach) a light observation helicopter, generally identifying the OH-6.

LP listening post.

LRRP or LRP (lurp) long-range reconnaissance patrol; members of it; also a light-weight freeze-dried meal designed for use by the patrols.

LZ landing zone.

M-35 two-and-a-half-ton cargo truck, the deuce and a half.

MAC Military Airlift Command.

MACV (Mac-vee) Military Assistance Command, Vietnam. The senior U.S. military headquarters in Vietnam.

MAD magnetic anomaly detector.

MARS Military Affiliate Radio System. Radio transmissions that linked U.S. civilians with soldiers calling from Vietnam through the use of Signal Corp, assets and volunteer amateur radio operators in the States.

MATS Military Air Transport Service.

medevac medical evacuation by helicopter. Also called "Dustoff."

MOC maintenance operational check, usually completed after an aircraft comes out of maintenance and before being released for operational flying.

motor pool section of a military organization assigned to maintain the motor vehicles.

MP military police.

MPC military payment certificate; scrip issued for U.S. Armed Forces to use instead of U.S. currency.

MTA military transport authorization, the military equivalent of an airline ticket.

napalm *na*phthenic acid and *palm*etate; jellied gasoline, originally designed for flamethrowers in World War II.

nape napalm.

NCO non-commissioned officer.

NDP night defensive position.

neutralize to render an enemy soldier, force, installation, or operation ineffective by use of military force; to kill.

NLF National Liberation Front.

NOK next of kin.

NVA North Vietnamese Army.

OCS officer candidate school.

OD olive drab; officer development (courses); officer duty.

OER Officer Efficiency Report.

OH-6 Cayuse, light observation helicopter produced by Hughes Tool Company, commonly called the LOH.

OH-58 Kiowa, light observation helicopter produced by Bell Helicopters. Originally used for command and control and VIP transportation, but used later in the conflict for observation.

opcon operational control.

operations section of a tactical organization in charge of planning and the conduct of tactical missions.

ops operations.

organics term used for an aircraft's organic weapons, those on board the aircraft.

OV-10 North American OV-10 Bronco, the aircraft that forward air controllers flew.

PACEX Pacific Exchange, mail order PX facility.

PAR precision approach radar, a ground-controlled approach conducted when in instrument meteorological conditions.

Pink team the operational section of the Air Cavalry Troop whose job is visual reconnaissance. Usually a LOH and a Cobra.

piss tube field urinal for male personnel. A fifty-five-gallon drum cut in half, buried in the ground, and covered by wire mesh.

platoon military unit formed of two or more squads or sections.

POL petroleum, oil, and lubricants; generally used to refer to the refueling point for aircraft.

"pop smoke" an order given when one wishes for a smoke grenade to be released.

POW prisoner of war.

prep preparation of a landing zone by artillery, airstrike, or gunship prior to insertion of friendly forces.

PSP perforated steel planking (plate); interlocking steel planks used to produce a hard, stable surface for runways, roadways, or flight lines.

PT physical training.
Purple team an LOH (White), a Cobra (Red), and a lift ship (Blue).
push radio frequency.
PX Post Exchange, a retail outlet run by the Army and Air Force Exchange Service.
PZ pickup zone for helicopter extraction of ground personnel.

QRF quick reaction force.
QSY the old Q code for changing frequencies.

R&R rest and recreation (or recuperation); out-of-country vacation taken during a military member's tour of duty in Vietnam. Out-of-country R&R locations were Australia, Bangkok, Hawaii, Hong Kong, Kuala Lumpur, Manila, Penang, Singapore, Taipei, and Tokyo.
recon reconnaissance, either on the ground (ground reconnaissance) or air (visual reconnaissance).
recon by fire a method of reconnaissance whereby fire is placed upon a suspected enemy position in an effort to give themselves away either by fleeing or returning fire. A common method used by First of the Ninth Pink teams.
Red the aerial weapons platoon of an Air Cav troop. The Cobra or Red platoon.
redball code name for a road.
regiment in the cavalry, two or more squadrons.
REMF rear echelon motherfucker. The guys in the rear areas.
revetment fortified protection for aircraft in forward areas; either parallel consisting of two parallel walls or L-shaped for gunships.
rigid litter a basket-type litter used to extract wounded personnel by rescue or medevac aircraft. The rigid litter allows the wounded to lie in a prone position.
rotorwash vortex given off by the rotation of the blades of a helicopter—usually referred to when the helicopter is hovering.
RPG rocket-propelled grenade; enemy anti-tank weapon also used effectively against helicopters. Variants were the B-40, B-41, and RPG-7.
RRF ready reaction force.
RSG Regional Support Group.
RTB return to base.
RTO radio telephone operator who carried the lightweight infantry field radio.

S-1 personnel.
S-2 intelligence.
S-3 operations.
S-4 supply.
SAB Student Activities Building at Fort Wolters, Texas. The social center where candidates met their wives and families and where social events were held.
SAC Strategic Air Command.

"Saddle-up" an order to put on one's field gear and prepare to move out. In the Air Cav it meant to board the aircraft.

same same the same as; to do it the same.

SAS stability augmentation system.

SCAS stability control augmentation system.

scouts name given to the pilots and crewmen of the aerial reconnaissance, or scout, aircraft. The White platoon.

scoutships LOHs.

SGLI Serviceman's Group Life Insurance.

shackle method used to encode numerical information.

shitter outdoor latrines known as two- or three-holers; fifty-five-gallon drums used as receptacles and usually burned off every day with jet fuel.

short term used by soldiers to describe the length of time they have left in-theater.

sit-rep situation report.

slick helicopter, usually a UH-1, used to airlift troops or logistics with only door guns for self-protection.

smoke grenades a hand grenade that when released produces brightly colored smoke; used to identify friendly force positions, enemy locations, or wind direction for landing helicopters.

Snake slang term for the AH-1 Cobra gunship.

SOI signal operating instructions. Radio code and frequency booklet carried by pilots.

SOP standard operating procedures. A unit's set of instructions covering standard and expected responses to given situations or circumstances.

Spec 4, 5, 6 specialist, a military rank, grade E-4, E-5, or E-6.

spider hole a hole in the ground dug by enemy soldiers that had a roll back or hinged cover. They would pop up from their spider hole to shoot and then drop down covering their hole and disappearing from sight.

squadron cavalry equivalent of the battalion.

SR5 subregion 5 of COSVN.

Stand-down period of rest and refitting when a unit is withdrawn from the battlefield—usually a cessation of all operations is implied. Also used to mean the final preparation of a unit to deploy back to the United States.

Stars and Stripes newspaper produced and distributed by the Armed Forces of the United States.

STOL short takeoff and landing.

tac air tactical air support, usually by fighter-bomber aircraft.

tac officer a tactical officer, usually a warrant officer or lieutenant assigned to a military school or academy.

TDY temporary duty.

TET Vietnamese Lunar New Year holiday period.

TOC tactical operations center.

TOP first sergeant of a military unit, the *Top* sergeant.

tracer a bullet that has phosphorus at the base of the shell used to visually track the flight of the bullet.

troop cavalry equivalent of the company.

UH-1 Iroquois helicopter manufactured by Bell Helicopters. Proper nomenclature for the Huey.

UHF ultrahigh frequency (radio).

Uncle Ho Ho Chi Minh.

URC-10 lightweight handheld survival radio carried by pilots in their survival vests. The URC-10 provided a beeper mode that enabled aircraft properly equipped to home in on the signal being transmitted and also a voice capability.

USAAVNS U.S. Army Aviation School.

USARV (Use-ar-vee) U.S. Army, Vietnam.

USO United Services Organization.

VC Viet Cong.

"V" device small metal device attached to a medal to indicate it was awarded for Valor.

VHF very high frequency.

VNAF (vee-naf) Vietnamese Air Force.

VOL INDEF voluntary indefinite. Terms of one's contract with the Army usually required for a promotion or advanced training; A person who would *volunteer* to remain on active duty *indefinitely.*

VR visual reconnaissance.

White the aerial reconnaissance platoon of the Air Cav Troop; Scouts.

White phosphorus an element that ignites when exposed to oxygen. It produces a cloud of billowy white smoke and is employed in artillery and hand grenades.

White team two LOHs, one would be armed with a minigun.

WIA wounded in action.

Willie Pete white phosphorous.

Wilson Pickett slang for white phosphorous.

WO warrant officer.

WO1 warrant officer, grade one.

WOC Warrant Officer Candidate.

WORWAC Warrant Officer Rotary Wing Aviator Course.

XO executive officer, second in command to the senior officer at company, battalion, and brigade levels.

x-ray call sign used by the First of the Ninth co-pilots. For example, co-pilot flying with Cavalier Two-Four would be Cavalier Two-Four x-ray.

Sources

The source of most of the material contained in the text came from letters and cassette tapes that I sent my mother and father, Etta and Joseph Zahn, between January 7, 1969, and March 10, 1971. Other useful sources follow.

Spec. 4 Robert Mantell, "Open New Frontier," *Cavalair,* First Air Cavalry Division. August 5, 1970.

Spec. 4 Robert Mantell, "Cav Earns Standdown, NVA Activity Stands Still," *Cavalair,* First Air Cavalry Division. July 22, 1970.

PFC Terry Turner, "Cav Captures Tons of NVA Supplies," *Cavalair,* First Air Cavalry Division. June 3, 1970.

First Cavalry Division (Airmobile). *Operational Report—Lessons Learned 1 May–31 July, 1970.*

Information Office, *First Team Magazine,* First Air Cavalry Division, APO SF 96490. "Red, White and Blue—the Real Cav." Winter 1970.

Headquarters Department of the Army. *Operator's Manual Army Model AH-1G/TH-1G Helicopter.* March 18, 1980.

Headquarters Department of the Army. *Operational Report—Lessons Learned, First Cavalry Division, Period Ending 30 April 1970* (May 15, 1970).

Headquarters Department of the Army. *Operational Report—Lessons Learned, First Squadron Ninth Cavalry (Airmobile), Period ending 30 April 1971, RCS CSFOR-65* (April 5, 1971).

Headquarters Department of the Army. *Operational Report of First Squadron, Ninth Cavalry for Quarterly Period Ending 31 October 1970 (RCS-CSFOR-65) (RI)* (November 1, 1970).

Headquarters, First Squadron Ninth Cavalry. *Operational Report of First Squadron, Ninth Cavalry for Quarterly Period Ending 31 July 1970* (RCS-CSFOR-65) (RL).

Shelby L. Stanton, *Anatomy of a Division, 1st Cav in Vietnam,* (Presidio Press, 1987).

Lt. Gen. John J. Tolson, *Airmobility in Vietnam, Helicopter Warfare in Southeast Asia,* (Arno Press 1981).

U.S. Army Missile Command, Rocket Management Office, Redstone Arsenal, Alabama. *Hydra 70 2.75-inch Rocket System Informational Handbook.* October 1, 1984.

Vietnam Helicopter Pilots Association, *Helicopter or incident 67-16193.* May 25, 1998.

Vietnam Helicopter Pilots Association, *Helicopter or incident 69-15138.* September 20, 1998.

Vietnam Helicopter Pilots Association, *Helicopter or incident 67-16547.* July 25, 1998.

Information and corroboration provided by:

Mrs. Nancy Buchanan   Larry B. Edeal
Ronald F. Beyer   Mrs. Irene Frye
John D. Craig   Samuel Hinch

Brian S. Holcomb
Frederick B. Joles
Walker A. Jones
Robert Lemaster
Rhett W. Lewis
John Mackel
Michael L. Poindexter

Ross A. Rainwater
Galen D. Rosher
John "Barry" Sipple
Michael E. Smith
Robert N. Tredway
Grover E. Wright
John "Mel" Wyatt

Maps kindly loaned by:
Walker A. Jones
John "Mel" Wyatt

Index

About the Author

Randy R. Zahn is chief pilot, Alaska Rotor Wing Division, for Era Helicopters in Anchorage, Alaska. He learned to fly helicopters while serving in the U.S. Army from 1968–1971. He served a tour of duty in Vietnam (1970–1971), earning two Distinguished Flying Crosses, a Bronze Star, two Air Medals for valor, and two Army Commendation Medals for valor. Vietnamese Cross of Gallantry with a silver star, Purple Heart, and 43 Air Medals. He lives in Eagle River, Alaska, with his wife, Kim, and sons, Brent and Kyle.